GW00363589

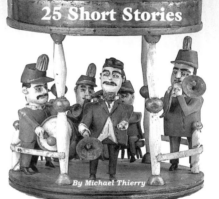

Bandstand Tales

25 Short Stories

By Michael Thierry

INDEX

FORWARD

Bandstand Tales, is a collection of 25 short 'brass banding' stories. Prompted and inspired by fact and embellished by fiction!

Brass bands bring together all age groups for whom the movement is a big part of their lives. Most towns, cities and indeed many villages have a brass band. Through their music-making, they serve the local community. Assisting at Remembrance Day Services, Church Fetes, raising funds through charity Concerts and bringing the spirit of Christmas to the streets.

Banding is strong throughout the UK. Village bands at one end and at the other, top contesting bands, Cory, Black Dyke and Brighouse & Rastrick amongst many others. Most bands are self-funded.

The Salvation Army introduced brass bands into their worship during the formative years. The premier band of the movement is the International Staff Band, ISB. Many centres have a band attached.

Some might argue that there is a third element, military bands. To the connoisseur, because they have woodwind, they are not purely brass band.

Brass bands have very rarely featured in books of fiction. Many technical books are covering just about every aspect of banding. Volumes offering advice on player improvement, articles which inform on the lives and work of composers, web sites which promote the various bands. Brass band fiction, on the shelves in the shop or at home is all but absent.

Most band personnel would readily suggest that there is a great deal of material from which fiction can be drawn. All bands have their anecdotal stories, incidents involving the band and members, some tragic, others humorous.

I hope readers will find the stories light-hearted and amusing, not to be taken to seriously.

Michael Thierry

Department
for Culture
Media & Sport

Regulation
Proposals
for
United Kingdom
Brass Bands

Scoping and Briefing Document
March 2020
Brass Band Section

ENVIRONMENTAL & COST SAVING MEASURES

INTRODUCTION

What is a brass band?
A brass band is a musical ensemble consisting almost entirely of a standard range of brass instruments played by people who want to make a loud noise!

Regulation

THE BRASS BAND WORLD WOULD APPEAR TO BE LARGELY UNREGULATED.

Clearly there is urgent need for Government regulation in respect of the Brass Band movement. It cannot be permitted for Brass Bands to continue in this totally unregulated manner. Regulation will be in the form of an Act of Parliament to be presented to the House of Commons as part of the Queen's Speech.

"My Government will bring in legislation to regulate and control Brass Bands."

Regulation Enforcement
However enforcement will be necessary. Local councils will have to make sure that bands comply with the new regulations. To enforce the regulations offenders will be brought before the courts.

Environmental and Climate Impact of the Brass Band

An environmental assessment and impact study needs to be carried out on Brass Bands, to make sure that Bands are compliant and conform to twenty-first century environmental standards. **Brass bands must make a contribution to climate change.**

The recent introduction of plastic trumpets, trombones and euphonium is a worrying development, doing considerable and lasting harm to the planet.

The Regulations for United Kingdom Brass Bands will introduce powers to make Brass Bands more environmentally friendly beginning with the mouth-piece.

LEGISLATION WILL BE TABLED IN PARLIAMENT TO COMPEL THE USE OF EDIBLE MOUTH PIECES.

Tests have been taking place in Government Laboratories and at other experimental facilities **USING FROZEN FRUIT, SHAPED INTO MOUTH PIECES.**
During testing fruit mouth-pieces lasted a full concert.

Bearing in mind the health of band members the use of non-healthy foods was not considered. For example mouthpieces made from Chocolate Gateau.

The Minister for Brass Bands is recommending the following fruits to be made into edible mouth-pieces, reflecting the characteristics of the instrument and the make-up of the average player.

Bass   Coconut
Simply expressed you have to be 'nuts' to play the bass.

Euphonium   Lemon
The term 'A right lemon' applies to most Euphonium players.

Trombone   Dragon fruit
A dragon is a legendary aggressive creature you want to stay away from.

Baritone   Nectarine
Nectarines are a very confused fruit.
A cross between a peach and a plum.

Tenor Horn   Pomegranate
The pomegranate is a boring, uninteresting over-rated, fruit. Difficult to stomach.

Cornet   Apple
"An Apple a day keeps the Cornetist away!"

Review of Brass Band

Review of Brass Band composition
The Minister for Brass Bands recommends a full review of banding. At a time when all Government departments and local councils are facing reduced budgets and therefore cut-backs, it is reasonable that Brass Bands should also come under scrutiny and face savings and cut-backs.

A panel of Brass Band experts have advised the Minister for Brass Bands.

The following cut-backs will form part of the **Brass Band Act of Parliament 2020**.
All Brass bands throughout the country will be compelled to conform.

Manifestly there is opportunity to make savings within the Brass Band world.
Savings will bring economic dividends.

The Minister for Brass Bands has indicated that the new measures will apply to all bands, non Salvation Army Bands and bands attached to the movement throughout the entire United Kingdom.

In coming to this decision, the minister based his consideration on an internal review of a number of bands throughout the United Kingdom. The fore-going is the confidential report of that review.

For the time being the minister is not minded to place an age limit on brass band players. An assessment of musical instability may be called for at a future date to access and establish suitability.

Brass Band experts have considered each Brass Band instrument and assessed their musical value in coming to their decision.

In their assessment experts used the standard, respected 'Doorbell' method.

The 'Doorbell' Test

Eb Soprano Cornet:

Plays too loud. Attention seeking. Plays to the audience. Seeks approval. Convinced he/she has the most difficult part to play in the band.

How do you know a soprano player is at the door?

The doorbell sounds in pain.

Recommendation - DELETE - Saving
Surplus to requirements. Only the musically illiterate would miss the Soprano. Re-arrange part for Bb cornets. (They mess about with the octave anyway).

Principal Cornet:

Feels over worked. Can be a bit of a show-off. A prima donna. Worries about triple tonguing. Feels unloved and un-appreciated.

How do you know a principal cornet player is at the door?

The doorbell shrieks!

Recommendation - RETAIN
But must be kept under review. Watch for signs of instability.

Second Cornet man down or 'bumper upper':

Often comes in at the wrong place. A bit of a flapper. Seeks to undermine the top man. Makes quiet under the breath unkind comments. Thinks he/she can play the solo parts much better than top man.

How do you know a 'bumper upper' is at the door?

The doorbell sounds rubbish!

Recommendation - RETAIN
Can remain a band member but needs a good talking to.

Third and Fourth Cornet man down:

Loud brutal musical thugs with lots of stamina and no finesse. The ugly twins. The trouble-makers on the cornet bench. Always up to no good.

How do you know a third or fourth cornetist is at the door?

The doorbell is unbearably loud and raucous!

Recommendation - DELETE - Saving
Major concern. If there was a Trade Union within the band they would be the Union Officials calling for occasional strikes. Leading disputes. Enforced retirement.

Repiano Cornet:

Really confused. Player needs counselling. Often misses an entry. Half asleep! Does a lot of looking around. Questions why she/he is there.

How do you know a repiano cornetist is at the door?

The door bell stutters!

Recommendation - DELETE - Saving
The entire part should be withdrawn and divided amongst the other cornets.

2nd and 3rd Cornet:

Hesitant, out of tune, but can play a bottom C with a wobble. Can also play lower G but can't remember the fingering. Has a musical fit when they see Upper Middle C.

How do you know a 2nd or 3rd cornetist is at the door?

The door bell tune stops half way through!

Recommendation - DELETE - Saving
Merge 2nd and 3rd Cornet and quietly drop the parts No-one will notice the difference.

Flugel Horn:

Complex players. Can't decide whether to be a cornet or a tenor horn. Feels they are mis-understood. On medication for spilt personality. Doesn't know where to sit in the band formation.

How do you know a flugel horn player is at the door?

The door bell sounds confused.

Recommendation - DELETE - Saving
Flugel horn is a German european instrument and cannot be used when the United Kingdom finally leaves the European Union. Leaving Brexit means disappearance of the Flugel horn.

Horn Section:

Often considered the 'girlie' entry into the Band. Unwise to upset the lady players or they might go home. Suggest a mirror, hair brush and make-up on the music stand. Can't start playing until they have painted their nails.

How do you know a horn player is at the door?
The door bell is temperamental!

Recommendation - RETAIN - Savings
One tenor horn is more than desirable.

Baritone Section:

Players want to play trombone - But can't remember the slide positions. The poor relations of the brass band world. On musical benefit. In a closing down sale the Baritone would be marked down 100%.

How do you know a baritone player is at the door?
The door bell stops and starts for no reason.

Recommendation - RETAIN - Saving
The pensioners of the Band, often away on cruises. Drain on the NHS system. Replacement glasses and dentures. Fails the medical. Opportunity for savings. One is more than enough.

Euphoniums:

The band 'big-heads', must be loved and always told how good they are. Big egos! Can blow longer and harder than any other instruments. Needs taking down a peg or two. They strut about full of their own importance.

How do you know a euphonium player is at the door?
The door bell increases in volume.

Recommendation - DELETE - Saving
Reduce the number to nil and make the world a happier place.

1st & 2nd Trombone:

The Al Capones of the brass band world, real musical bandits. Would you trust them with your wallet?

How do you know a trombone player is at the door?
The door bell sounds pathetic.

Recommendation - DELETE - Saving
Trombones should have been outlawed years ago and banned. A public offence in the hands of misguided exponents. All trombones should be licensed and only sold with a seven day permit.

Bass Trombone:

Sounds like a chainsaw with loose cogs. A car exhaust pipe trailing on the ground. If the Bass Trombone was a clapped out car you would take it to the crusher.

How do you know there's a bass trombone player at the door?
The door bell sounds like a road drill.

Recommendation - DELETE - Saving
The Music Hall stand up comic upsetting ladies of a gentle disposition. Very intimidating. The sound is grossly obscene.

EEb & BBb Bass:

Often bass players play what is not written and in a different key. Have been known to exchange bass band parts without noticing.Nearly always half a beat behind the rest of the band.Very suspect.

How do you know a bass player is at the door?
The door bell sounds like a factory hooter.

Recommendation - RETAIN ONE BASS - Saving
Playing every third note would improve appreciation.
Every fifth note would be better. Just an occasional
bass will do.

Percussion:
Has lots of noisy toys used in the most inappropriate
manner possible. Plays instruments more in keeping with
their character. Like toddlers. Nothing more than skin
bashers. Guilty of assault on a musical instrument.
How do you know a percussionist is at the door?
The door bell melody just gets faster and faster,
no sense of rhythm.

Recommendation - DELETE - Saving
Room for cut-backs. Remove the sticks for an
enhanced musical experience.

Under the new regulations the national
composition of a UK brass band would consist
of:

CORNET
HORN
BARITONE
BASS

Bandmaster or Musical Director

Normally devoid of much musical ability but still conducts. The brass band movement went down hill when the term Musical Director was introduced. Nothing more than banding social snobbery. Think they are better than anybody else and wanted a new posh title. The most ignored member of the band. Advisors consider that the conductor was largely a 'relic of the past'. The role needed twenty first century assessment.

> *How do you know a Musical Director is at the door?*
> *Silence. The Musical Director does not know how to press the bell.*

Recommendation - DELETE - Saving
The panel of experts advising the Minister for Brass Bands finally concluded that perhaps the time had arrived to dispense with the role of Musical Director and to explore other methods.

PERHAPS THE BANDMASTER COULD BE MADE REDUNDANT AND REPLACED WITH A CONDUCTING ROBOT.

In the basement of a secret government facility, under strict military guard, work was commissioned on a design and prototype of a Robotic Computerised Conductor.

The project was given the title

ILLUMINATING LIGHT
OSCILLATING DEVICE

Replacing the Brass Band Conductor would be a light bulb. Single changing coloured bulbs are now available. The bulb could be used in two ways. Large main bulb on a stand central to the band. Individual bulbs positioned on music stands. The bulb would take the place of the baton. Computer software would direct the musicians, using the colour changing bulb.

General lighting would be

Amber	Get ready to play
Green	Commence playing
Flashing Amber	Prepare to stop playing
Red	Stop playing
Flashing Red	Emergency Stop

The flashing bulb would replicate metronome markings. Dynamics would be indicated by colour.

Flashing Yellow	pp
Yellow	p
Blue	mp
Orange	mf
Brown	f
Purple	ff
Brown & Purple	fff

CONCLUSION

Government Brass Band proposals are to go out for consultation.

Members of the public and those actively involved in the Brass Band movement are asked to respond to this consultation.

As is the usual practice. HM Government will take no account of the consultation.

Regulation Proposals for United Kingdom Brass Bands was presented as after-dinner entertainment for the Ringwood & Burley Band Christmas Dinner 2018.

Trombone Trouble

(2)

RIVALRY has always existed, and there are numerous examples. In sport the 'Old Firm' rivalry between the two football teams in Scotland, Rangers and Celtic. Fast-food, McDonald's versus Burger King, in the upper echelons of education, Cambridge versus Oxford, and in movie-land, Batman versus Superman. The rivalry between the various capital cities of the globe, London versus Paris and rivalries within families. But perhaps one of the least known rivalries is that between cornets and trombones within a brass band.

The Battle of the Brass Band is nowhere better to be found than the competing troops of the cornets versus the trombones. The Cornetites versus Tromboneians! The trombones are normally outnumbered by the cornets, perhaps as much as two to one, but what they lack in numbers they make up in trombone tenacity. They are fearsome warriors. They are the cavalry of the brass band world, using trombones like lances. It is for a very good reason that trombones normally lead a band march, and the cornets bring up the rear.

"Do you think I would put my life in danger by marching in front of trombones," a cautious cornetist Chris asserted, "We've all heard stories of band caps being tipped off heads by an extended trombone slide". There were nodding heads. They recalled the Annual Whit Friday Band Contest. Bringing the event to mind, Chris related, "Do you remember that nasty piece of work in one of the northern bands, a big chap, he made Desperate Dan look like a midget. In one deft movement he had the cap off the head of a rival bandsman as they were marching by. That following bus made a right mess of the cap. They lost points for that".

A typical seating arrangement for a brass band ensures that

the two sections are kept as wide apart as possible, with trembling tenor horns and brave baritones creating a musical buffer zone, the back row basses at the ready should the big guns be required to act as peacemakers.

So many things can create tension leading to conflict; both sections want extra platform space, a turf war begins with the positioning of the first chair. In some bands the chair setting has to be protected. Bandits from the cornet section have been known to sneak up and rearrange the seating for the trombones. "Why do they need all that space, have you noticed they only play half the time, and then not all of them together", voiced the shop steward of the cornet section.

Representing the trombone club affiliates was the bass trombone player. One time he had been end man of the trombone section, but over the years had found himself chair by chair moving south. "I've been saying it for years, you've heard me say it before, and I'll say it again, there's only one way to sum up the cornet section. With cornets it is simply, 'all blare and no flare' - you know what the dictionary says, blare - 'to make or cause to make a loud, harsh sound'. That's cornets for you, take my word for it".

The intersection war could sometimes turn really nasty, tit-for-tat excursions, equivalent retaliation, were planned. The three man raiding party for the cornets in the town band was spearheaded by Chris, second cornet, Stephen who played soprano, and Roger deputy principal solo cornet. Stephen was the one who always wanted to administer the most damage, and who had come up with a 'wheeze'.

It involved sneaking into the band library cupboard and doctoring the second trombone part with the second horn part. 'The Hallelujah Chorus' would just not sound quite right, or so he hoped.

The next band engagement was to be a shared concert with the local Choral Society, the evening ending with the rousing Hallelujah Chorus.

The second trombone was feeling a little bit tired, he'd spent the afternoon in the garden, mowing the lawn and trimming the hedges. "Retirement is for spending time in the garden and keeping out of the way of the wife". A relaxed and part sleepy Derek, sat in his position on the platform, and scanned through the programme finding the music for the final piece, 'The Hallelujah Chorus'. Ever trusting, he checked the title of the piece and noted it was marked 'trombone'. Happy with that Derek lifted the trombone in the start position and awaited the downbeat of the conductor. Up to that point in the joint concert the programme had gone rather well, both Choirmaster and Musical Director were pleased and congratulated each other.

Over the other side of the platform cornets also awaited the downbeat. Had their plan worked? Indeed it had. One-nil to the cornets! Second trombone was reduced to making his part up as he went along. "I thought second trombone was a vast improvement!" reported a jubilant Stephen. Close examination of the trombone part revealed the copy tampering. Smirks on cornet players' faces confirmed the music tampering culprits.

Time for retaliation. A trombone council of war was called. The atmosphere was tense and threatening. "No, we can't torture cornet players even though we might want to and they certainly deserve it, thumbscrews is not the answer", said Derek, the offended party. Triple strength laxative in their pre-concert cup of tea was dismissed as being uncertain of success. Principal trombone, Simon, posh bank manager, sat back and pondered as if he was considering a bank loan he was going to refuse. "We know that all cornet players are dim but who is Mr Big Dim in that lot over there?" The four were silent, in their minds they reviewed the dimability of each of the cornet players. Almost in unionism, they shouted "Nervy Nigel".

Nigel was one of those players who you had the feeling was never quite sure where he was and what he was doing, often agitated. He'd forget his tie and turned up for a concert without one; he was always the last player to find the music, on one occasion he found it after the piece had ended. It was a miracle if he ever arrived at rehearsal before it had started, and when he did put in an appearance he was greeted with decorous comments. He was the band standing joke. 'Nervy Nigel' was ideal.

The proposal was daring, daring and cunning. If the trombones could pull it off it would certainly be game set and match to them. There was no way the Cornetites could retaliate, they just could not come back. The effect would be seismic. "This is just brilliant, well done Simon, it's a winner", an exuberant Derek exclaimed.

The big event in the band's calendar was the prestigious Town Mayor's Gala Concert. Preparations for the programme took place well in advance. Details of the suggested pieces were sent to the Town Clerk for approval, who always checked to make sure that the final item would be, *Land of Hope and Glory*. "The Mayor is insistent, *National Anthem* to be played once the Mayoral party have taken their places. His Worship would like to meet some of the band during the interval. This year the Council has invested in some Union Jack flags, although flags of other UK nations will be available, which we will be asking people to wave in time with the music".

The programme was billed as *'The Wartime Spirit'*, included in the lineup was a three-piece girl song and dance group, *'The Bell Bottom Belles'*, sailor suits, peroxide blondes, fire engine flame-red lipstick and a repertoire of wartime melodies.

To revive the war-time musical spirit, a comedian had been booked. Noting the band, he asked the audience, *"What is a gentleman? - Somebody who knows how to play the trombone, but doesn't - Boom! Boom!". "Why can't a gorilla play the trombone? He's too sensitive - Boom! Boom!"!*

"Don't worry about that", said the bass trombonist under his breath, "I'll speak to him in the car park afterwards and enquire if he's got a good dentist!"

The interval was the opportunity for *'Operation Cornastrophe'*. Each of the trombonists had a crucial and critical part to play in the exercise. Derek was tasked in making sure that Nervy Nigel went off for refreshments at the interval. "Don't bother to bring your cornet with you" said Derek to Nervy Nigel, in a kind and friendly manner. "Just leave it on your chair, it will be quite safe there, as you can see others are going to leave their instruments on the platform whilst the refreshments take place".

Innocent Nervy Nigel did as he was told and trotted off behind Derek heading towards the refreshment room. Part one of the plan executed. "I wonder what it's like sitting on the cornet bench", queried Simon as he made his way through the band chairs. His number two suggested that they give it a try, "Seeing things from another perspective is always a good idea", he said. The second part of the plan was activated. Choosing the back row of cornets, the trombonists occupied cornet seats, including Nervy Nigel's. "I don't know if this is a good idea", said Simon lifting Nigel's cornet, "I don't want to be contaminated with Cornetitis!" With the pretence of playing the cornet, Simon moved into phase three of the operation.

Simon gave the cornet a thorough inspection, pulling out the slides a little bit one by one and opening the water key, for good measure he thought he ought to look down the bell. Simon then extracted the middle valve from its casing; he looked at it as if under a microscope. "I often wondered what a cornet valve looked like, how it was constructed. Just look at the spring mechanism", Simon said to number two, as he offered him the valve, "I suppose they're all the same", suggested Simon, "Let's have a look at the third valve", removing the same from its casing.

Now came the conjurer's trick, with sleight of hand, the extractions part hidden by the back of the chair in front, Simon exchanged valves two and three. He was impressed, both valves still fitted in the incorrect casing, they popped up and down as if they had always been there. Snug and tight fitting. Nobody could possibly know there was any difference, and certainly not Nervy Nigel.

Inspired and elated by success, Simon thought why stop at one cornet, next to him on either side were a couple more cornets. Taking the valves out and swapping them round had been all too easy, he could do it again, and again. Encouraged, number two, seeing what Simon was doing, 'adjusted' the soprano and the repiano cornets. That was the back row done. Did they have time to sabotage the front line of cornets? Would anyone notice, certainly not the public, they would think it was something that happened during every band concert interval. Simon considered that it might depend on the length of interval speech of the Town Mayor.

Simon looked at his watch; timing was everything, did they have the opportunity to lean over the chairs and capture and sabotage the solo cornets? It must be a risk worth taking. He looked around him; he could still hear chatter and the clink of cups from the refreshment room. Rising above that social hub was the voice of the Town Mayor, "Now, I just wanted to say to you all, as I've just been saying to the Bandmaster, sorry Musical Director, how very much the town appreciates the service of you good folk. You're a credit to our community, and I know where ever you play people are entertained", pausing for breath, and changing the subject, he added, "Times are hard, and money is tight, we've got to keep the rates down, but I'm sure we can find a grant for the band from next year's budget. Not as much as last year mind you. Anyway, well done".

By the time the Mayor had uttered "Well done!", all cornets had been successfully 'doctored' and the trombonists were back in their rightful seats. The rest of the band wandered onto the platform and sat in their places; the Musical Director already had raised his baton.

The Town Mayor took his place, adorned in Mayoral robes and chain. Gesturing towards the band he indicated that he was ready, he smiled a smile of appreciation and consulted the programme: Opening number, the March of The Royal British Legion, a nice steady 6/8. With no time for the players to really get ready, it was up with instruments and down came the first beat.

MAYOR'S GALA CONCERT ENDS IN BAND AFFRAY

POLICE were called on Saturday night to the Town Hall in Mayoral Way to break up a disturbance which had broken out during the Town Mayor's Gala Concert.

Inspector Gray called for backup to deal with the affray, describing the scenes at the Town Hall as "disgraceful". There are ongoing enquiries, "From what I can ascertain a confrontation took place between various personnel of the town band".

"The allegation is that members of the trombone section mucked about with instruments of the cornet section. Whilst I know very little at all about brass band instruments it would appear that the cornets were tampered with, indeed the word 'sabotage' has been freely used and the incident has been described as an 'outrage'", said the Inspector.

Continuing the Inspector said, "A person or persons unknown had 'nobbled' the cornets so that they were unplayable. Every member of the band is to be finger printed, and statements taken from those who have any evidence to give. I do feel that charges will follow".

As one witness said, "It was tribal warfare on the platform. The cornets raised their instruments to their lips to play, puffed out their cheeks, and nothing happened. The gala concert descended into a pub brawl".

"Over went numerous music stands, music went flying all over the place. The cornet players were jumping out of their seats and were waving their fists at the trombone section, who in turn were laughing their heads off. Yes, I did see one or two fists flying, but nobody was really hurt, just a bit of instrument cases!".

Through the Town Clerk, the Town Mayor issued the following statement:

"On behalf of the town I want to say how appalled I am at the behaviour and conduct that I witnessed at my Gala Concert Evening. In all my years on the council I have never known such a public disturbance, even on election night".

"Residents must be assured that they can safely attend any band concert organised in the town. The safety and well-being of townsfolk is vitally important, and it is my public duty to take such actions as necessary to ensure the maintenance of good public order. People must be protected from brass band hooligans - indeed they were band hooligans - no other name for them. The local football supporters do not act in such a fashion".

'The town brass band is immediately suspended and barred from playing within the town boundaries. The council is not prepared to licence any further concerts. We have done this to protect our citizens from harm'.

The police decided not to press any charges; gathering evidence proved far too difficult, neither side in the affray wanted to testify against the other. With the lack of evidence the police just issued a stern warning and a caution.

The band committee gathered together. Officers were all for putting the incident behind them, there is nothing to be gained from raking over previous events.

The Musical Director reported that all band instruments were now in good order, no real damage had been done to any of the cornets. Going forward is what needed to be decided. The committee wanted the band still to function and looked at ways in which that might be achieved. A 'peace' Bar-B-Que was organised, with 'special terms and conditions' applying. The Mayor was invited, but he said he was 'otherwise engaged'.

Not only was the band able to play an arrangement of 'Deep Harmony', but they were able to demonstrate that a new level of harmony now existed between the two tribes. "Play nice now you lot", was the instruction of Mrs Musical Director. A refreshing 'esprit de corps' prevailed throughout the band.

It was to be expected that the Gala Night affray would appear in the pages of the newspapers, even local television managed to give the incident a brief spot, accompanied by an old 'clip' of the band.

A documentary on the band was suggested by Channel 5. The idea was turned down because the television company insisted on a re-enactment.

What was unexplained was that now the band was functioning, invitations to perform were arriving from all over the place. One town had the band billed as the *'Fighting Band'*, the publicity for the concert suggesting that a brawl could break out during the concert at any moment and that there would be an extra charge for front row seats.

A grovelling letter of wholesome apology was dispatched to the Town Mayor, included was a Town Council Grant Application Form asking funding for the band. It was immediately returned, marked 'Rejected!'

Clippertone Antique Cornet

(3)

ROY'S grandparents lived in a double-fronted Edwardian house in one of the more salubrious roads of the town. The property set in its own grounds, had a number of outbuildings which were mainly used for storage. It was a house that Roy knew well, he spent almost as much time with his grandparents as he did with his mother and father. Roy was a sensitive child, rather bright and intelligent; he was a child who was confident in what he said and in what he was doing. "He is far too advanced for his age", said his grandfather, "I don't know where he gets it from, but he keeps on asking me things and I haven't got a clue how to answer him. The other day he asked me, "How did the Queen become Queen?" When I asked him why, he said that at school they were studying the British monarchy from 1900 and as I was alive during the abdication period, what were my thoughts and feelings about it?".

"I had to tell him that I was only a youngster myself in 1937. I seem to remember the radio broadcast from the King telling us that he was giving up the throne, 'for the woman I love'. The next minute we had Bertie, the Duke of York, becoming King and his eldest daughter would become Queen Elizabeth II. Then he asked me, did I think that Mr Baldwin, the Prime Minister, acted correctly. I didn't even know Mr Baldwin was Prime Minister at the time. I just don't know what's going around in that lad's head".

Roy was twelve years old and for the past two years had lived with his grandparents following the tragic death of both his parents in a motoring accident. The family of three had been on a touring holiday in France and on one of the mountain passes, they had come face-to-face with an oncoming tractor. Roy was thrown from the back of the open-top tourer and landed in the soft verge. He suffered no injuries. He recalled seeing the backend of the car as it disappeared from the road down the ravine where it burst into flames.

Grandparents, Frank and Mabel Harrison travelled to France to bring their grandson home. Roy was a resilient lad and grandfather Frank thought that, so often, Roy coped better with the loss of his parents than he did on the loss of his son. The parent's home was cleared and sold. Everything from Roy's bedroom was transported to his new home. Even everyday utensils of his parents were now to be found in the kitchen and dining room; the grandparents felt it important that Roy should see around him items with which he was familiar.

Roy knew the Edwardian house very well. He would love to go to the house for one of grandma's cream teas. He enjoyed helping grandad in the garden, but best of all he loved the summer picnics. From on top of one of the kitchen cupboards, grandad Harrison would lift down the picnic basket. Roy marvelled at how everything was so neatly packed away in the basket. Melamine crockery with cutlery to match, dinky little pepper and salt. Plenty of room for sandwiches, cake, a flask of tea for the adults and a bottle of pop for Roy.

Off they would set out in grandad's ancient Ford Prefect and head for the coast just seven miles away. Where they parked there was a lovely wide expanse of grass on top of the cliffs. "Do we go for a walk first and then come back for a picnic, or do we do it in the reverse order?" asked grandad. Grandma Harrison always said the same thing, "Walk first and then we will build up an appetite for our picnic".

The three of them would make their way down the tiny winding cobbled streets into the town centre. Both his grandparents were window shoppers, Roy, for nothing better to do would sometimes count the number of shop windows that they gazed into. It could take ages to get down onto the seafront and the small fishing harbour. Roy was patient, he knew that he'd be able to spend all the time he wanted looking at the boats, watching fishermen with their fishing rods trying to catch fish, often mullet. Grandad had suggested that perhaps he might buy Roy a fishing rod, but Roy thought not.

The old Edwardian house and the outbuildings were great places for Roy to explore. Upstairs above the main house first floor bedrooms, was a full-length attic which ran from gable to gable, large enough that if they wanted it could be converted and divided into rooms.

Over the years it had been the family 'dumping ground'. "We will put that in the attic, then we'll know where to find it when we need it", said grandma and so up into the attic went all manner of things, just in case.

While searching about in 'his playground', Roy unearthed a very old black-and-white television, a child's pedal car, rather nice dolls house, an old suction carpet hoover, with a very old-fashioned plug which had circular terminals. Upstairs was also a number of trunks and suitcases, one trunk seem to contain nothing other than curtains, another trunk contained cricket bats, pads and tennis rackets. Each trip to the attic was an adventure. He would come across old family photographs. Roy brought them downstairs wanting to find out from his grandparents who they might be.

The outbuildings also proved interesting. Grandad had a medium sized shed, he called it his PR, 'potting room', whatever that meant, where he kept all his bits and pieces, paraphernalia to do with gardening, decorating and things that grandma wouldn't allow him to have in the house. Roy was intrigued by the fact that grandad had installed in the shed an easy chair, table and on one of the shelves there was an electric kettle, couple of mugs, which needed an urgent wash, and three packets of various biscuits, and in the corner a one bar electric fire, propped up on an old box. Occasionally a large slice of grandma's lemon drizzle cake would find its way into the shed. Not for Roy the armchair, he had to sit on an old orange box, to listen to grandad's collection of stories. "You know it's a funny thing, but I can never hear grandma calling me when I'm sitting in the shed. I've had many a good nap in this chair!"

One of the other buildings was a large barn which now served as a garage. At one end grandad 'stabled' the family Ford car always covered by a large tarpaulin and at the other end, the lawnmower, one of those sit on jobs, which annoyed grandma because of the noise that it made.

Roy knew he couldn't go exploring in grandad's shed. But the big barn looked terribly exciting. It did look as if at one time it might have served as a stable; there was a central gully running down the middle of the building out of the entrance and into the yard. Also, Roy noticed some very large round rings, which had been driven into the wall as if to restrain perhaps cows or even horses. The building had a loft, Roy imagined that maybe it was up there that hay and straw might have been stored. There was a ladder giving access to the loft. To Roy's disappointment, the loft yielded nothing. He couldn't even find one of the gold pieces of eight that he dreamt about finding.

Never mind he still had the house attic, and there was loads of stuff up there that he had yet to have a look at. It was at weekends that Roy was able to climb the ladder into the loft space, "I'm just going up to the attic grandma to see what I can find", "Now you be careful, some of those floorboards may not be as strong as once they were, and I don't want you coming through into one of the bedrooms, thank you very much indeed, and put some old clothes on, we don't want you messing up your new stuff", cautioned grandma.

While part of the attic had an electric supply there were just one or two lights spread throughout the length of the attic, they were not enough to fully illuminate the space. For Christmas Roy had asked for and been given a really bright big torch, the size of a lantern with a beam that seemed to go on for miles. Up he went, opened the attic door, switched on his new torch, and prepared for his adventure. He could not believe how much of a difference the new torch made, it floodlit the area.

It has been a little while since Roy had investigated the left-hand side of the attic and certainly not with his Christmas searchlight. The way in which things had been stored allowed him to walk up a central aisle, either side of him things were placed in storage, a carpet and for some reason or other an old washing mangle was propped up at a funny angle. He tried to turn the handle, but rust had made the machine inoperable. "That really should be in a museum, like most of the rubbish up here", thought Roy. Continuing along Roy came across some old photos which he'd looked at previously. "Now this looks interesting, not spotted this before", Roy bent down and underneath the legs of the old carver dining room chair, with an arm missing, was a small, attache case, about two foot long, eighteen inches wide and about the same in depth. Dusting off the top of the lid appeared the words Hawkes & Son - Piccadilly Circus - London embossed in gold lettering. "What have we here?", queried Roy resting the case on one of the trunks. The two catches were not going to be moved - time for Roy to visit grandad's shed. "I shall have to wake him up and get him to apply a squirt of WD-40". Roy gave the case a shake and found it rattled; there was definitely something in there. It was a bit too heavy for pieces of eight unless there was a huge stash of them.

Roy made his way down the attic ladder and the flight of steps to the ground floor, back through the house, passed his grandmother who was in the kitchen getting the evening meal ready, "Tell grandad he needs to come in for about half-past six", "OK", he said as he went through the back door on the way to the shed. Looking through the window, Roy could see that grandad was having a snooze, he gently tapped on the window and with a start grandad looked up and motioned him in. "What have you got there young man, been exploring?" asked grandad noticing the case. "I found it in the attic underneath the battered dining room chair. It's got something in it, but the catches are a bit stuck, so I thought if I came to see you, using your magic WD-40, we could see just what is inside".

Grandad took the case and found a space on his work bench, turning around to look for the WD-40 he didn't have far to look, Roy had already got it in his hand. The WD-40 performed the magic and within no time at all both locks sprang open, and the case could be opened. Inside was a silver instrument, clearly a trumpet or a cornet but, at that time neither knew what exactly it was, evidently it had been made by a company named Hawkes & Son. Some paperwork in the case revealed that it was a Hawkes Clippertone Cornet Outfit. Amongst the documents was a copy of an advertisement for the Clippertone. *'This world-famous cornet outfit already in use by practically every soloist of renown is now made available to every bandsman under a new extended payment plan. Full details with handsome new catalogue'*. The cornet appeared to be complete although it had been knocked around a bit.

"I wonder how it got to be stored in the attic, have you any idea grandad?" asked Roy. "When your grandma and I purchased the house, it was a bereavement sale. The previous gentleman owner had just died. His relatives failed to completely clear the house of his affects, they just wanted the house sold as quickly as possible. I suppose the case and contents ended up being included in the house sale, along with other items in the attic".

"Well before you can do anything with it it's going to need a clean and that won't take place till after dinner and grandma is prepared to vacate the kitchen, because from my little knowledge of brass band instruments this needs a jolly good wash and rinse through".

Mrs Harrison was not best pleased with the idea of using her kitchen sink. "Kitchen sinks are not made to clean brass instruments in, just you two be careful what you're doing mucking about with that bit of old scrap metal". To ensure the protection of her kitchen surfaces Mrs Harrison disappeared into the scullery and came back with a bundle of newspapers and a couple of old towels. "If I find so much as a mark anywhere I shall have you two put away!" threatened grandma.

"This WD-40 stuff is good", said grandad as they began to dismantle the cornet. They managed to get two of the four slides out, they were both a bit green from age. Without letting grandmother know they boiled the two slides in one of her saucepans, adding the mouthpiece and the long shank in with the mix. "I think we're going to need to put the pliers on those valves they're just not budging", said Roy. "I don't think that is a good idea it will end up leaving teeth marks on the metal which is a little bit soft. Let's try some WD-40, and wrap a leather belt round to get a purchase on them. With time and patience, little by little the valve tops began to move, and one by one the valves popped out of the casings. Into the saucepan went the valves to have a little boil up.

"On Monday after school, I'll meet you and we will pop into town to the music shop in Cow Lane. We will tell them what we have found and see if they can help us to get it going. We could always take it with us and the bits from out of the saucepan!"

Seeing the case, the owner of *Music for all Times* said, "I suggest you need the antique shop next door!" "I think you may be right", said Mr Harrison, "but we'd be ever so grateful if you could have a look at it for us. My grandson found it tucked away in the attic; it must've been there for years, I've never seen it before. I suspect perhaps the previous owner had just left it in the attic", said grandad.

The owner of the shop was only too happy to tell them what little he knew about their instrument. The cornet, they knew, was a Clippertone, made by Hawks & Son from the early 1900s. In its day it had been a very popular cornet, and the range continued for quite some time. The model that Roy had found dated from 1906, identified by the instrument number.

"Well you're very lucky everything is just about there, in fact, I can't find any bits missing, often you find that the long shank has been removed or that the additional tuning slide has taken a wander, but in this case everything looks complete, even the mute appears as if it was the original one which came with the cornet", said the music shop owner.

Roy who had quietly listened to the conversation now asked the question that had been going through his mind long before they came into the shop, "Can the instrument be repaired so that it can be played again?". "No problem, young man, we would have to send it away to an instrument repairer, but it could be refurbished. New springs and felts; the water cork needs replacing. There are one or two dents, and the bell does appear to be a little twisted, but all those things can be put right. If you wanted, you could also have it re-plated".

"Let's have it done", said grandad without a moment's hesitation. "This cornet is over 100 years old and it deserves a new lease of life. Just think, all that time up in the attic, lying there waiting for someone like you and me Roy to unearth it and make it playable once more". The owner of *Music for all Times* asked, "Don't you want an estimate for what it's going to cost?" "No", said grandad, "the government is going to pay for it from out of my pension!"

Six weeks later, on a Saturday afternoon, Roy and grandad called into the music shop. A beaming owner placed the case, which had also received a spruce up on the shop counter, and invited Roy to flip the catches and open up the lid. Both were totally amazed at the transformation before them. The Clippertone just was not the same instrument. "This is just so wonderful", said Mr Harrison, "What a brilliant job they've done on this old cornet, it looks as perfect as it must have looked way back in the Piccadilly Circus shop of Mr Hawkes & Son in the reign of Queen Victoria".

Mrs Harrison had prepared one of her picnics, ham sandwiches, a bit of salad, plain crisps and currant rock cakes she had made that morning. With cornet still on the back seat they drove the seven miles to the seaside. Before Mrs Harrison could utter the usual, Roy said, "Walk first to give us an appetite!". Grandpa questioned in his mind why Roy was carrying the case with the cornet. He let it pass.

As they approached the promenade, they could hear the strains of brass band music, playing the *Light Calvary Overture*. The local band was giving a performance in the bandstand, part of the summer programme of entertainment for residents and visitors.

"Grandad, let's go and have a listen to the band. I noticed that the poster said the programme began at 2:30pm and it's not yet 2:45pm, so they still have quite a bit of the programme to go through".

Along with the holidaymakers and locals, they stopped to listen to the band enjoying a varied selection of brass band music. At about 3:10pm the conductor announced that there would be a short interval. "Then we will come back for the last half an hour", he said.

Making the most of the opportunity Roy approached the seated band's principal cornet. "Hello young man, what can I do for you, how can I help you?", expecting that Roy was going to produce a programme and a pen and would ask him for his autograph. "Well I wonder if you'd be so kind as to have a look at my cornet?" With that Roy placed the cornet case on the ground opened up the lid and took out the Clippertone cornet.

"Do you know I haven't seen one of these cornets for years and years", said the principal. "When I first started playing, in the training band, it was on a Clippertone cornet I was taught, it was my first cornet. I really loved it. It was a bit old and worn then, but to me, it was the best cornet in the world. I practised and practised on that old Clippertone. I might have played on a few cornets since, but I doubt anything better. I always think back to the Clippertone."

The principal cornet checked over the recently refurbished Clippertone. "It's a weighty, solid instrument. No cheap inferior brass used on this instrument. The valves have got a nice action, lovely and smooth. The one I played had a felt missing on the second valve and as a result used to get a bit clanky. The restorers have done a really first-class job on this instrument, it's as good as the day it first came out of the factory".

Roy explained the story behind the Clippertone. It had been hidden away for nobody knew how long, it could be decades since someone last blew a note through the instrument. "Well with your permission, young man, I think it's time we rectified that situation. In the second half I've got a tricky cornet solo to play, I would love to play that solo on this instrument". "Would you?" said Roy, "that would be absolutely marvellous. Thank you so much". Turning to his grandad excitedly, he said, "We're going to hear the cornet played!".

The principal cornet player used the first piece after the interval to warm the cornet up and to get a feel of it. The conductor introduced the principal cornet player and the piece that he was going to play.

Stepping up to the microphone, the cornet player related the story of the cornet. "We know how old it is but not when was the last time that somebody played any notes on it. For decades, perhaps, the cornet was stored in an attic, undisturbed.

The principal called Roy onto the stage. This young man here, Roy, unearthed the cornet and with the help of his grandad they have had the instrument completely refurbished. I assure you as good as new. It was on the same model of cornet that I was taught to play; therefore, what a great thrill it is for me this afternoon to once again be able to play a Clippertone cornet. I owe a lot to the Clippertone cornet."

"Young man sit on my chair whilst I play your cornet".

Teething Trouble for Bert

(4)

In memory of Bert Hodgetts
The Salvation Army - Guernsey

IN Bert's own opinion, there was nothing special about himself. Bert was the original Mr Average. Average in height, average in size, average in expectation. At school his marks were always average, sometimes a little above, sometimes a little below, but always average. When it came to romance Bert knew he could never date the most beautiful girl in the class, and so he looked for Miss Average, and finding her proved to be a solid basis for marriage. And so they enjoyed year after year of being just average. There was something very comforting, for both of them, in being average.

Bert was never destined to be a star; he acknowledged that and was content. When he joined the local Salvation Army band, not for him the dizzy heights of the cornet section, or seeking to be a show-off euphonium player, even playing the trombone was a step too far for Mr Average. People in the congregation and audiences seem to spend a lot of time staring at the trombone section he noticed.

He settled for a homely baritone, knowing he would never have a solo to play, in the knowledge that he could be part of the band and at the same time be hidden away. Second baritone really suited his profile. The Bandmaster never expected too much musically from Bert, and Bert never delivered much.

Bert was completely average, boringly in comparison to other band personnel, or so it seemed. But Bert had a quirk and not your average quirk. A quirk, very much out of character, a quirk which, unbelievably, drew attention to himself,. In this respect he was no longer Mr Average.

We all do funny and strange things from time to time, but with his quirk, Bert was in another league altogether. He may well have been the only exponent worldwide of this quirk. When 'quirking' he was for a few moments the star of the show, he was in the limelight, it seemed that all eyes were upon him. Was he the star of the show?

Summer months involved outdoor engagements for the band. Regularly the local bandstand was one of the venues. Another activity was the traditional Salvation Army open-air meetings taking place along the seafront, the band standing in a semicircle, Bert in amongst the other baritone players. Ministry through music.

On occasions without warning, Bert could be seen standing in his place, not with the instrument in hand but, his upper dentures being cradled in his left hand. With a sense of occasion, Bert would extend his right hand into the inner pocket of his uniform jacket, Napoleon like, and extract what was obviously a shaker, the sort of thing you might find on the fish and chip counter containing salt.

Bert, with seasoned expertise, would gently shake the shaker over his false teeth. This was something Bert had done on a number of occasions before and felt no embarrassment whatsoever in doing so in public.

Indeed, when he did it, Bert had attracted a number of interested bystanders. One youngster grabbed his mother's arm and gesticulated towards Bert, not wanting his mother to miss this particular performance.

For other members of the band, they had seen it all before, and they had witnessed Bert's right-hand slip into his jacket, false teeth in left hand awaiting the Bert shake. As soon as Bert laid his baritone on the ground, the whole band and the Bandmaster knew exactly what was to follow.

For Bert, it was no more than normal banding behaviour. You sorted out your music, made sure you had your music stand, double-checked you had the mouthpiece - but in Bert's case, it went one step further. Final check before leaving home ensuring that in his inside pocket he had his precious shaker, just in case of need.

Over the years Bert had utilised a number of containers, all had done faithful service, they were just as important to Bert as valve oil for his baritone. If the instrument needed 'servicing' then so did his teeth.

The Bandmaster, Harold, was a very accommodating fellow. He just accepted that Bert had his peculiar ways; he had spoken privately to Bert about the ritual; it made no difference whatsoever. When Bert judged the moment was right, just like emptying water from your instrument, out came the teeth accoutrement. The fact was that, often, Bert was unable to go through a band performance without the procedure.

Asking Bert what exactly he was doing was fairly pointless. It was obvious. Bert shrugged off any enquiries over the exposed teeth and the shaker. "Bert does what Bert does", seemed to be the excepted stance amongst the other members of the band, it was private; it was personal.

Bert knew that at some point in the programme, he might need to put down his baritone and substitute the shaker for the instrument. The sight of Bert's dentures in one hand and shaker in the other was mesmerising; it had more impact than a conjurer pulling a rabbit out of the hat. Bert stood in his place in the band for the rendition, he knew it made him different, but it didn't matter

It was alleged that following one performance, a ripple of applause went around the crowd; evidently, somebody had thought this was all part of the band's repertoire. Just another solo item. Of course, this was quite understandable because there were occasions when the shaker emerged whilst the band was playing, when this happened Bert would shake in time to the music, carefully following the Bandmaster Harold's beat.

Knowing what was coming next in the programme, Bert would await a suitable march. Out of consideration and respect for the band, Bert would not begin his routine until the band had played the introduction to the march, and then at letter A, in rhythm to the music, Bert would shake away. Not that he had a favourite piece of music, but a good old-fashioned Salvation Army march certainly worked a treat.

The percussion section was not happy. Bert knew it was a mistake to make enemies in the 'kitchen department'! They felt that Bert took some of the glory away from them, rattling away on the side drum was no competition for Bert and his tin shaking. Bert considered himself a little musically aware, and so when it came to the bass solo in the march, he would, in sympathy to the music, cease shaking and await the final section of the march before commencing again.

Over the years Bert had developed a very fine art of finishing the march at exactly the right moment with a tremendous flourish, extending his arms as wide as they would go before bringing the applicator down to teeth level in a strong, precise movement.

Such was his reputation that the Bandmaster was once approached by a couple who requested that perhaps the Bandmaster would ensure that Bert was on the programme for the next band event. They had some friends visiting and felt that the sight of Bert was something that they would remember from their holiday, something to go back home and tell their friends.

"We were down in the area for a holiday," they would relate, "it was absolutely marvellous, the weather was perfect. We were particularly told to look out for one of the town's main tourist attractions. We were not disappointed. We witnessed the 'shaking bandsman'; it was magnificent the way that he handled a lookalike salt shaker, not part of his instrument — pure artistry. On the way back to our hotel we bought some fish and chips simply so that we could see if we could handle a salt shaker as well as Bert, although he was our inspiration I have a sense that we failed. We took a little clip of Bert on the mobile phone as a precious memory of that evening".

One day disaster befell Bert. With baritone on the floor in front of him and a good sized crowd, in his left hand his upper dentures, he reached into his inside pocket. A look of horror spread across his face, utter disbelief, quickly he tried his trouser pockets, patting himself down. But the truth had already registered on his face; his shaker was not to be found.

For years Bert had suffered from very ill-fitting dentures, they were his demob set. As with many things in his life, he put up with things how they were, non-Salvation Army teeth included. Ill-fitting teeth did nothing at all to improve Bert's playing ability, he was average and would always remain so. The way he played, the harder he blew, the looser his upper dentures became.

The solution was to deal with the matter in hand immediately. He needed to once again secure his teeth in their correct place. For Bert, the only teeth fixative was the tried and tested powder, powder which he carefully sprinkled on the upper set before, with a sense of dignity, he replaced them. Bert needed help.

To his rescue came a Mr Davies, a dental surgeon, who had recently opened a private dental practice within the town.

Mr Davies loved brass bands. If he came across a band playing in the street, in the pleasure gardens, or in the promenade bandstand he just had to stop and listen.

Not a player himself, there was an aspect of his profession which had a linkage with brass band players. Over a number of years Mr Davies had been working on and researching the effects of dentures being used by brass instrumentalists when playing. It was clear that here was a wide field of research, what could be done?

People often had two pairs of glasses, one for general use and another pair for reading. Mr Davies considered that there was a merit in applying the same principle to dentures. Dentures for general use and a separate set of dentures for when the user was playing a brass instrument. Mr Davies recognised that a different pressure was being exerted on false teeth when blowing through an instrument, apart from other factors and considerations.

Bert came to the attention of Mr Davies going through one of his performances one Sunday afternoon. Mr Davies standing nearby was fascinated by the teeth routine.

"I think I may be able to help you", said Mr Davies approaching Bert. Mr Davies explained who he was and invited Bert to visit him at his dental practice. Bert was to become a 'case study', written up in a number of dental journals, with graphic photographs of his teeth and mouth structure. Mr Davies was continually tweaking Bert's dentures until he felt that he had got them right and more importantly Bert was happy.

Bert was very grateful to Mr Davies, but there were unforeseen outcomes. Bert was now a minor town celebrity, he was stopped in the street and impertinent individuals would ask what set of teeth he had in today. Youngsters would shout at him in the street, "Show us your nashers!"

With quiet reserve, Bert, as he had done just about all of his life, accepted he would always be Mr Teeth.

Treasure Trove

(5)

IT was the beginning of the summer season of bandstand concerts. The bandstand was circular in design constructed of wrought iron with a cantilever canopy, it had been built on the town's wide promenade directly overlooking the sandy beach.

During the winter months, the council had redecorated and refurbished the bandstand which had been erected by public subscription to celebrate the Jubilee of Queen Victoria, in June 1887. Miraculously the structure had been overlooked during the second world war when wrought iron was collected to be turned into munitions.

It was a magnificent bandstand allowing the audience an elevated view of the band and other performers using the stage. Surrounding the bandstand on three sides were public seats, which had been dedicated in memory of various folk and organisations; supplementing the benches the council hired out deckchairs.

Seafarers Brass Band performed once a fortnight on a Sunday afternoon during the season. The Musical Director prepared a varied programme of music from traditional brass band marches to music from West End shows and music from the classics, drawing from a wide selection of music to entertain. Some of the dates coincided with national events and so the MD 'customised' the programme to suit the occasion.

The first June concert the band would celebrate both D-Day and Dunkirk with guest vocal soloists singing some of the wartime songs, with which the audience could join in heartily.

Seafarers Brass Band, like most bands, comprised of volunteers, men and women who just enjoyed getting together to play brass band music. Not being one of the top bands, Seafarers were always on the lookout for new players, and financially it was a struggle. Raising money to keep the band going exercised the mind of the band treasurer continuously, always thinking of ways to bring in additional funds. Each of the players paid an annual subscription; the band had a supporters' club, they also received an income from engagements, for example playing at fetes and garden parties.

Another source of income was the Christmas Carol playing programme, and whilst the council did not pay them to play in the bandstand, they were able to take up a collection, and folk could be quite generous. The council also made a grant in recognition of the band providing supporting music for Remembrance Sunday and other town events.

Once a quarter, the treasurer presented a financial review of just where the band stood to the committee. "We're doing OK", announced the treasurer, Neville Ireland at the January meeting. "Carol playing was good this year, in fact, we took more than last year's figure by over £200, the better weather helped us. We do need to bear in mind that what we have in the kitty has got to last us until the early summer months. As you know, to help bridge the gap, we begin to collect the band subs in April and we have to decide whether or not the subs remain at last year's figure or should we make a small increase".

The band secretary said, "At the moment the subs are £15.00 per year and if I recall it was the same amount the previous year. I really do feel that we can justify a small increase, perhaps taking it up to say £17.50 per year, that is still not a lot of money when you consider what some people pay for a gym membership and to be a member of the golf club".

"I tend to agree", said the Musical Director, Andrew, "Neville just remind us of some of our expenditure". "Well, of course, there is the hire of the rehearsal room, there is always an annual increase in the hire fee, we have to insure instruments and music, once again we can expect an increase in the premium. Fortunately, quite a number of the bandsman own their instruments although we have always paid for any repairs. The deputy Musical Director and I had a look at the instruments that the band own, and quite frankly many of them are in a very bad state. Had we the money we would replace them, perhaps not with brand-new instruments but much better second-hand ones. It's strange, but most cornet, trombone and euphonium players have their own instruments, not so many tenor horn players but you don't often come across a baritone or bass player owning their instrument."

"At the moment we are doing quite well and subject to no disasters we should get through the year and, as in previous years, a small surplus of income over expenditure", reported the treasurer. "Of course, it would help if we could attract a major sponsor, we really could do with a new set of Fisherman's Guernseys, a number of the Guernsey sweaters have seen several wearers. I know other bands have jackets, but because of our nautical connection we have always worn Fisherman's Guernseys as our uniform. A new traditional original Guernsey can cost over £80.00", observed the treasurer, "I can't keep asking Mrs Ferbrache to darn the holes much longer".

The summer season commencing the Seafarers Band began playing in the bandstand, it wasn't long before seat benches, and the deckchairs were occupied by both locals and visitors. It was perfect weather for giving an outdoor band concert, lovely sunshine, tempered with a cooling breeze, ideal playing conditions.

"Good afternoon, ladies and gentlemen, what a glorious sunny afternoon and welcome to the first of this year's season of bandstand concerts, which we hope you will enjoy. We've got a varied programme of music to entertain you", introduced Andrew. "Do we have any Canadian friends with us? Well just to make you feel a bit homesick we're going to play, as our first item, a very popular Salvation Army march entitled *Montréal Citadel*". Clearly there were some in the audience, perhaps Canadians, who applauded loudly at the end of the march.

"We might not be able to go to West End theatre this afternoon, so we're bringing the theatre to you. For a second item, we have a selection of melodies from various West End shows so if you know the words, please help the band and sing along".

"Time for us to go on our musical travels again. The Swiss are not famed for their brass bands. But for anyone who has visited that delightful country here is a collection of Swiss folk tunes. Now, you can join the band for this item, so can I hear you yodelling?", invited the MD. Whereupon he began encouraging the audience to yodel. "When I give the instruction to yodel, let's give it all you've got. If it helps you can take your false teeth out and hand them to the band secretary for safekeeping".

"Before we conclude with a march and the national anthem, we are going to play you *'Jerusalem'* the anthem of the Women's Institute. We have room on the bandstand to enable WI ladies to sing along with the band. Any Institute ladies out there, perhaps a soloist?", encouraged the MD.

"It was a good crowd this afternoon for the first concert of the season", remarked Joe the principal euphonium player, "I thought my *Carnival of Venice* solo was a success, up to my usual high standard". "I thought the band played moderately well for a first outing, a bit rusty in places, but overall a good performance, I was well satisfied", said Andrew. "That 'old bird' certainly really sang *'Jerusalem'* well, gave it all she had, she was belting it out towards the end, went a bit red in the face with a final note", said a disrespectful Jeremy, one of the younger cornet players who received a playful 'clip' around the ear from his father. "You wait until we get home and I tell your mother", threatened Jeremy's father.

"I noticed one or two familiar faces in the audience, local people who seem to make their way down to the seafront. I'll tell you who was there, that elderly gentleman who always likes to get one of the bench seats, he props himself at the end of the seat with the armrest", observed Neville, "He's always very generous when the collecting box goes around, I saw him pop a fiver in at the last concert. I really must go over and say hello to him. I don't know if any of you know who he is?"

At the next bandstand concert, the elderly gentleman was in his usual place. There was a slight chill in the air, he was wearing a military camel double-breasted overcoat, with epaulettes, trilby hat, grey flannel trousers and brown shoes, highly polished. "Good afternoon", said Neville approaching the gentleman, "I've noticed you before, you seem to be at just about all of our bandstand concerts". "Indeed, I do, I have my Sunday lunch at the Conservative Club and then take a gentle stroll along the promenade to the bandstand. I always like to get here early so I can get a seat on one of the benches, corner position if possible", the elderly gentleman replied.

"You enjoy the band? What do you like the most marches or the more modern West End shows stuff?", enquired Neville. "I enjoy all music, but I prefer the sound of a military band over a brass band, I think the woodwind adds something which the total brass is lacking", said the old gent. "As I'm walking along the promenade, I often have march melodies playing in my mind, of course, these days they have to go much slower, they need to keep up with my legs", he joked. "I will ask the Musical Director to slow down the speed on the opening march, get the band to play it more sedately, just for you", offered Neville.

"I notice you usually play marches from The Salvation Army repertoire, why is that?", the gentleman asked squinting into the sun, which was getting a bit stronger with the clouds moving away. "To be honest, Sally Army marches are just about the best. There are so many really cracking ones, with different degrees of difficulties. I think most Salvation Army marches simply play themselves. A number of players in the band are members of the Salvation Army and play with the local SA band as well as the Seafarers Band", said Neville.

"I also noticed that some of your instruments are beginning to show a bit of age. A couple of those basses have more dents than I had in my old car, and the music stands are quite an assortment. I suppose running a band is a bit demanding financially".

Captain Herbert Cornwall Stanwick MBE, named after the county of his birth, had completed more than thirty years of military service. For most of that time he had been stationed with one of the minor regiments and had been appointed Assistant Director of Music with British Forces Germany (BFG). As band number two much of his duties where administrative and occasions to conduct the band were limited. He had written two or three military band pieces of his own and had arranged and scored some other pieces.

While in Germany he had married a local girl. Tragically in very much less than a year, he was a widower. His wife, Greta, was killed in a climbing accident. Herbert never married again, as with so many the army became his life. In retirement, he had taken up residence in sheltered accommodation for retired military officers.

Over the course of Sunday afternoon bandstands, other members of the band got to know Captain Stanwick. "What have you on the programme this afternoon?", he would ask, "So we are to be treated to a bit of Mozart and Handel". By now the band were very fond of their Captain Stanwick, he was like their mascot at each concert. Young second cornet Jeremy, wanting to make amends for being so nasty about the lady who sang Jerusalem, asked a couple who were sitting in Captain Standice seat, "Would they mind moving to make way for the old gentleman because it was his normal seat. He has a regular booking!".

Somehow the band got to know that during the week it had been Captain Standwick's 85th birthday. "I've arranged for the confectioners in the High Street to make a special birthday cake for him, and they're going to decorate it with musical symbols and three pips for being a captain", the band secretary told the Musical Director.

On the following Sunday afternoon, there was Captain Stanwick in his place awaiting the band concert. The weather was so much warmer that he was able to leave off his military overcoat and sat there in his smart blazer, still with grey flannels and highly polished brown shoes, even the trilby hat had been given a day off.

Once again, Andrew was the compere. Just about halfway through, Andrew announced, "During the week we have had a very special birthday. Celebrating his 85th birthday is our very good friend Captain Herbert Stanwick". Leaving the bandstand, Andrew went down to the captain, shaking him by the hand and led him up the steps onto the bandstand. Immediately the band struck up Happy Birthday. Quick off the mark, the audience picked up the refrain, 'Happy Birthday to You, Happy Birthday to You, Happy Birthday Captain Stanwick, Happy Birthday to You'. A beaming Herbert acknowledged the clapping and good wishes of the audience.

He was about to leave the bandstand, Andrew gently needing to pull him back, when from the wings two young ladies from the tenor horn section came forward with a birthday cake and kissed him on his cheeks. Andrew told the audience, "Captain Stanwick has been a great supporter of this band, attends every single bandstand concert that he possibly can. The band knows that when Captain Stanwick is in the audience, they have got to play their very best".

"Captain Stanwick was for many years attached to the military bands, so he knows full well when the trombones are making a mess of it". Turning to Captain Stanwick, Andrew said, "Captain Herbert Stanwick MBE would you do the Seafarers Band the great honour of conducting them in a march you must have conducted many times over your years of service, the March of the Royal British Legion".

Captain Herbert straightened his back, turned towards the band and with a baton in his right hand, pointed to the percussion section to begin the march. Behind him, the audience began to stand, other joined them, and before the march was less than halfway through, clapping in time to the rhythm broke out.

Finishing the march with a flourish Captain Stanwick placed the baton on the rostrum, turned around, with tears running down his cheeks smartly gave a salute. With that final tribute to

Captain Stanwick, the summer season series of bandstand concerts concluded.

Browning, Curtis and Browning

Band Treasurer
Seafarers Band

Dear Sir,

Captain Herbert Cornwall Stanwick MBE

As executor, it is my sad duty to inform you of the death of Captain Herbert Cornwall Stanwick MBE, late of British Forces Germany (BFG) and more lately of the Seaview Retirement Home for Military Officers and Gentlemen.

Captain Stanwick died on Saturday, September 15th, 2018. Captain Stanwick died without any living relative.

We were instructed to act according to his wishes. In his last will and testament, Captain Stanwick made a Specific Legacy in respect of the Seafarers Band, of which you are a named trustee. The bequest is that the Stanwick Collection of Walking Sticks be used in the best interest of the Seafarers Band.

I am Sir,

David Browning,

Solicitor.

Herbert Stanwick was an acknowledged expert on walking sticks. He had written a number of reference books on the subject and had acquired a significant collection of walking sticks. His field of expertise was in the gadget walking stick and canes. These might hide a weapon like a sword or a gun; canes could also conceal cigarettes, a pipe, smelling salts, or makeup. Other canes contained useful tools like microscopes, barometers, horse measures, and fishing poles.

During his period of service in Germany it gave him the opportunity to buy walking sticks and canes not only from Germany but when he travelled to other European countries. In his army quarters he had a display of sticks, they were to be found in just about every room in the house. Herbert also had made custom-built storage boxes a bit like ammunition boxes. The collection was collated not by country but by the additional purpose of the stick. Over the period of time he had amassed quite a number where the handle became a telescope, and so all those walking sticks were stored in the appropriate box and labelled.

In retirement he had found himself speaking to various groups, giving a talk on his passion. The Rotary Club and Probus got him back on a number of occasions. Antique Clubs also found him a very acceptable speaker. He even did one season as a speaker on cruise ships. He made a couple of appearances on television when the topic was Victorian walking sticks. Because of his expert knowledge he was often asked to give valuations. "Tonight, giving us what will certainly be an interesting talk, is Mr Stanwick or perhaps he should be referred to as Mr Cane. Please welcome Mr Stanwick". Talk over, then came questions from the audience, ever ready for the old favourite. "Did you ever get the cane at school, and was that when your interest in canes first began?"

Altogether Herbert Stanwick had a collection of more than 190 sticks and canes. Each had been well recorded, the day and the place from which they were purchased, the cost and Stanwick's estimate of what the item was worth. The advice from Mr Browning was that the entire collection should go to a London auction house, he felt that the sticks and canes would attract interest worldwide.

A London auction house was very interested and agreed that

they would act as auctioneers on behalf of the band. "Our estimate, having looked at Stanwick's catalogue, is that they should realise, after commission fees et cetera, something in the order of £9,000. I know that Stanwick has put a higher figure than that on his collection, but it is the fact that most people think what they have is worth more than it actually is", noted the expert.

The band committee travelled up to London to attend the auction. Excitedly they listened as each lot was called, sometimes an individual cane, other lots were comprised of walking sticks grouped together. The band treasurer found it impossible to keep a running order of the auction total. Up the bidding went with some items being sold at the top end of the estimates and above, one very ornate 18ct gold-topped, banded cane, with provenance linking it to a minor English Royal sailed past £1,000.

There was one walking stick which did not go to auction. The committee retained the walking stick. It was the walking stick Captain Stanwick used on his walk from his home to the bandstand. A special cabinet was made to display his walking stick, certainly not the most valuable but the most personal.

Following the auction, the band committee met. They were all of one mind. The Seafarers Band would, in honour of Herbert Stanwick be renamed, The Captain Stanwick Band. From the proceeds of the sale was purchased a new set of jackets. A crest was designed to be displayed on the jacket breast pocket depicting crossed walking stick and cane!

The council agreed to a new promenade seat close to the bandstand. A single person high-backed seat with arms. The Captain Stanwick Chair!

Flugel Horn
Faye

(6)

FAYE always wanted to play in a brass band, as long as she could remember that desire was always there. She wanted to follow the example of her father, who for many years had been a bandsman, playing in the local village band. What dad played Faye wanted to play, and her dad played the flugel horn.

"The flugel horn is the finest instrument in the band", maintained her father. If that was good enough for the family patriarch, then it was certainly fine by Faye.

Her father, Philip, had been born during the first world war, in a small Cornish village, remote and isolated from the struggles of the conflict. The family owned the only shop in the village, a shop which sold just about everything and anything, meeting the demands of villagers, with wartime shortages always a challenge. The Post Office and combined grocer/hardware store sustained the village community.

In 1934, upon the death of his father, Philip took over the running of the village store. Two years later, Faye was born. In September 1939 a declaration of war was announced. Philip should have been conscripted into the forces but a serious road accident had made him unfit for military service. "We will do all we can to help the war effort on the home front", he told his wife.

To compliment the village store was the one and only village pub, peculiarly named *'The Brass Band Inn'*. "I'm off to band practice", Philip would call out to his wife, it sounded a bit more cultured for people listening in the shop, than, "I'm off to the pub!". But Philip wasn't kidding anybody. Actually, both were correct, because the village band held their rehearsal in the bowling alley of the Brass Band Inn, a happy and satisfying congenial arrangement.

It was difficult to keep the band going during the war period, practices became a little irregular, but Philip as a member of the band, was doing all he could to maintain the village tradition. The changed circumstances involved alterations within the band, and to maintain a balance, bandsmen (for in those days females never played in a brass band), had to move around a bit. One week bass, the next baritone.

The band was not as big, numerically, as pre-war. Roger, who played euphonium, had quickly volunteered and joined the Royal Air Force as ground crew. One of the solo cornets, William, had enlisted into the Duke of Cornwall Light Infantry. In July 1944 the village was to receive the news that William had been killed in Normandy in the battle to capture the French town of Caen. Where previously there had been three tenor horn players, the band was now reduced to one. Although the loss of the drummer was not considered dramatic, not every band part could be covered.

In many ways, the war had very little effect on the village. Some of the village girls joined the Land Army, the village being surrounded by farming land. Occasionally a military vehicle might drive through the village and stop for refreshments in the Brass Band Inn. Such occurrences were very rare; the village was on the road to nowhere.

In 1945, the war ending, village 'worthies' planned a street party, bunting and band were demanded. "This will be the best party the village has seen. Every villager is invited to the celebrations to be held in the Market Square; folk are asked to share, we'll beg the ladies to make cakes and sandwiches, jelly for the children and using our ration coupons we'll have a communal 'knees-up'. We must do something really 'top table' to celebrate the end of the war in Europe," said the Chairman of the Parish Council.

And so the village people set about organising the celebrations with vigour and enthusiasm. On the Victory Celebration Day in early August, the day was blessed by summer sun. Sunshine promised by the Chairman. The Market Square was heaving with euphoric people, dancing and singing. The war was over, and it was time to have a party, even though the Council Chairman insisted on making a speech, which seemed to go for ever.

Later it was long argued that the Chairman failed to finish his dissertation because the band suddenly struck up, and played, *God, bless the Prince of Wales*. Being born north of the border, the Chairman was offended. The village band was central to the festivities, so much depended on them. They borrowed a couple of players from a nearby town to supplement the seventeen players they had. Music was a little limited; not all the band parts could be found.

The Salvation Army Band, just up the road, agreed to loan the village band their tune books for the day, provided they were back by Sunday.

The band secretary managed to locate the wicker basket, stored for the duration in the loft of the bowling alley, which contained the band's red showman tunics. The tunics were, 'hook and eye', a bit like ladies corsets. Stand-up collars were the order of the day, tunics fully decorated with braid, and lion tamer stripes, not the best for playing in on a hot summer's day. It was noticed that not every bandsman had a fitting uniform; some jackets were looking decidedly slack on their wearers.

Whilst rummaging around in the wicker basket, the band secretary felt something solid, tubular, it was going to be an instrument. Mixed in amongst the uniforms was the band's flugel horn. Last time that instrument had seen the light of day was a couple of years before the outbreak of the Second World War.

The flugel horn had been purchased by the band, as the inscription on the bell noted, "In memory of Jeremiah Pengelly - He blew to the end - 1864 to 1934".

One of the slides was determined not to be pulled out, and the valves had decided, amongst themselves, that without suitable lubrication they were going to remain passive, unmoved even by world events. "A good bit of spit will soon get those valves moving again", ventured the band secretary'. So it proved to be the case. (Valve oil was considered only to be used by 'softies').

Chairs from the Village Hall were purloined and arranged in band formation in the bandstand situated in the centre of the Market Square. The village programme included dancers from the Tap Step School of Dancing, organised by the matronly Miss Dorothy Monmouth, hair in a bun, dress length to the floor, pince-nez glasses suspended from a ribbon, late of London and Cheltenham, and now retired to the village.

A wind-up 78rmp gramophone had been found to assist the dancing; the records were old and worn, the scratching of the gramophone needle was audible above the music. One of the scouts was delegated to keep the gramphone wound-up.

The Vicar was at odds with the choir; he had a rebellion on his hands, the Reverend Bertrand wanted the choir to sing *Jerusalem* with members of the Women's Institute, the boys in the choir had elected to 'belt out' *Boogie Woogie Bugle Boy*. Bill, in the bass section, always one to run a 'book', was giving odds of 2 to 1 on the choirboys and 20 to 1 on the Vicar. Bill's boy, Arthur, sang in the choir and Bill had inside information. That Bill encouraged the rebellion was never in doubt. "I'll give what I make to the band fund", announced a pious tuba player.

The afternoon would be nothing but a great success. As and when required the band filled in with suitable music. The landlord of the Brass Band Inn, never one to appreciate band music, but having a sense of occasion, and wanting to do the right thing plied the band with a round of drinks. Calling everyone to attention, the parish clerk announced the singing of the *National Anthem, 'God Save the King'* to conclude the event. Playing his father's flugel horn was Philip Pengelly.

At the back of the store, a day or two before, he'd found a half-used can of 'silvo' polish, and a new yellow duster taken from stock, with newspaper carefully covering the kitchen table Philip had given the flugel horn a bit of a refurb. He ran a goodly amount of water through the instrument using the tap in the backyard, splashing his trousers and shoes in the process. With a bit of persuasion, one by one, the valves were removed from their casing. Years of neglect was evident, but Phil soon had them in playable order. Watching his every move was his daughter Faye.

During the afternoon festivities, Faye had positioned herself immediately behind her father, resting on the back of his chair, she scrutinised everything he did. Not only did she love the look of the flugel horn, but the sound was just magic. Not for her the shrieking cornet, or the overloud euphonium, and she considered the tenor horn not 'showy-off' enough. She looked at the length of her arms and immediately dismissed the trombone. It was the flugel horn then and would always be the flugel horn. The flugel horn was ladylike, genteel; it had social graces, you could take and play a flugel horn anywhere, from pub to palace, a flugel horn would always be welcome. It was the high society of the band.

Perhaps that day was the turning point in the band's history. Faye, now a little older pestered her father to teach her to play an instrument, it had to be the flugel horn. "You know that we don't have women in the band", said her father. "Well don't you think it's time you did," his daughter replied sharply. Faye was an apt student, fingering presented no problem at all, she studied the rudiments of music, Faye was well versed with the construction of scales, she knew what a tetrachord was, minor and major keys were second nature to her.

The pressure was mounting on the band committee to allow her to join the band. It was argued that she could play very well indeed, above standard. Dwindling band numbers forced the issue.

With one or two coughs and splutters from the 'old school' members of the band, Faye attended her first band rehearsal. Her father, with due ceremony, presented the family crested flugel horn to Faye.

Two things were later to coincide. The first was that Faye was awarded a university place. It meant leaving the village. Everyone said Faye would be the first village child to go to university. "It might not be Oxford or Cambridge, but Bristol has a very fine university," Mrs Pengelly was anxious to tell her customers. Mrs

Pengelly knew, all but for a few visits, Faye, now twenty, had left home.

Matters were also becoming critical for the band. Numbers were dropping to an exceptionally low level. Engagements were getting more difficult to fulfill, and they were not as plentiful as previously. The band still managed to accompany the hymns on Remembrance Sunday; Tom still sounded last post and reveille as he had done for many years, at one time it was a perfect note rendition, but with the passing of years that top G was a struggle, one or two 'duff' notes crept in. Tom admitted he was well past his best, his playing days were over, and indeed so were the band's.

A change of landlord at the Brass Band Inn hastened matters. Holidaymakers were finding the village, "Isn't it quaint?", they expressed. And for the first time in the entire history of the village, there were postcards of the Market Square with the bandstand in the background, delightful shots of the little stream which meandered through the village. The Parish Church with its Norman tower featured. There was talk within the Parish Council of the need to create a car park.

The bowling alley at the pub, now renamed and rebranded as the Cornish Cutlery had been converted into a multi seated café/restaurant, with take-away option. Decorated in a nautical style, sails and rigging hanging from the roof beams, anchors and ships bells attached to the walls. The staff were attired in little sailor uniforms topped off with straw brimmed hats. Planning permission was needed for the voluptuous mermaid figure-head which looked down on patrons as they entered the eatery. The Vicar declined to give his blessing at the opening.

The village band was now homeless and also out of money. Instruments needed repairing; the blacksmith did what he could, he could only solder and patch so much. Committee decided the instruments were a little more than scrap. The unanimous decision of the committee was to hold one valedictory concert in the bandstand before disbanding.

Mustering as many players as they could, a Sunday

afternoon final concert was advertised. Invitations went out to former players asking if they would like to come and have a final blow with the band. Faye responded, and drove down from Frome in Somerset where she then lived. She still loved her banding and had joined the Lees Lane Silver Band in the town.

The Truro Metalworks Company came down to the village to have a look at what was the remnant of the instruments. "It's a sad day", said Mr Benson from the company. There was no sincerity in his voice. It was what you said on such occasions. "Let's see what we've got here then - there's not much call for brass instruments these days. Everybody wants a guitar and a skiffle board", he said seeking to ease the pain.

Mr Benson, without much feeling took the lot, throwing instrument after instrument onto the vehicle."It will be scrap!", and with that, nearly one hundred years of banding disappeared on the back of the Truro Metalworks Company lorry.

During one visit back home, Miss Pengelly, referred back to the days of the village band. In reminiscing, she asked her father if he knew what had befallen the Pengelly flugel horn. "I'm sorry to say it went with the other instruments to Truro. We were away at the time, on an extended holiday. When we arrived back in the village we discovered the fate of the flugel horn. By then it was too late. We later found the old wooden instrument carrying case, and if you would like that you're very welcome to it".

At her home in Frome, Faye tried to make a feature of the instrument case, it was nicely tampered, lined with purple velvet, frayed in places, with a solid brass military flush chest handle, and a bonded keyhole. Its stood in the fireplace; it was for her a reminder of things she treasured. With the missing flugel horn, Faye felt she had lost part of her family heritage, made all the more painful because of retirement and advancing years.

Glancing through the local newspaper her eyes were drawn to the announcement of a Bank Holiday Monday Car Boot Sale in Bradford-upon-Avon. Sellers pitch £10.00, buyers car parking £2.00. That might be fun she thought, strolling around from pitch to pitch, seeing what people no longer wanted.

On the day the weather was damp, rainy and completely overcast. Did she forget the car boot sale and settle for a quiet day in, finishing her current library book and watching a few pointless bits of television? The adverts had said over 130 traders, a play area for the children, a burger van and a pop-up café. She had loads of stuff she could take to a car boot sale and certainly didn't want to bring anything back.

She searched for the newspaper and re-read the advertisement. She spotted something she had missed the first time reading through, a school band was promoted to play for an hour commencing at 2.00pm. Youngsters needed encouragement and support and so she would go.

Parked up, as she opened the car door she could hear the sound of the band; they were playing something she recognised from one of the musical shows by Andrew Lloyd Webber, *Any Dream Will Do*. With quickening step, ignoring the sales pitches, she hurried towards the band. A family of two adults and two youngsters were heading towards her the children jumping about, getting underneath their parent's feet.

Faye stopped, and stepped to one side to let them pass. Her heart missed a beat, she looked down and just within a couple of paces, on a pitch, tarpaulin partially covered up by a pair of faded curtains, was the 'crook' end of a silver brass instrument! The shape she recognised at once, it could only be a flugel horn. Bending down, she picked up the instrument. The first obvious thing was that the mouthpiece was missing, and the screw from the tuning shank had disappeared. Two valve cap tops were lacking, as was one of the bottom valve casing covers. Dents, there were aplenty.

"Where did you get this from?" she enquired of the seller. "I clear out houses which is where I get some of this stuff". "And the instrument?" "To be honest with you, I think it came originally from a metal scrap merchant down in the West Country - thought it might make a bob to two". "How much do you want for it?", an edge creeping into her voice. "It's yours - if your name is Pengelly and in your family you have a Jeremiah."

Conductor's Cunning Plan

(7)

THE postman walked up the drive, rang the doorbell, in his hand he had a large, weighty registered package. The label was marked Anniversary Brass Band Championships. Stan opened the door and extended his hand to take the parcel. "Good morning Stan. I think this might be what you're waiting for", offered the postman. "Indeed so. I hope you haven't had a little sneak look?" replied Stan, "You will have to wait until band rehearsal to know what the test piece is and how difficult. Meet up with you later". Over the postman's shoulder Stan could see coming up the drive was Pauline, one of the band's tenor horn players and the band librarian.

Stan ushered her in, extending a 'Good morning', ripping open the parcel as he walked up the passageway to his living room. "Make yourself a coffee and one for me", Stan instructed Pauline, "Well, the waiting is over. What have they come up with this year?", asked Pauline. "In a moment or two we will know the answer to that question", replied Stan.

On to the coffee table, Stan dropped the full score and the band parts. Pauline shuffled through the individual copies looking for the first horn music. "Well that's an interesting title, a bit more challenging than what they came up with last year", said Pauline. "I never understood what 'Opus for Tubes' was all about".

Stan considered the Full Score cover. "It would be helpful if composers tried to dovetail the title of a piece with the musical content", remarked Stan. "Do you remember the year we had, 'Vignette for Moving Valves'. More than half the band couldn't pronounce 'vignette', and the trombones maintained they had never heard of valves!".

Stan was the Musical Director of the town band, and had

been for a good many years, a good band trainer. Whilst Stan might have dreamt of a Royal Albert Hall appearance in the National Championships, that was beyond the capabilities of the band. His band could never compare with any of the top premiere bands. For Imperial Infirmary Band, they might get to sit in the Royal Albert Hall but never have the honour of playing on the stage. But every year they hoped.

Like many towns, in Victorian days, people who were ill and poorly became patients in an infirmary. The use of the word imperial was in recognition of the great Imperial Empire over which Queen Victoria reigned. In 1888 the foundation stone of the Imperial Infirmary was laid, a small brass band made up of infirmary porters supporting the unveiling. The Imperial Infirmary Band quickly followed, commenced from that small group of infirmary porters. The early records of the band indicate that for a few years the band's title was the Porters Band. But by the turn of the century, the band became the Imperial Infirmary Band. Newspaper cuttings of the time reported that, in the view of the band committee, the name Porters was restrictive and prevented other sections of the infirmary like ambulance drivers and kitchen staff from joining.

Sometimes, looking around the band personnel in front of him, it was difficult for Stan not to come to the conclusion that many in the band were musically infirm. How many more times did you have to tell the band when they saw *ppp* underneath the bar it meant to play very softly. The baritones could be merciless in respect of dynamics. A fortune could be saved in printers ink if only they printed the music without dynamic marks, thought Stan.

Reg, a member of the offending baritone section, advocated the proposition that dynamic marks were there purely as a suggestion, they were not mandatory like traffic lights. "It's all a matter of interpretation, the Musical Director thinks one way and thinks he knows best, but I've got every right to make my own mind up. Anyway, why should the MD always decide either *f* or *fff* and things like that? What we need is democracy in this band, we should be able to vote on dynamic marks", stated Reg.

Reg for many years had been a trade union official and, although now retired, sometimes his former union role crept in. Reg knew the band's rulebook inside out and what he didn't know he would make up.

Looking at Pauline, Stan took a sip of coffee and said, "This year we are going to be playing a piece entitled, '*Stratosphere*'. I have never heard of this composer before, Zulfeker Pogrebnyakov", Stan could not pronounce the name and pointed it out to Pauline, "evidently he, I say he, could be female, comes from an East European country. The programme notes say, he or she will bring a flavour of traditional East European folk music to the concert hall through brass", noted Stan opening the pages of the full score.

From anticipation and excitement, Stan's demeanour changed to horror and disbelief. The piece began with a cornet and trombone full-blown fanfare feature which extended for sixty-four bars! The dynamic marking was all that the baritone section could have desired. The soprano and solo cornets were asked to commence with top C, remaining up there for sixty-four bars of sustained, tongue killing notation. Meanwhile, the trombones were required, continuously to glissando through thirty-two bars. The programme notes helpfully suggested that the opening bars musically represented the taking off of a rocket, stages one and two, ascending into the stratosphere, hence the imaginative title of the test piece.

"I've been looking at my 1st horn part, and it seems I've got to sit there, doing my makeup, whilst either side of me I've got the Blastaway Battalions thumping about for sixty-four bars!", moaned Pauline. "I think it gets a bit better", a pacifying Stan retorted, "the more sedate middle section looks much easier on the ear. Once en-circling the earth the astronauts have a longing for home, it is suggested they break out singing folk songs which is reflected in the music, played entirely in a minor key, although the basses will not be happy, it appears that Pogrebnyakov", again Stan stumbled with the name, "let's just call him 'Pog', requires the basses to play nothing more than a pedal note, to break the monotony from time to time he scores in a couple of quavers for a crotchet. The bass drum has a single tap on the first beat of the bar".

The band gathered for the Thursday evening rehearsal, knowing that the MD would bring the test piece with him and all were keen to see their band parts. The band librarian, Pauline, with raised eyebrows, making funny faces, passed Pogrebnyakov's test piece around the band. Whilst the players considered and studied their part, Stan introduced the music. "This piece is definitely different. One or two tricky bits, but then the composer, 'Pog' has to test us, that's why it is called a test piece. I've studied the score very carefully, it is a challenge, but I am sure it is one we can meet". At this point, the MD was sounding very unconvincing even to himself.

Already dissension was building within the band. The postman who was principal trombone picked the sheet off the stand to examine it more closely. "I want danger money if I'm expected to play this musical mess. I'd sooner be bitten by a dog then try all those glissandos, that's one too many for me, and to think I actually delivered this stuff to you!"

By now, the basses were looking at the quiet passage. "What is all this crotchet after crotchet followed by crotchet, is this a one-note composer?" moaned the Eb tuba player supported by his colleagues. Get ready thought Stan, any minute Adrian on the euphonium is going to chip in, he was not disappointed. "I've got musical diarrhoea. Any more runs and I will be playing my part in the toilet, of course behind a locked door", joked Adrian, after a quick laugh.

"Look we really must give this piece of music a run-through, you just can't dismiss it by looking at it. I'm sure as we get going, it will be one of those pieces of music which at the beginning was grim but ended up as a masterpiece", pleaded Pauline supporting the Musical Director. The principal cornet player speaking, he felt on behalf of the entire cornet section, pleaded, "This introduction is nigh on impossible, it's not the top C, it's what the composer wants to do with it when we are up there that presents the problem. The adjudicators will expect us to represent music just as a composer intended, I'll give it a go and so will the entire cornet section, but this is the brass banding equivalent of Chinese or should I say East European water torture".

Meanwhile, the trombones decided to practice glissandos, not the ones written by the composer, but glissandos of their own. One of them scraping the slide up-and-down might have been tolerable, but with all three, the sound just accentuated how problematic the test piece was.

The Musical Director was all for accepting defeat, "Perhaps it would be better if we didn't enter the Anniversary Championships this year", suggested the MD. "We don't want to go to Bournemouth just to make a complete fool of ourselves in front of the other bands". By now one of the front row cornets, taking a wrong turning, had found his way up to a top C. With foolhardy ambition, he tried the opening bars of the piece, though a noble effort it came far short of what was expected. He quickly got tongue-tied, and his top C slipped down to a G. The exercise produced a letterbox red face. "Can't be done!", he whispered exhausted, trying to regain his breath. But he did get a round of applause, not for his performance but for his musical courage.

Soprano, with a reputation to maintain, was the next up, he blew his instrument through three or four times, his left hand covering the bell end, did some shoulder shaking exercises, flexed his arms, gripped the soprano, wiggled the valves, all this as part of his big build-up. He reckoned the previous attemptee had got to about bar twenty. He thought the attempt was pretty poor; he would consider himself a very disappointing soprano cornet player if he could not manage at least twice as many bars. He also considered cornet player number one was lacking in volume - time for a bit of musical welly.

He hit the note top G, the equivalent of top C full on. Principal cornet sitting in front received the note like the condemned prisoner being told that the executioner was now very much better and they could meet in about half an hour if that was convenient. Adrian on euphonium had already decided what he was going to do, he began counting the bars as Sop played, "One, two, three, four, five, six, seven, eight", counting bars suddenly became a united band activity. The side drummer added a tap to the counting. By bar twenty-six the soprano player could go no longer, he ended by blowing an embarrassing raspberry.

Thinking of his position, the principal cornet player had no option but to enter the fray as number three. Whilst the other two had set out thinking that perhaps it might be done, the principal decided he was going to prove beyond a musical shadow of a doubt that no cornet player was able to last all sixty-four bars. The band noticing they had another entrant in the competition decided to give him some encouragement, mild clapping went around the band. Finally, after a struggle principal, overcome by nerves, managed to pitch an uncertain top C. Now began the difficult bit, the notation was a killer, either that or cornetist suicide, he didn't need the rest of the band to count the bars he was already counting them in his head, whilst at the same time giving full concentration to the opening bars of the Stratosphere. Actually, the Principal cornet player surprised himself and, in fairness, the rest of the band, not only did he pass number one and sail ahead of the soprano player he also managed a couple of bars more. Thinking that he had done enough, he relaxed, and took the applause as if he had just played 'Golden Slippers'.

Fearful that the trombones might have a go at their glissandos routine, and mindful that Pauline had indicated she would do her makeup, Stan decided to commence the piece from bar 65. "Right ladies and gentlemen I think we've had enough fun and games, time to get down to the serious business, let's see what we can make of this piece by our East European friend".

"Evidently, the East Europeans love to march, lots of swinging of arms, parading up and down on special days and not so special days. At bar 65 the composer introduces a well-known East European march melody, this is to inspire and encourage the astronauts, it's music to lift their spirits. The percussion section leads the way, just for four bars, then the horns introduce the melody".

Drums abeating the 'kitchen department' drummed out a frenzied rhythm, the first beat of the bar demanding clashed cymbals. "Yes, I think that will be fine and we don't need to suffer . . . I mean to go through it a second time", announced Stan, stopping the band. "They like a bit of drumming in Europe", offered Adrian, "I nearly went there once on holiday, but I didn't much like the sound of their food, mainly because I couldn't pronounce it!" Pauline, and her two tenor horn companions, were poised ready for what they took to be their highpoint in the anniversary test piece. Following the first run-through, Stan commented, "I think the horns need to project themselves more and the rest of the band, please play more sympathetically, and I'm looking at you baritones". The march tune theme was now taken up by the euphoniums, with a 'side order' of off the beat by the trombones and baritones. Pausing the band Stan observed, "I think it's going quite well, I know we will need to work a bit on the opening 64 bars, but quite frankly I'm quite encouraged".

The folk tunes section in the minor key ran through with wrong notes here and there. Stan asserted, "Some of you need to go back to basics and revisit your fingering".

The final section of 'Stratosphere' was brisk and lively, and would present no problems for most competent bands. The cornets concluding with a cut down version of the opening fanfare. The composer in the grand finale had left the trombones in a completing chord mood, long semi-brieves. Euphonium had a run of ticky triplets which jumped around all over the place, "I must represent a bumpy landing", suggested Adrian.

"Time for a cup of tea and then we will tackle the opening", said Stan resting his baton on the conductor's stand.

The tea break quickly developed into a moan and groan session. Shop steward Reg was leading the moans and encouraging the groans. Sounding forth, he bellowed, "This composer chap. They're all a bit strings and woodwind over there. Comrades I know relationships with our European cousins are to be welcomed, and in the right place under the right circumstances, I encourage it and support it, but not in the venerated world of brass banding. Brothers and sisters, I believe that this imposition composition calls for, and demands immediate aggressive action. I am asking solidarity in this matter. We will put our case to the Musical Director. I will certainly make him aware of our concerns and that unless these are met forth-with, it is our intention to restrict our musical labour. I shall be calling for a band vote".

With that, Reg headed towards the Musical Director. Reg couldn't on the spur of the moment think of what he was going to demand. The band could hardly go on strike; they could not demand better working conditions; they could hardly lobby for reduced hours. He needed to think fast. Chocolate biscuits instead of boring rich tea biscuits for a tea break that would be his demand.

Heading off Reg, Stan shouted across the room, "Right now everybody let's get back to rehearsal and have a go at the introduction. If we can make some headway with that, the piece might 'come together'". "Sailing right in the face of a gale, the man is musically, optimistically deluded", said Adrian.

"Two elements to this introduction one is a high note and the second is the notation. Let's deal with the first one, I suggest that we go for middle C for rehearsal and concentrate on the notation, are we all agreed?", asked the MD. One or two run-throughs and the cornet section was showing improvement, the pace was pedestrian, but they did get the notes in. "Now I know that we need to play an octave higher and we need to get near the metronome speed, notes first, speed later".

Stan suddenly stopped the band. For the first time that evening, Stan actually looked happy, with the end of the baton between his teeth, he was in deep contemplation, occasionally he would nod his head, cast his eyes upwards in concentrated thought. Looking at the front row of cornets, finally, he finished pondering. the band was hushed sensing something dramatic.

"Now, there is a way we might be able to play the opening introduction as written. It's a long shot, not exactly in the competition spirit, but we could just get away with it", Stan said trying to sound confident. "If we accept my suggestion, this will need to be an Imperial Infirmary Band secret not to be revealed to any other person outside of this band. It can only work if we ensure that we have total security". Stan outlined his plan.

"It's a cunning scheme, right enough," said Adrian in his best Baldrick voice. "It's very devious, it's disgraceful, it must be a betrayal of the brass band code, in all my years as a trade union official I've never come across any plan so underhand as this, it is unethical. Jolly brilliant gets my vote", added Reg.

Like all plans, it was amazingly simple, and like all such plans could fall apart at a moment's notice. Getting noticed, or not noticed was the basis of the Grand Stan Plan, and a bit of luck in the draw.

"On contest day, adjudicators will be locked away in the box, they have no idea which band is playing, and neither are they able to see which band is on the platform", confirmed Stan, "We have four cornets on the front row with backup from behind. I want principal and number three cornet to play the first four bars of the introduction, then deputy principal cornet and number four takes over for the next four bars giving principal and number three a couple of bars or so to recover. Then we just repeat the pattern for 64 bars!".

"I'll check the rulebook just to make sure that nowhere does it say that all players have to be playing when they should be", a helpful Reg offered.

The Grand Stan Plan seemed it might work, the cornets quickly got accustomed to the two on and two off arrangement, the two having a rest, giving the appearance that they were still playing, and from a distance, it was hard to tell differently. Each rehearsal the cornet section got better at it, using soprano to bridge the 'transfer' if necessary.

The anniversary contesting day arrived, and with it the

invasion from bands across the region arriving in Bournemouth. Registered and signed in the band awaited the draw, when it came it was announced that Imperial Infirmary Band would play last. First part of the plan was successful. What an omen, luck was on their side.

First to play was a middle-order band who had come in from Andover way. The introduction proved too much, from a good start, halfway through the 64 bars the cornets were already reduced to three cornet players, by bar 48 it was two players. The final player gave up around about bar 56. The band tried to continue playing but filled with embarrassment fled from the platform, a couple of players not even awaiting the cut-off from the conductor. The applause was muted, even shouts of, "Well done!", sounded patronising and insincere.

The first band to play set the pattern for the remaining bands. The introduction was the stumbling block, even the band, which was hot favourite to take the title made a mess of the introduction. They broke down and were forced to pick-up from bar 65. "We did manage it in rehearsal", the principal cornet was heard to say as with cornet and stand in hand he left the platform, "I think I've had a bit of an upset tummy", reversing around to go back onto the platform to pick up his mute.

One band barely managed to get the first note. Made a false start and never recovered. The conductor had to spend a minute or so consoling his front line of cornets, one of whom had burst out in floods of tears, "I can't do it, I can't do it, I want to go home, don't make me try and play that again, I feel a nervous breakdown coming on!". No-one was able to console him.

Another promising band, who, at contests, always displayed a bit more confidence than they should have, from near Dorchester, informed the competition secretary that they would not now be taking part, evidently the A31 was a bit heavy with holiday traffic, and they wanted to get on their way on the advice of the coach driver. The relief on players' faces was palpable. "See you next year," said the secretary. "Not if it's the same test piece", said their Musical Director.

It was pitiful to see band people so depressed and dejected, in the bars and foyer. There was universal sympathy for the cornets, even the trombones found it in them to be kind and conciliatory. "This really is a 'pig' of a piece", David from near Portland asserted. Groups of cornet players stood around voicing opinions that the introduction was, "Simply crazy, I'd like to hear the composer come along and play the introduction to Stratosphere", said an emotionally recovering cornet player.

The time came for Imperial Infirmary Band to take to the platform. Some people only stayed in the auditorium out of politeness. The band had never been placed in the top half of any competition. Without any shadow of a doubt, this test piece was well beyond them. Supporting family and friends wished them well, with not much enthusiasm or conviction.

The Grand Stan Plan could not have been better executed. The cornet section performed magnificently, better than they did in rehearsal. Buoyed up by the confidence of the cornet section the band just went through the test piece like a knife through butter. Prolonged applause greeted the final sweep of the Musical Director's baton. Congratulations on the band's performance came from all directions. Other bands were gracious in their praise. "What a marvellous cornet section you've got there", one of the other musical directors said patting Stan on the back and shaking his hand.

However, very quickly, how the band had achieved their success was spreading amongst the other bands. The reaction was mixed; some considered it a great cheat. "Did you notice that only half the cornet section was playing in the opening section, from where I sat they certainly fooled me", an irate cornet player from near Salisbury complained. "That's not playing the game, let alone playing the test piece", voiced another complaining competitor. "In my book it's not great, however you try to wrap it up, I'm calling it a big banding foul. The playing field and platform must be equal to each band. None of this play when you like attitude. I am asking the organising committee to declare the Imperial Infirmary Band's entry null and void, they must not be allowed to win a competition by unfair means, no matter how clever. Furthermore I believe there should be a significant points reduction for bringing a 'scam' into the competition, 'sharp' practice". "Actually I don't think 'sharps' were involved in the test piece introduction", suggested a youngster, about to have his ears clipped, figuratively speaking.

Others, were full of admiration. "That's the point of a test piece, it is to see how a band tackles and overcomes the trickiest sections. The challenge, being set by the composer was surmounted in an imaginative way by Imperial Infirmary. Nowhere on the score did it say at the introduction 'all players playing' you have got to give it to them it was a very smart move!"

An emergency meeting of the organising committee was assembled to examine and debate the rules of the County Competition. Outside the committee room the issue was still being fiercely debated. Not quite to blows but it was certainly getting heated and at one point a little nasty. "It's not an adjudicator we need but a wrestling referee", voiced someone from the crowd.

A lady front row cornet player, from a mid Hampshire band, known for being a bit fiery, considered Stan had pulled a fast one, "It was thoroughly underhand and the next time I see that Stan from Bournemouth, I'm going to knock his block off, or perhaps I'll do something worse which converts Stan from a bass to a soprano!". The listeners to a man squirmed. "She's got a grip like an industrial vice", whispered one of them.

The committee searched through the rulebook, made one or two telephone calls to experts and people with a great deal of experience in brass band competitions. The conclusion was no-one could find any regulation in the current rulebook or any other which prevented players from having a 'break'.

Stan, avoiding lady front row cornet player, from mid Hampshire, accepted the Winners Shield. Finally, the Imperial Infirmary Band had their name on a shield. Winners!

Composing Challenge

(8)

DAVID looked at the collection of items on the dining room table. Things which were so familiar to him. A group of family photographs spanning several decades. A boxed chess set. Half a dozen long-forgotten books, school prizes. A pair of old-fashioned lace-up football boots. A metronome. On the floor alongside the table was a large box.

David's parents had decided to move from the four-bedroomed house which they had lived in for many years, a home in which they had brought up the family, to move away to the seaside and to join the happy residents, as they said in 'bungalow land'. Their choice was Swanage. The moving day had arrived, and David, along with his sister, were there to assist with the move. David had thought he had removed everything from the family home, bit by bit during his college days. His mother, in one of the final round-ups of the house, had come across the items now placed on the dining room table and the box on the floor.

The items could go in the boot of David's car; he could decide what to do with them later, they needed to concentrate on the move. His mother found another box and packed the items away for him. Outside in the road, one of the large removal vans loomed. "They're here", chorused father and son together. "I suggest we keep out of their way and simply let them get on with it. They are the experts, and we followed their instructions. Everything is labelled so when we arrive at the new bungalow each of the rooms should have what it is supposed to have in it", said dad.

The plan was that the parents would go on ahead and be a reception committee at the new property. Brother and sister would ensure that the old house was secure once the removal men had finished. They expected to be in Swanage ahead of the removal people. They would be on hand to help out where needed. The drive down to Swanage for brother and sister was a conversation filled with memories.

The family reassembled in the new bungalow in Swanage. Mother had pre-prepared a picnic, and while awaiting the removal van, the family shared in their first meal in the garden of the new home.

David wanted to know what was in the box that he had put into the boot of his car. His father said, "I suggest you wait until you get home, and when you've got a quiet moment, sit down and open the box. It may have one or two surprises for you, because as I recollect, it is literally years and years since that box was last opened".

Back in his own home David was able to examine the box, with an interested wife and a couple of curious children. The contents took him back to when, aged nine, he was a member of the Salvation Army Young People's Band. As a family, he, his parents and sister had attended. In the box was a photograph of the boys' band taken not long after he had joined. "What a smart lad I look", thought David, with nicely combed hair and wearing what would now be considered old-fashioned, a red jersey with the Salvation Army Crest evidenced on the front, which was buttoned along one shoulder. Short trousers, knee-length grey socks, even the shoes look polished. Across his knees was the Tenor Horn he played at that time.

His eyes now alighted on the Scale and Fingering Card that was given to him by the bandleader. He looked at the C scale, under each note was the fingering. He considered the F scale and noted the change from B natural to B flat, from the second valve to the first valve. The card explained to him how a semibreve could be divided into two minims, two crotchets to a minim, four crotchets to a semibreve. He had yet to get into quavers and the sub-divisions of quavers. David considered it must've taken him a long time to learn all that was on the card as the card was so well used. "I wonder if they still print them?".

Now a Bandmaster himself there were more than one or two players in his band who would benefit from consulting the Scale and Fingering Card.

David recalled the exercise book for 'home-work' which was issued at each practice to be completed during the week. Music exercises aimed at extending and improving performance.

The Young People's Band Leader was keen on introducing musical appreciation to the youngsters in the band. The world of the classics was revealed, Beethoven, Mozart, Haydn and Elgar were discussed and debated. David remembered that another series featured Salvation Army composers, Dean Goffin, Leslie Condon, Norman Bearcroft, Eric Ball and George Marshall were just five Army composers featured. Hunting around in the box David came across a couple of photos of staff and students at National Schools of Music. He sat for a while with the photo in his hand recalling people who had attended.

David pulled out a book entitled 'composition'. David now remembered what this book was all about. The YP Band Leader introduced composition. One of his interesting exercises was to ask the senior members of the band to have a go at writing a tune. The band members spent time studying hymn tunes; they were challenged to write an essay on a hymn tune of their choice, discussing the structure and timeline of the melody, suggesting changes to the tune. David ran through his melody, his attempt at writing a hymn tune, in his head. He was interested in reading the comments from the bandleader. It was always a mixture of encouragement and praise. Negative comments were identified as positive, learning by error approach. One tune developed into more.

His first effort at composition was pretty dismal. He used just about every possible note from semiquaver up to semibreve and all notes in between. The tune from first note to last appeared to have no idea where it was going, wandered around the scale like a ball in a pinball machine. The band leader's comment had been Hymn Tune 41. The tune was Tallis. David recalled the bandleader saying, "Have a look at Tallis, consider the structure of the tune. Eight bars, 32 notes, Tallis keeps coming back to the Key signature note, and of course, the first thing you would have noticed was that Thomas Tallis only used crotchets. The crotchet is your bread-and-butter note, the one most used in hymnology. You can't go very far without a crotchet!" Observed the bandleader.

From writing a simple tune, the next stage in their musical development was harmonisation. Very simple two-part harmony, the bandleader encouraged the youngsters to work in pairs. With his pal they tackled two-part harmony, writing and playing. David recalled much discussion between himself and his pal, it seemed to him every note ended in an argument. Did they ever finally agree?

It was David's choice to try and cope with four-part harmony. In the box was his attempt to bring together a simple hymn tune arrangement on the tune St Agnes. David could not remember why he had chosen the Hymn Tune St Agnes for his first attempt at a Hymn Tune arrangement.

Later David was to study at Durham University and visited the St Oswald Church in the city where John Dykes the writer of the tune was the Vicar.

David had not long been transferred to the senior band when The Salvation Army Music Department introduced The Bandmasters' Training Course, to which David signed up. In the box was the coursework along with a copy of the Rudiments of Music written by MacPherson. David spent some time flicking through the pages reading the side notes he had written all those years ago and the comments by his tutor. David remembered passing the course, he searched around for the certificate without success.

All this seemed such a long time ago. Having qualified he had entered the teaching profession, his main subject music. The experience he learnt from the Band Leader paid dividends in the classroom.

The Salvation Army was a major influence on his life. His father, grandfather, and great grandfather, had all been members of the movement. Any family gathering was going to be Salvation Army orientated in each of the family homes.

Where he wondered had all that composing ambition gone, did he no longer have a tune in his head? Where was the St Agnes enthusiasm to write an uncomplicated Hymn Tune arrangement? Was it all left in the box?

Perhaps it was the realisation that having composed music, getting it published within the Salvation Army, in a very crowded market, was notoriously difficult for new and non-published composers. As Bandmaster, he was always conducting the composition of others. He wondered what it would feel like to conduct the band in something he had put down on manuscript paper.

In that moment he decided that one of the 'must do tick boxes of life' was to either write a brand new piece of music or arrange the work of a composer. He felt he would need some drive on this project. He set himself a goal. It was now early May, more than half a year away was December, the season of Christmas pudding, mince pies, Christmas crackers, gifts and carol concerts. He would give himself six months to write an arrangement of a popular Christmas Carol. David accepted that most of them had received, 'musical adaptations' already. But he was not first and foremost doing this for others, he was doing it for himself.

It seemed odd to be thinking about Christmas and having Christmas carol melodies pervading your mind in summer. 'Oh I do need to be beside the seaside', was pushed from his mind in favour of, 'When Santa Got Stuck Up The Chimney' or 'Santa Claus Is Coming To Town'. Neither carol seemed a suitable carol. David was attracted to the very simple but well loved Carol, 'Away in a Manger'. The final verse of the carol David had often used as a prayer at various carolling engagements.

Be near me Lord Jesus; I ask thee to stay,
Close by me forever, and love me I pray,
Bless all the dear children in thy tender care,
And fit us for heaven to live with you there.

David was aware that there were a number of musical settings for the words, 'Away in a Manger'. The popular tune 'Mueller' known as 'Luther's Cradle Hymn' is much used in America. *'Away in a Manger'* also entitled *'Cradle Song'* was more favourite in Britain. He could use the tune *Spilman*, known as *'Flow Gently, Sweet Afton'* with the interesting metre of 11.11.11.11.

On a visit to his parents to see how they were getting on, David discussed the project with his father. The box had been the spark to get David going. Thinking back to YP Band days, David could now see and appreciate the dedication of the band leaders, the members of the senior band who came into practices to mentor the youngsters. His father reminded him of how there would be groups of two or three playing over their parts in various corners of the hall. In one 'conclave' the baritone part could be heard, in another the horn section. The band had four players on the melody line, each, in turn, would play through the melody. After a while, the band would come together to judge how much progress had been made.

His father recalled the Bandmasters' Training Course, that had been an ambition some years ago as a youngster. "Your grandfather could recall the days when they used to hold International Band Music Competitions. Many notable Salvation Army writers entered with great success, including a former General". "There is no way I could write anything to submit to a music composers' competition", a sadly expressed David said.

"Come on then Beethoven", said his father, "I suppose you're going to write the music for the Festival Series. Something big and bold and lasting for half an hour and more, and in the modern idiom having some ear-splitting sections!" "Possibly not, I know my limitations, I also know the expertise required to have a piece published in the festival series, and that is well beyond me".

"I'm aiming to be more inclusive, so I'm planning to arrange something for the other end of the scale, the unity series. I know it's a cut-down version and it's basically four part harmony, but when you listen to some of the music it can be dynamic, challenging and interesting to hear", suggested David. "Wise choice", said his father, "I remember when the first unity book in the series was first published, the cover was coloured orange" recollected his father. "Many top composers in the Salvation Army world submitted an item. I may be wrong, but I have a feeling that the International Staff Band held a festival to introduce the new Unity Series".

"The Advent of the Unity music greatly enlarged the repertoire of so many smaller bands. I bet many band cupboards still have set of the orange ones, later a blue book and a green book where added to the Unity collection ending up being tucked away somewhere", said his father. "One Bandmaster was totally dismissive of the series calling it 'baby music', however it wasn't long before he had his band in musical nappies".

Father and son discussed the route of the arrangement, from start to end. David was in favour of a brief introduction. "Two quaver upbeat before bar three, three crotchets, and pausing the following minims, repeating the notation in the minor key, and then again in the major key, running into the presentation of the melody for the first occasion is my idea to get the piece moving". "You will need to link verse one and two with some chord progression if you are planning a key change for the second verse. Moving between verse two and three can easily be achieved by playing around with the pedal note. Finally, it's how you wrap the whole thing up", his father concluded.

"Thank you", said David, "all we need to think about now is variation in harmonisation, and that's it".

Over the succeeding months David studiously worked on his 'Away in a Manger' project. The musical route he commenced with was not quite the one he finished. Changes here and there, a fresh idea for different cord progression. What sounded quite good on the piano one-day seemed less pleasing when he visited the arrangement again.

By October David was ready to run the piece through with his band. He had kept his arranging a secret. He felt that to get an honest appreciation it would be better if the band did not know he had written the arrangement. His piece was never ever going to be the most difficult his band had tackled, they pretty well ran through it sight reading, and immediately guessed that David had written the arrangement.

One clever youngster in the band asked, "Was this piece passed by the Music Editorial Board?" "No!", shouted his pal, "the Water Board!"

In mid-November David and Band Secretary considered the carolling programme for December. It was the usual mix of Christmas engagements, visiting one or two elderly residents' homes, providing music for the local Women's Institute Christmas dinner, participating in the Town Mayor's Christmas Gala Concert and playing carols in the town centre on Christmas Eve, followed, on Christmas morning by, playing carols around the wards of the local hospital.

A couple of engagements presented David with the opportunity to play his arrangement of 'Away in a Manger'. Folk were complimentary about his arrangement. It was one of the pieces he elected to play in the Mayor's Gala Concert. In the printed programme it said Carol arrangement - 'Away in a Manger' – arr David Weston. That was the nearest his work got to public acknowledgement.

Right from the beginning David knew that he would never feature as a composer. He had dissected the work of top Salvation Army composers. He could never come anywhere near emulating the skill they displayed. He was content in what he had done, thanks to a box of music paraphernalia which belonged to his youth and challenged him in middle age.

Bandstand Postcards

(9)

RAYMOND lived in The New Forest; he had moved there in semi-retirement. Raymond and his wife, Pamela, had been frequent visitors to the area, in the beginning as campers and more latterly in their motorhome. They knew and loved the area. With their children having moved away from the family home, and now being just the two of them, they took the opportunity to consider where they might spend, as Raymond said, "Their twilight years". The New Forest was a natural choice.

Raymond worked for one of the major national charities at their head office in Staines or as it became Staines-upon-Thames, in Raymond's view a decision which led to a lot of confusion. Colleagues were forever telephoning for directions to Staines-upon-Thames. The reply would always be, "Make your way to Staines; the place has gone all snobby, councillors wanted to improve the image of the town, for Staines to become a bit like Henley and Kingston. I still call it Staines".

It might well have been the council's decision to rebrand Staines which influenced Raymond and his wife that it was time to 'reposition themselves'. Raymond was always doing things a bit differently, he persuaded his wife to put their house on the market immediately. "Let's get things moving", asserted Raymond. "What if we sell next week, perhaps to a cash buyer?", his anxious and more cautious wife asked. A one-word reply came from Raymond, "Motorhome". "Raymond you're just being stupid as usual, sometimes I lose all patience with you. We will do this 'repositioning' properly or not at all". That Raymond accepted was the final word.

Weary of potential buyers marching through their house, Raymond and Pamela elected to have a break. They loaded the motorhome to drive to The New Forest and their usual camping site, often with a stop at Winchester. M25, M3, M27 and then picking up the A337 to Hollands Wood, their campsite of choice, situated on the road between Lyndhurst and Brockenhurst.

The price of property in The New Forest was always above the average, particularly in some of the more sought-after locations. Raymond observed any place in The New Forest beginning with the letter 'B' was going to be on the more expensive list. Brockenhurst, Barton-upon-Sea, Beaulieu, Burley, Boldre. He called them 'Bank Balance Busters', and the 'L' was just as bad, Lyndhurst and Lymington, 'Loot Losers'.

Raymond estimated that they had about £700,000 plus to do the New Forest 'repositioning'.

Searching properties online they found that one of their favourite New Forest towns had the kind of house featured they were seeking and well within budget. They found a very suitable bungalow, with parking for the motorhome, in Broadshard Lane, Ringwood. Completed a couple of viewings and put in an offer.

Ringwood was a town they always visited on their trips to The New Forest; it was ideally located, they liked the High Street and the natural amphitheatre which formed the Market Place, The Furlong Centre and the Meeting House. Ringwood was on the direct route to London and in the opposite direction the west country. Raymond could still commute to Staines, and with more homeworking being introduced, he could probably reduce the number of hours at head office.

Matters took a significant turn when the director of the charity, knowing that Raymond was preparing to move to The New Forest, asked Raymond if he was interested in the vacancy as County Organiser which had occurred within the organisation. The job could not be better; it had Raymond's name all over it. The three counties were Hampshire, Dorset and Wiltshire.

"The interview will be nothing more than a mere formality, as they say, I can confidently assure you that the appointment is yours", confirmed the director, "And we will even help you with moving expenses".

'Repositioning' moved quickly, the house in Staines was sold to a young family who were in a position to move immediately, the bungalow offer in Ringwood was accepted after some negotiation, and everything came together just as they wanted. In next to no time they were New Forest bound, and Ringwood was their new home.

Raymond transferred his Rotary Club membership to the Ringwood Club, and found himself acting as a Carnival steward for the annual September Ringwood Carnival. They both joined the Ringwood Musical and Dramatic Society and very quickly settled into the forest way of life. They suddenly found 'friends' they had not been in touch with for decades who were just aching to come and see them. "I don't suppose we would have heard from them had we moved to somewhere like, with all due respect, somewhere north of Gateshead", Raymond mused.

Before he met and married Pamela, Raymond had, as he said, "learnt to salute", he'd entered the army for military service, on what he maintained were his terms. None of this crawling on his belly through muddy fields, neither was he prepared to jump out of an aircraft. "I have very little faith in string. Just think of how long your shoelaces last. The world is full of two pieces of string which once were one!"

He had taken lessons on the trumpet as a youngster. When he enlisted he took his trumpet with him, it was his 'announcement card'. The trumpet case was soon noticed by the Warrant Officer in charge of the regimental band. Raymond was 'captured', and a cornet put into his hand. Thus, commenced his years of army banding, mainly serving in the UK. It was a life he greatly enjoyed. The most enjoyable time was during the summer seaside engagements when the band went on tour. Admittedly there was a bit of marching up and down to be done, but in the main he had a sit-down job.

At his first seaside engagement he met Pamela. The band was booked to do a three-day stint at Eastbourne, on the East Sussex coast, the band playing in the unique semi-circular design and blue domed roof bandstand. Friday evening the band was to give the first of the three concerts in Eastbourne. The programme for the evening was primarily popular dance pieces. Raymond was called upon to do a 'bit of jazz'. "I want you to try and sound like Glenn Miller's band, give us a bit of swing", demanded Warrant Officer".

Completely contrary to military band practice the officer allowed some of the bandsmen to jump down from the bandstand stage to dance with the local girls. As Pamela said "It proved to be, 'A bandstand romance'. Although I was a bit disappointed, I was hoping that the trombone player would get to me before Raymond did!"

Next morning they met during Raymond's free time. Parents came to the Saturday afternoon bandstand concert and were introduced to Raymond. Sunday morning the band had Church Parade, then one more concert Sunday afternoon before returning to the band depot to get ready for the following weekend.

Bandstands were to play an important part in their romance. Replacing love letters, Raymond sent Pamela picture postcards, which always included a photo of the bandstand in which the band had played.

Pamela had kept all the postcards, the date postmark ensured that she was able to keep them in order. Unpacking in Ringwood, she came across the postcard album in which the cards were kept.

There were a couple of postcards from Scarborough, sometimes known as the Spa bandstand. Raymond wrote about the first concert in Scarborough. "It was blowing a gale. Hardly anybody about and virtually nobody was sitting in the deckchairs. "We were playing to ourselves; it was very miserable. The concert should have been cancelled. The sergeant suggested that the bracing air would do us good. I have caught a cold along with a few others. No sympathy from the sergeant, he called us sissies!"

The second Scarborough postcard was much better. Sun was shining, blue sky, people on the beach and folk sitting on deckchairs enjoying the music of the band. Raymond mentioned the rather pleasing chequered floor part of the bandstand apron. Band items included, *The William Tell Overture, The West Riding March, The Floral Dance* and the *Post Horn Gallop* with Raymond as soloist. "The warrant officer is a sadist when he takes the piece, he goes so fast it just about kills me", complained Raymond.

Raymond only sent one postcard from Scotland. It came from St Andrews. Message on the card, was simple, "No golf clubs – so no clubbing!" Raymond wrote about the great scenery and how he wished he could spend more time in Scotland. "We must come up here one day, just the two of us, it would be great".

The regimental band was booked to play in the St Andrews bandstand adjacent to the Royal and Ancient Golf Club. Positioned very close to the coast, the bandstand comprised of base, topped by a simple canopy supported by a series of pillars. It was completely open all the way around offering no protection. It was as one bandsman observed. 'A cloth peg job', the only way to keep the music from flying off the music stands towards the golf course was to pin it down with pegs. The concert was performed on Sunday afternoon. The weather was excellent, and a good crowd turned out to listen to the band. The programme was the usual concert mix-and-match, of popular and military band music.

The Saturday night previous the band had given a band concert at Dundee. On this occasion, the Warrant Officer chose a programme featuring Scottish music. "Got to keep the locals happy". A bagpipe band supported the event - lots of flag-waving. The concert over-ran some-what and it was decided to drop the Post Horn Gallop. "We might include it on tomorrow afternoon's concert", said the sergeant thinking he had disappointed Raymond. "It was either you or *Scotland the Brave*".

The weekend in Scotland was one of those occasions when one thing after another just simply went wrong, nothing major but enough to be annoying.

One of the tubas was unfortunately left behind at the depot.

Fortunately, the fact that the tuba was missing was spotted at a motorway service station comfort stop and a frantic call had the tuba being 'jeeped' up to the band.

The sergeant in charge of the band coach, in the absence of a more senior officer, who would be joining the band in Dundee, was always keen to put people on a charge. He decided to play Sherlock Holmes but ended up playing Inspector Clouseau.

Admittedly trying to conduct an investigation on a 53 seater coach on the motorway was going to prove demanding. By the time the coach had reached the Scottish border, the sergeant had accused four members of the band of being implicated. On the outskirts of Edinburgh, the sergeant produced his conspiracy theory. There was plotting afoot, and the missing tuba supported his allegation of a conspiracy to discredit him. The whole charade came to a conclusion when one of the bandsmen had a look at the weekend inventory and spotted the missing tuba was not on the list prepared by the investigating sergeant.

The stage in the Dundee church hall was a tight fit for the band. Conditions were cramped, ideal for an outbreak of 'musictipitus', stands toppling over. "When one goes over the rest are sure to follow", observed the clarinet player. The officer was able to make light of the incident. "Please don't worry ladies and gentlemen - at the last concert we dropped a couple of grenades, like one or two chaps in the band they were duds!" (The band had heard that joke before. Rank demanded that they laughed!).

"Bournemouth has a boring Pine Walk Bandstand", Raymond noted in his Bournemouth postcard, following the band's visit. "It is a simple three-sided building with an open front, the two sides are filled in with glass, and the rear has folding doors which can be fully opened. The whole structure is topped by a pent roof which has a single slope creating an incline, with its highest point at the front of the bandstand. Frankly, my garden shed is more attractive".

A further minus point is that the public is some considerable way from the bandstand, separated by a river called the Bourne Stream. The distance makes communication just about impossible without the aid of a public address system. All that said it was noted the band had a thoroughly good weekend.

"To compensate there is the really exciting nightlife in the town. I can tell you that most of the band were 'reviewing' or revelling in the nightlife after our Saturday evening concert. Not me, of course. Straight back to my billet! Travelling to and from Bournemouth we drove through The New Forest on the A31 bypass that cuts Ringwood in half. Actually, our vehicle broke down on the steep hill going out of Ringwood, Picket Hill, it might have been a dual carriageway, but we still held the traffic up".

Pamela received a colourful postcard from the Island of Jersey, again a photo of another boring bandstand. The band was invited to take part in the Jersey Battle of Flowers. The islanders ensured that they got their money's worth out of the band's visit. It was one of those engagements when the band was on their feet marching as much as sitting-down playing. For the first engagement, the band marched through the town of St Helier to give a pre-battle of Flowers concert in the Royal Square during the morning. The evening concert was held in the Howard Davies Park, in a rather non-descript bandstand, basic and utilitarian. All visiting bands draw crowds, opportunities to hear bands on the island being rather limited. The concert was billed as music from the West End shows. It was a good opportunity for the public to get involved and Raymond remarked how well they joined in.

Battle of Flowers day was march time for the band, given pride of place as the lead band. For most of the band, it was a completely fresh experience. The day was blisteringly hot with little or no breeze whatsoever. Musically it would be a series of military marches. The Battle Day concluded with an evening parade and fireworks display, again the band was on duty. It was estimated that there was close on 48,000 people watching the parade.

The next afternoon the band, with all the equipment, was to sail from Jersey to the mainland harbour of Poole, in Dorset. Under different circumstances it would be a very pleasant journey, a relaxing time in the lounge, drink in hand, a spot of duty-free shopping before the boat reached Poole. What greeted the band was a complete reversal in the weather. Raymond noticed that the vessel was wobbling about just a little bit in St Helier harbour whilst still attached by ropes to the quay. The wind was high and very strong and dark clouds above indicated heavy rain.

"This is Captain Blake", the onboard tannoy system announced, "All vehicles have now been loaded, we have secured the vessel for sailing, first to Guernsey and then onward to Poole. Sea conditions are pretty grim, and whilst the run-up to Guernsey should not be too unpleasant, we do expect difficult and challenging, possibly gale weather conditions, once in the English Channel, past Alderney. We do advise you not to move around the public areas unless you have to do so and move with extreme caution, things may be flying around a bit. Because of the sea conditions, we will not be able to open the bar or the duty-free shop. We apologise for the inconvenience and disappointment. Please do now take to your seats and try to relax; Crew members will be coming around with sick bags." They could still see Jersey's Elizabeth Castle when the first bandsman made use of a sick bag!

Raymond didn't tell Pamela that while in St Helier he had been window shopping. In one of the jewellery stores, he spotted an engagement ring which caught his eye. A large deep blue sapphire stone mounted with four diamonds. He went back two or three times to look at the ring and also at the price tag, priced at more than all he had on him. He went back for another look, this time a gentleman sales assistant invited him in. "Is there something in the window which has attracted you?" he asked. "Yes, but it's a touch over what I can afford". "Never mind let's have a look at it, I think it might be the sapphire ring". The assistant opened the protective glass panel, reached in and lifted out the ring. "I imagine you want the item as an engagement ring". "Indeed, that is what I had in mind". "I am the owner of the shop, and the ring you are looking at is actually a piece of jewellery which I recently purchased, I suppose you could call it second hand. Over the years it will grow in value, particularly with that setting. I am sure we can do something". It was a bit of a blur, Raymond left with 95p, all the notes had gone, but in his hand was the ring.

One engagement which the band looked forward to was the couple of days in Stratford-upon-Avon. This was a prestigious 'gig'. Sadly the bandstand was less than prestigious. The bandstand at the bard's birthplace was the base, pillars and canopy design, but it was in a very nice park setting. There was nothing taxing about the programme. A concert in the bandstand, the organisers had requested music nothing other than English composers, a bit of *'Hearts of Oak'*, not a piece the band played on a regular basis. The band was more comfortable with *'It's a long way to Tipperary'*, *'Pack up your troubles in your old kit bag'*, *'Keep the home fires burning'*, excerpts from *'The Planet'* and *'I Vow to Thee my Country'*, tunes suggested to the officer.

One of the nice things about the bandstand engagement was the number of former military personnel, wearing their regimental ties and badges, who wandered over to have a chat with the band members, an occasion for them to share their memories. Raymond always made time for the veterans, particularly those who had served during both of the world wars.

Just about everybody wants to see a band on the march, no less the good people of Stratford-upon-Avon increased in number by numerous tourists. As was expected a route was mapped out for the band to march through the town. Click, click, click went the cameras. "Goodness knows how many countries have sent representatives to be tourists in Stratford-upon-Avon this weekend", offered the euphonium player. "We expect to get photographed but do they have to put their camera up your nostrils?"

Not only did they want photos of the band marching but also they wanted to be in photos with members of the band. It might not have been Stratford-upon-sea, but it had the feel of a tourist destination. The band completed the image which so many people had of Stratford-upon-Avon, thoroughly English. As for Shakespeare, judging by the number of young couples Raymond observed the spirit of Romeo and Juliet was very much in evidence.

During a bit of free time Raymond purchased his bandstand postcard of Stratford-upon-Avon. He wrote Pamela's name and address and on the correspondence side of the postcard simply wrote. "Will you marry me?"

A Multitude of Mouthpieces

(10)

Inspired by George Blackwell
The Salvation Army - Willenhall and Ringwood
and The Bournemouth Area Fellowship Band

GEORGE always enjoyed a good hearty meal, at home or dining out, and as a result, he had become rather plump and cuddly. Now into his early 70s, the youthful man of yesteryear had long since disappeared and been transformed into a slightly overweight, slow moving, but lovable figure. Age had elevated George into being a two pair of spectacles man with a walking stick and a modest saloon car.

George had been a member of a brass band for decades. His father taught him to play and encouraged him to join The Salvation Army Young People's Band, red jersey and short blue trousers. From there, the journey into the senior band was a natural progression. George was a faithful and diligent member of the Corps band, although once he was told to 'sit out' because he forgot to change his socks and the Bandmaster couldn't possibly have one of his musicians wearing multicoloured socks.

George, front row cornet in the Fellowship Band, had buttonholed David, a member of the horn section, in the band room. From out of his pocket George produced his latest acquisition, yet another cornet mouthpiece. 'How many more is he going to buy?' went through David's mind. If George ever jumped off a bridge, with all his mouthpieces attached to him, he would surely sink to the bottom of the river; the weight would be more than any diver's set of "Frankenstein Boots". This interest in mouthpieces had laid dormant for years, and yet at pensionable age, George was seeking the acme of perfection in cornet mouthpieces.

David had heard it all before, many times, but there would be no halting George, he would just have to run through the parts of a mouthpiece. Just like reciting a nursery rhyme, George could name them one by one. "Inner rim: Rim: The contour, or shape of the rim: Rim edge: Cup: Throat: Backbore and finally the Shank."

For David, rescue was at hand, in the distance, he could hear the euphonium player going through his arpeggios. Never was he more grateful. "Time for rehearsal George", said David heading for the door.

George had a fixation, there could be no other way of putting it, and whilst other people collected postage stamps, Minton china, comics, for George it was cornet mouthpieces. He could quite easily bypass a mouthpiece for a tenor horn; trombone mouthpieces had no interest for him whatsoever. He could never recall having even looked at the mouthpiece for the flugel horn. For George, his sole interest in mouthpieces centred on the cornet variety.

George was seeking the holy grail of mouthpieces. He was convinced that there was a magical mouthpiece, somewhere, that would enhance his musical performance enabling him to play some of the most difficult cornet solos published with the greatest of ease. He had visions of himself playing 'Golden Slippers'. If David Daws and Martyn Thomas could play the cornet solo, with the right mouthpiece, so could he. The fact that he had never played a 'stand-up' difficult cornet solo in his entire life made no difference to his Walter Mitty fantasy.

George had purchased and tried many of the main brands. Vincent Bach, Besson, Warburton, Al Cass, Dennis Wick, Yamaha etc. A 'blow' in the shop was all part of the process and pleasure. He could linger over decisions; it took him longer to make his mind up on the mouthpiece than some people took to decide on a house purchase. Knowing sales assistants would dread the sight of George coming through the door, they fled fearing the worst.

In fairness, he did use all of the mouthpieces he spent money on, but they didn't last very long, George was never satisfied, he suffered from an acute case of mouthpiece disappointment. The next one was always going to be the one, the last one, but it never was.

As to how many mouthpieces he currently owned, George was never precisely sure, he had the uncomfortable habit of finding mouthpieces in the most unusual places, mainly because he had hidden them away from his wife.

Also hidden, at least from Mrs George, was just how much he had spent on his obsession. She was convinced that it was certainly more than the price of a decent weekend away. She was at a disadvantage, unfortunately she could hardly distinguish one mouthpiece from another, and George could easily convince her, "It's an old mouthpiece, I've had for years", when challenged.

In his defence, he often said, "Once you've collected one you might just as well add another one, why stop"? It was no good telling George basically all mouthpieces were the same, a crescent cup mounted on a shank. Although to be fair, as George pointed out, there was a little bit more to a mouthpiece. Mrs George struggled to see it. Perhaps it might have been easier had Mrs George been a member of a brass band, but sadly she was a brass band widow!

"What are Saturdays for? - it's a shopping day", he would suggest. Sadly for Mrs George, not for her, wandering around departmental stores, kitchen ware and china in the basement, perfume on the ground floor, always as you entered the store, ladies fashion the first floor above that, the next floor a mixture of gentlemen's outfitters and furniture and right at the top of the store the restaurant.

Such retail outlets held no interest for George. He judged places visited by the quality of their music shops. Holidays were no different, just another opportunity to seek out and locate a music emporium which might have a stock of mouthpieces. Wherever they went on holiday, George checked, beforehand, to make sure there was a music retailer in the vicinity.

"It's just down here, look you can see a treble clef sign

hanging outside the shop over the door," exhorted George during one of their holidays. A quick look in the window and once inside George came straight to the point addressing the sales assistant, who foolishly had come forward and asked, "Can we help?". "Can I see your range of cornet mouthpieces please?" In the background, the patient, despairing, waiting Mrs George.

Leaving a non-mouthpiece establishment in disgust, George would declare, with some outrage, "Do you call that a music shop?. That snooty salesman saying there is little call for mouthpieces in Cheltenham, and that they only stocked the high end of the musical instrument market, like grand pianos and five-figure costing guitars". Affronted George would immediately dismiss the shop and the town. George knew the topography of the entire UK by its music shops, and in his mind, he graded each and every one of them by their stock of mouthpieces.

In his search for the elusive Prix d'excellence mouthpiece, George resorted to browsing the mouthpiece listings on eBay. Here he was in his element. Before him on the screen, tantalising mouthpieces of all makes, sizes and models and all available to purchase. When he found a mouthpiece which took his fancy, he would decide in his mind just how much he was going to bid. He told himself he would be strict, whatever amount he decided that would be the limit, that and no more.

When you're addicted with mouthpieceitis, that little button marked 'BID' just leaps off the screen. Desire triumphing over common sense. Mrs George got used to occasional small packages being delivered by the postman. George was as excited as a six-year-old on Christmas Day. "It's arrived!", shouted George. Mrs George knew what it was!

Mrs George never needed to ask, "What are you doing on the computer George?" Looking over his shoulder, all she ever saw was the listings for mouthpieces. A gentle suggestion that he might look for a much-needed kitchen utensil was re-joined by, "What do you need that for?". Mrs George usually turned away; she admitted defeat. If it came down to a choice between her and a mouthpiece, Mrs George was never convinced of the outcome.

It probably wasn't the continual sourcing and purchasing of mouthpieces which upset the equilibrium of the household. She always knew what was coming, when a new mouthpiece came in through the door, the cornet came out of the case. "Mrs G, how do you think it sounds, I'm sure it's an improvement, my lips don't appear to be quite as tired, and high notes, I seem to be getting high notes much easier". "Who does he think he's kidding?" thought Mrs George.

Was an obsession with mouthpieces serious grounds for divorce Mrs George mused?

David, his band colleague, had often made the very obvious observation, that regardless of how many mouthpieces George owned, he could only play them one at a time. George had to concede that David had him there; here was a weakness. He had actually seen 'trick instrumentalists' who were able to play two instruments at the same time but perhaps not successfully brass instruments.

There must be a solution, having all those mouthpieces and only able to blow one at a time, it was depressing. It was like having a box of the finest mixed chocolates, and all you can have is one!

Suddenly he was inspired. A Damascus Road experience. The answer to the multi-use of mouthpieces had been staring him in the face, on his music stand, he just had failed to see it. There was a solution. Oh, glory be! Why had he been so blind? His band music folder had the answer, it had been there all along, and he'd failed to comprehend it.

The band repertoire included Marches, Hymn Tune Arrangements, Meditations, Air Varie. The whole gambit of brass band music was in the band folder. The style of music was different for the various pieces; George realised he could take advantage of the differing musical styles. It seemed logical to George that if the pieces of music could be catalogued under general headings, for example Marches, Meditations and Song Arrangement and required being played differently the same principle could be attributed to his collection of mouthpieces.

George elected to have a special mouthpiece for when playing Marches, a different mouthpiece would be utilised for the more gentle Meditations, and so he would continue through the various musical categories with a dedicated mouthpiece for each one. Brilliant!

The theory may be correct - but George had to put the theory into practice, or perhaps rehearsal. George worked out that probably five or six mouthpieces would be needed to cover a full band programme and a rehearsal. He knew there would be time to change mouthpieces between band items.

That was not his problem. You could buy holders, which attached to the music stand for mutes et cetera, but not a holder for mouthpieces. Again the solution was simple, he would lineup the required mouthpieces on his music stand. Exchanging mouthpieces was a simple operation. Laid out in military precision George stood the chosen mouthpieces. Like sentries on duty, ready for action, awaiting the call to serve.

George thought he could be clever and take things a step forward. George noted that one piece of music, perhaps a Selection, may have a number of different mood passages. Perhaps a martial introduction, followed by a slow, softly played melody, concluding with a treble forte grand finale. George was ready for the change in musical moods, and quicker than you could give the fingering for lower D flat, George would change his mouthpiece as the music went along. George just couldn't work out why the members of the band didn't follow his mouthpiece strategy.

Did continually changing one's mouthpiece make a difference to your performance? Perhaps George thought it did, others were far from convinced. They remained happy and content with mouthpieces they had been using for years. A change of mouthpiece would make no difference, as experience confirmed. As the old proverb notes "It's easier to blame the tools used rather than the tool user."

Then George came across an advert for coloured plastic mouthpieces!

Adjudicator Anguish

(11)

IN one of the pretty parishes near to the River Piddle in Dorset, surrounded by daisies, buttercups and primroses lived Adam Perceval Stubbington-Harris. 'Stubbs', a nickname from public school days, who would say, "I own just a little bit of Dorset, you know, I like to think of myself as a gentleman farmer. I've got a couple of sheep and a small herd of pure Guernsey cows. I like fresh milk in the morning on my cornflakes, don't you know". A couple of sheep was a small flock, and the herd of Guernsey cows comprised of six.

Wednesday market day, you would find him in Dorchester. A larger than life character dressed in a three-piece Harris Tweed suit with plus fours and brogue shoes. An enormous handkerchief would hang down from his breast pocket, used to mop his sweating forehead on hot summer days. It was the animal section of the market which interested 'Stubbs'. He would always bring at least one sheep to market to sell, and might end up buying a couple more. Most of the deals were settled in one of the adjacent public houses where 'Stubbs' would hold court.

Often he would be addressed as the King of Dorset. He was there to receive due homage and if colleague farmers wished to 'touch the forelock', bow the head or in the case of female farmers curtsy, why should he object?

Truth to be told he was considerably less rich than he made out. It was inherited wealth and not a great deal of it left. Over the years his Kingdom of Dorset had been sold off, field by field, plot by plot. The land his animals grazed on was no longer his. He had become a tenant farmer. No matter he could still play the part of Mr Bountiful. He still had a fair sized manor house to live in.

Another market day ritual was his parade around the Duke's

Auction House. He was not a buyer but, he had been known, quietly selling off items of family interest. The auction house was very discreet and, would describe the item as 'the property of a gentleman'.

He was a character, and all markets need such a flamboyant personality. Everybody knew 'Stubbs', and called him by that name, from the youngest to the oldest, it was, "Hello 'Stubbs', 'Stubbs' took no offence, he exchanged the greeting. Recognition ensured that the 'Stubbs' legend continued. One of his funny little quirks, was to pull out from under his overcoat a pocket cornet. Trumpet tunes were heard all around the market, 'Stubbs' liked to play sea tunes. *'Blow the man down', 'Rule Britannia', 'The Sailors Hornpipe', 'Lady of Spain'* and popular favourites like *'Oh Shenandoah'*. As in most things 'Stubbs' had an immensely high opinion of himself. He would assert that had he not been a gentleman farmer he most certainly would have been a professional musician, a trumpet player, one of the best in all Europe in demand by the top orchestras.

"Sir Adrian Cedric Boult", a name he just picked out of the blue, "was always asking me if I could play in one of his orchestras, as a favour mind you to help him out".

At boarding school, it was obligatory for pupils to choose a musical instrument to learn. 'Stubbs' dismissed all instruments other than the trumpet, he was not a woodwind man. His reasoning very simple. He chose the trumpet on portability and weight. His first choice, for volume, had been a tuba, you could make quite an impression with the tuba. "With a tuba I would have needed to have employed a manservant to carry it around for me. I've got the frame, the physique for a tuba, but not the inclination", opined 'Stubbs'".

In an effort to keep up appearances, 'Stubbs', occasionally had dinner parties at the manor house. His favourite themed evening was Tudor, he thought he had the figure of Henry VIII. While the dining and wining was being enjoyed, above them in the minstrels gallery a group of musicians entertained. In Tudor times the musicians would have played a lute, the forerunner of the guitar. Other Tudor instruments included the keyboard and recorders.

On the menu was traditional Tudor fayre and like the diners of Tudor times no cutlery was provided. "Use your fingers", prompted 'Stubbs'. Dancing formed part of the evening's amusement for the guests. Never one to miss an opportunity 'Stubbs' would always have his pocket cornet near to hand.

'Stubbs' had a collective mix of guests to his parties. One was a local car dealer and his wife, Mrs Car Dealer was a member of the hunting and shooting brigade. They could always be relied on to come if asked. A councillor, noted for having his snout in the trough, who 'Stubbs' always addressed as 'Piggy'. The President of the local Musical and Dramatic Society, whose teasing wife was aware that she could suggest naughty! The National Trust regional fundraiser was a very welcome guest. ('Stubbs' hoped that the trust might take an interest in his pile of bricks).

Then there was his brother, Anthony Antelope Stubbington-Harris, who came down to Dorset from London for the weekend from time to time.

His brother was a music composer, arranger and at times conductor. Not for him the Grand Opera or four section symphony. He specialised in what he called 'non-existent light entertainment'. He was never more happy and content then when he was commissioned to write a jingle for a new television show. He only watched the final moments of a television programme so he could see his name rolling through the credits. "Do you know the most money I made from just a few notes", he asked other dinner guests at a 'Stubbs' party, "it was a dull and meaningless note clip of music for a television commercial. I'm sure you've heard it many times, it's that one for Argentinian Corned Beef".

Trying to lift the tone a little the president of the Musical and Dramatic Society politely enquired, "What are you working on now, is it something that the Society might be able to put on in the Corn Exchange Assembly Room in Dorchester, if it's not too difficult?" Leaning across the table and looking directly at Mrs

M&D Society, and at the same time gently touching her hand said, "That little trumpet fanfare, of mine, in the corn beef advert appears to have got the attention of a couple of fellas in the brass band business", said Anthony,

"Evidently", explained Anthony, "they have some tremendous brass band blowout, bands from all over the country converge on the venue, trying to damage the building like bringing down the walls of Jericho. All the bands play the same piece, it's called the test piece. Somebody, perhaps a committee decide which is the best band and they are the winners and get a cup or a shield or something. Anyway, it's quite a hoot, very popular, although, for my money, listening to the same piece of music umpteen times must be a little bit draining. My thought was once you've heard one band play the test piece you've heard them all. I assume you're just sitting there waiting for one of the bands to drop a clanger, or for bits to fall off the concert hall!"

"It's a bit like golf", Anthony further expanded. "Why do golfers pop that little white ball into the hole and then not leave it there. No, like the test piece they keep on doing the same thing time and time again, sometimes doing it eighteen times, day after day. I can understand putting the little white ball into the slightly larger hole the once, but once you've done it, leave the jolly old ball in the hole, it's done nothing to you which warrants you continually giving the ball a tremendous whack. Ball in hole it's a case of job done, and off to the club house for drinky poos".

"Well imagine my total surprise", said Anthony, "when about a week ago I got a very official letter from this brass band organisation inviting me to write the next test piece for the brass band championships. My initial thought was that they would want it to be a little bit longer than the Argentinian Corn Beef Advert clip, perhaps a full two minutes plus rather than the 45 seconds for corn beef. My second thought was that at the moment I appear not to have as many coloured pictures of Her Majesty the Queen on varying sizes of paper with the figures on them like five, ten, twenty and the joy of great joy fifty".

"That's why I've come down to Dorset, to spend some time

with you, oh brother of mine, you've got loads of room. I can set myself up in the music room, with the grand piano and compose away to my heart's content. The organisers know I'm here, I've given them the address and a telephone number. Staying in London would be just too much of a distraction", Anthony said, pointedly looking directly at Mrs M&D Society.

Mr and Mrs Brown, the housekeeper and handyman were told of the temporary new arrangements, over dinner. Never one to appreciate music Mrs Brown declared that under no circumstances was she prepared to put a single foot inside the music room. "And please, would Master Anthony keep his own bedroom and music room tidy. I shall not be at your beck and call".

As the evening broke up Mrs M&D Society slithered up to Anthony and resting her hand on his arm offered, "If I can help you in any way, perhaps copying or writing out parts, that sort of thing, please do give me a call, I would find it fascinating to work so closely with a famous composer", she purred. Anthony smiled, a lying smile that said, "Don't wait for the call".

Anthony was not the musical dunce he liked to pretend. In his early days, as a student, he had studied composition at the Royal Academy of Music and also at the Conservatoire in Berlin, the home of the Berlin Philharmonic.

The area around Bournemouth was a home for quite a number of good brass bands with varying degree of excellence. He took the opportunity to attend one or two rehearsals, he wanted to be sure in his mind of the different tonal qualities which the instruments provided and also to better understand what limitation they might have. Reading a full score demanded that you were fully acquainted with how the various individual and family groups of instruments interact with each other.

Anthony had his extended keyboard and computer brought down from London. Around the house 'Stubbs' and the housekeeper could hear a progression of chords, the construction and reconstruction of the melody often just a small number of bars. Anthony would go over the melody and then begin the process of harmonisation. Composing moved away from the piano to the synthesizer keyboard and the computer was now utilised with sophisticated software. Now he could more closely hear what the finished piece would sound like.

His brass band bosses in the capital were absolutely delighted. Anthony had kept them well informed of progress and had outlined the scope of the test piece. Anthony recalled the 1973 Hovis advert which featured Gold Hill in Shaftesbury and the music played by Ashington Colliery Brass Band. He would draw inspiration from the music of Gold Hill in Shaftesbury. He would give a musical salute to the Tolpuddle Martyrs. Music identified with Thomas Hardy would be featured in his test piece. Anthony succeeded in finishing the test piece entitled *Dorset Dowry*, without the assistance of Mrs M&D Society, packed up his belongings and moved back to London.

'Stubbs' was surprised to receive a letter a week later from the brass band people who had engaged Anthony. The letter was clearly addressed to Mr Adam Stubbington-Harris at the Dorset address. The substance of the letter was an invitation to be one of the adjudicators at the brass band championships.

Clearly this was an error, the invitation letter should have been sent to Anthony at his London address, but the administration still thought that Anthony was living down in deepest Dorset and hadn't updated the address records and for some unexplainable reason the two brothers had been mixed up. Adam with Anthony.

The matter is easily resolved, thought 'Stubbs'. I'll give Anthony a telephone call and explain the letter and then he can sort it out with the organisers because, quite clearly, they want him to be an adjudicator for his own piece, but I do quite like the idea of being an adjudicator myself. It appealed to his vanity.

Later that evening 'Stubbs' telephoned his brother. "Look Antelope, you lovely chap, there's been a frightful mix-up by your brass band fellas. They have been blowing trombones when they should have been blasting away on trumpets. I received a letter today inviting me to be an adjudicator at the brass band bash, the one you are writing the test piece for. Well, obviously it is wrong, the intended recipient of the letter is your good self, younger brother. I'll leave you to sort it out. Oh! by the way Mrs M&D Society is so sorry she couldn't catch up with you while you were down here composing".

"I think I should also let you know that for a bit of fun, nothing more, I've sent off my letter of acceptance to be an adjudicator!"

"Yes, 'Stubbs' leave it with me and I'll have a word with them the day after tomorrow. I'm sure it can be quickly sorted out. Rather wish you hadn't sent off the acceptance letter. Not much point you sitting as an adjudicator, you were an utter disaster at the County show judging the cows and the sheep. How could you have declared that old mingy looking animal 'Best in Show'. The only person who valued your judgement and thought you were right was the owner of the beast. The other shepherds were all in favour of shearing you!".

Anthony popped into the organisers office and explained the mix-up. "Oh dear", said Jeremy, handling contest arrangements, "that is most unfortunate. Let me just check and confirm". Jeremy reappeared with a copy of the letter in his hand. "Indeed, it does appear as if we've invited your brother to be the adjudicator". "Well I'm sure it's no problem", said Anthony, "just switch the names over, and it will be as you intended". "It may not be as easy as all that", with a shaking of the head Jeremy said, "We are going to have to consult the governing laws of the contest. The problem may be that once an invitation has been sent out and has been accepted, it may not be possible to uninvite your brother. I don't recall this situation before. Many of our laws go back decades!"

"Is it not the rule that adjudicators have to be members of the Governing Body or Institute. Surely, the judges have to prove that they are capable of serving as an adjudicator. You just can't pull anybody off the street who happens to be walking around with nothing much to do, stick them in a box and ask the 'kidnapped' to adjudicate", Anthony advanced.

By now Jeremy was treading water. "Yes indeed, that is the case and all the adjudicators that we use have the correct professional qualifications, without that there would be no trust and confidence at all in the result".

The organising committee met to discuss the impasse. They could write a letter direct to Mr Adam Perceval Stubbington-Harris withdrawing the invitation. The organisers solicitor cautioned against such action. Mr Stubbington-Harris had sent a second letter confirming that he was not prepared to withdraw and fully intends to fulfill the role as adjudicator on the day, as legally offered to him, the solicitor pointed out.

"The fact that he is not an accredited adjudicator does not preclude him from acting as one. The history of the competition has a long list of men who served as adjudicator, yet had no qualifications or membership accreditation. I fear if Mr Stubbington-Harris was to challenge our decision to remove him as an adjudicator in a court of law, he would most certainly win his case with costs".

A member of the committee noted, "We have had for many years, as long as I can remember, a very firm unwritten policy of only using adjudicators who have passed the appropriate examination and are members of the governing body, that is our policy now and we cannot go against it. If it goes to court then it goes to court, I am not so sure that the courts would find against us!"

"You've touching faith in the law and the courts", said the advising solicitor. "There are three little words with which Mr Stubbington-Harris can successfully defend his position". All eyes turned towards the solicitor. Sensing an audience, the solicitor sat back in his chair, appearing to be deep in legal thought and prompted by, "Come on man, what are these three magical words?" said slowly and with meaning, 'Exception to Policy'.

"You may have a policy, we will need to check that, but Mr Stubbington-Harris will be able to assert that an 'Exception to Policy' is warranted in this case. Your letter to Mr Stubbington-

Harris confirms and validates that exception. The letter did not state any conditions".

"If we do go ahead with this mad scheme, we are going to need an excellent public relations exercise to sell this one, not only to the bands, their conductors but also the band going public", noted the chairman. "Anybody got any bright ideas?"

Hazel James put her hand up to speak. Hazel was the newly appointed public relations officer for the organisation, the chairman saying 'good public relations exercise' made her realise that this was her moment. Hazel was a bright, quick thinking young lady. A little nugget suddenly dropped into her brain.

"I think the fact that the composer and adjudicator are brothers gives us something to work with; it's an angle which we may be able to turn to our advantage. The notion of choosing a non-qualified adjudicator demonstrates the forward-thinking of this committee. It can be seen as quite inspirational, taking the competition into new and exciting possibilities. We can sell this, not as a mistake, but something that the committee, after deep thought and consideration fully intended". With that an exhausted Hazel stopped and slumped into her chair.

The air of desperation was immediately lifted. "I think you've come up with something young lady; I think you can turn the negative into a positive. Now all you have to do is go away and write a press release. Jeremy you can explain to Adam and Anthony what we are proposing", concluded the committee chairman. It did not take long for Hazel to come up with the first draft of a press release.

New Adjudicator Announced

The Brass Band Championships have already announced the list of adjudicators for this year's competition. While two adjudicators are accredited, the additional third choice has no brass band experience whatsoever.

Already announced the test piece has been written by Anthony Stubbington-Harris, drawing inspiration from his home county of Dorset. The third adjudicator will be Anthony's brother Adam. Anthony spent much of his composing time in the family home in Dorset, and his brother was a listener to that composing technique and shared with Anthony the ethos of his music, Adam Stubbington-Harris has a unique insight into the test piece.

The chairman of the organising committee, Mr Jonathan Wellworthy, said, "This is an exciting departure for the competition, it is a demanding challenge to introduce a non-professional into the adjudicators' box. Support for brass bands and competitions comes from members of the public, some of whom play in brass bands, but others who enjoy listening to brass band music. For the first time, an adjudicator will be representing those thousands of people.

The press release was signed off and made available to the media, the music press and a copy sent to all band secretaries. The national media was cautious and had very little comment to make. Musical directors and contesting bands expressed dismay, dissatisfaction with the new proposed arrangement. "The contest could be decided by somebody completely outside the brass band world", emailed one MD, "The idea is totally insane and utterly flawed, there would be a miscarriage in deciding the ultimate winner. We may have to rethink our participation in this year's contest". Members of the public were largely supportive, "It makes the outcome considerably more democratic, let's see how it works out", wrote Tubby Tuba from Tooting!

On the day of the competition, the two brothers entered the auditorium together. Anthony to receive public recognition of the test piece he had produced. Adam as an object of some curiosity. He dressed as he would have done had he been going to Dorchester Market. With the same flamboyancy Adam acknowledged, what he took to be the adulation of the audience. Halfway down the aisle, Adam had to stop and wave to his 'fans' who had taken up the chant, 'Stubbs', 'Stubbs', 'Stubbs', 'Stubbs'. From out of his breast pocket, he took his large silk handkerchief, in the design of a Union Jack flag and waved it vigorously. With a final wave on the steps, 'Stubbs' entered the adjudicators' box to join his two colleagues. Now, all three incarcerated, the main business of the day, the adversary contest could begin.

The competition committee was greatly relieved to announce a unanimous winner, all three judges agreeing. When asked how he came to his decision, Adam replied, "My right foot – I found myself tapping away to the rhythm of the piece with my left foot and that applied to all the bands, with the exception of one. That band had my right foot tapping, told me all I needed to know".

Always Second!

(12)

MARK Stewart seemed destined to always be second. Second, proved to be a re-occurring pattern in his life. The second son in the family. Hand me down clothes from his brother. If he went out in the car with his father, it was always his brother who got the front seat.

He noticed that mealtimes his mother would always ask his brother first if he wanted another helping, that did not mean to say that he did not get an additional portion, it was that he was always asked second.

Summer holidays spent at Weymouth, camping, to begin with, and then in a caravan, always included a family game of cricket on the sands. First to bat, first to bowl was his brother. There was no resentment on Mark's part; he simply accepted that he was number two.

The big change came when elder brother Simon left home for university. Now it was just Mark, no longer a second, in the family order he had been elevated to number one spot. Mark also went to college but failed to get into the cricket first team, ended up playing for the second XI, he didn't open the batting and was quite some way down the batting order. Second choice to bowl.

He took some solace from the fact that the former president of the United States John F. Kennedy had been a second son and of course the second son of George V had become George VI. Most of the research did concede that being a second son did bring with it some fairly unusual problems mainly in the field of self-identification. The deputy leader was the second choice of his political party. There was a lot of commonality between being a deputy and being a second.

As part of his coursework at college, he produced a paper on being second best. He noted the dictionary explanation of being second. "Not as good as the best and therefore not wanted as much." It seemed rather harsh to him, but at the same time, it had a ring of truth about it. He recalled at junior school when they were making up 'teams', he was never picked to be captain, and was never the first choice of the captain, sometimes not even being picked at all until there was nobody else left.

His grandfather, to whom he was close, had encouraged him to study music or to be more precise an instrument. Grandfather pushed Mark to learn the flute because he considered it a gracious instrument from a bygone era. "It's got a lovely sound, has a flute, your aunt Mary used to play the flute; she was quite good at it actually, I think she played at your mum and dad's wedding".

Mark was going to disappoint his grandfather, not for him a flute. While at college he had attended a number of jazz clubs and was smitten by the sound of the trumpet and to a lesser extent the trombone. He thought if he was going to 'do an instrument', it would be one of those two but certainly not the flute.

While at college, passing one of the city's many second-hand shops, Mark saw in the window, hanging from a rail, a silver trumpet, a bit bashed and very grubby, he just couldn't resist going inside and having a look at it. The shop owner got it out of the window and passed it over for Mark to examine. "I've not had this trumpet long, probably been in the shop about a couple of weeks. We often get musical instruments in here being sold by students from the music department. Once they leave college, they come here to see if I'm interested in buying their instrument".

"You'd be surprised what we've had in this shop. About six months ago we had a really fine bassoon, that didn't hang around very long". "How much do you want for the trumpet?" Mark enquired.

Knowing that most students were fairly hard up, the shop owner was realistic with his prices. "I'd like to get thirty quid for it; it comes with a case and a couple of tutor books and a mouthpiece, oh and I'll throw in a music stand". Mark, in the traditional way of all buyers, pulled a face and wrinkled his nose. "How does £25 seem?". "OK, I can see you want it". With that, Mark handed over the cash and walked out of the shop with an instrument he didn't know how to play.

Fortunately, he had made a friend of a student who was taking a degree in the music faculty. The student was happy to give Mark some trumpet instruction, and quite quickly, Mark got to grips with the instrument to the extent that he could go along to the evening jazz club and join in when they held a 'free' session.

While he got through college without problems, he left with a decent degree, not the best. The next question was employment. One thing was very clear in his mind he did not want to go into an office situation. In fact, to be brutally honest he didn't want to work with anybody else, whoever he worked with and whatever he did he would end up being the second. He was fated.

That only meant one thing, and that was he was going to have to work by himself. A number of suggestions were presented, on the labouring side he could be a gardener, window cleaner, plumber or electrician, it was possible to do all those jobs as self-employed. None of those appealed. He considered collar and tie jobs; he could be an accountant, working from home, with that profession he could almost work in total isolation.

He quite liked the idea of being a book shop owner, whilst the world, at one time, appeared to move away from the printed word, there had been a resurgence in book buying and book owning.

His second hand bookshop would specialise in expensive and valuable first editions. He could visualise himself in the bookshop, folk would saunter in. "I wonder if you've got any Baedeker travel books, you know the really old ones that were clothbound in red?" "I collect Agatha Christie first editions". "I'm going on holiday on Saturday and want a couple of paperbacks for some light reading whilst sitting out in the sun.". Such charming enquiries would while the day away in a very pleasant convivial atmosphere, intermingled with tea and cake.

Mark could see himself as a bookseller. He would have sections on all topics, geography, topography, biography, musicology and the collected works of Enid Blyton for children, Catherine Cookson would meet the literary demands of the ladies, Dick Francis and Leslie Thomas were writers which mainly appealed to gentlemen readers.

However, for the time being, he took a number of temporary jobs. Everyone he knew at one time or another had worked for McDonald's. Shelf stacking for Tesco was another evening job. The Further Education College was looking for tutors to teach more adult students in the evening. Mark got a job there.

In another building on the campus, the local Old Comrades Band held their weekly rehearsal. On his way, home Mark stuck his head in through the door. There were some seats by the wall, and Mark went over and sat listening to the band. It turned out they were running through the last piece. Rehearsal finished the Musical Director came over, straight to the point, "Good evening, nice to see you, do you play an instrument?" Mark thought if I say 'no' he will tell me to, "Shove off!" "I've been learning to play the trumpet, mainly jazz when I was at college", Mark offered. "If you join us, I will get you out of those bad, wicked ways. Come back next week and I will sort you out a cornet, we don't like strange things like trumpets in our band".

The next week, his teaching tutorials with Further Education having finished, Mark entered the band room. "Good evening young man, good to see you again", said the Musical Director, "Now remind me, you have been messing about with the trumpet, well we've got a lovely silver cornet already for you. Best we start you on the second cornet and see how we go from there". "Here we go again", thought Mark, "second place once more". "Hello!", said a lovely pretty young lady introducing herself. "My name is Lauren. I think you're going to be sitting next to me. I'll be able to help you along, get you used to things". Perhaps second wasn't all that bad after all, considered Mark.

"The Musical Director can sometimes be a bit abrupt, direct

and grumpy, but don't be offended that's just his way. He's a jolly good chap really, and I should know he is my father". Mark nodded his head, understandingly.

The band was what you would expect to find in most towns, always anxious to recruit new players and with a need for funds to be able to keep going. Mark looked around the band at the first rehearsal, one or two 'old stagers' certainly, some in their 40s and 50s and others like himself and Lauren just into their 20s. They seemed a very happy bunch, and Mark warmed to them and Lauren in particular!

She too had just recently finished her college course after three years away. She had no difficulty in finding a suitable placement with one of the local solicitors. She rather frowned when Mark revealed that he had worked for McDonald's. Was Lauren a bit of a snob regarding McDonald's, or was she trying to tell Mark she was a vegetarian?

It wasn't long before Lauren and Mark were, as grandfather remarked, "Stepping out!", much to the delight of the whole band. Having made up their minds to get married, it was not going to be a long engagement. A date was quickly set for the wedding. A full band occasion. The bride, accompanied by her father wearing his Old Comrades Bandmaster uniform, entered the church to Felix Mendelssohn's 'Wedding March', played by the band with the church organ. As the couple exited the church, the band played 'Trumpet Tune' by Henry Purcell. Outside, sitting on some of the tomb stones, the band played some suitable music while the wedding photographs were being taken; the final one being of the bride and groom surrounded by members of the Old Comrades Band.

Mark still did not have a proper job, and the pressure was on for him to find one. Lauren had a well-paid job and Mark his temporary work, but it was just that, temporary. That situation could not last forever. He must find a permanent position, renting was expensive and they needed to get a foot on the property ladder.

A surprise offer came from his new father-in-law. Mark's first thought was that once again, he would be a second, again second fiddle. The prospect did not appeal, however, the job did. It was a job he didn't really realise existed. "You'll never be out of work, and if you're good at it there is a fine living to be made", said Lauren's father. "There really is something Victorian about him", thought Mark, "It's just as well he's not a chimney sweep otherwise he'll be pushing me up or dropping me down!".

Lauren was all keen on the idea, "This could really work out very well for you Mark, my dad is not a bad person to work for and with", suggested the musical director's only child. "He always wanted me to join him in the firm, but in that respect as a girl, I represented an enormous disappointment, 'I've got nobody to hand the company over to when I want to retire', dad would exclaim with bitterness and regret in his voice. You could just make him happy".

Lauren's father was the sole director and sole employee of Malcolm Dewhurst (Brass Band Repairs Ltd). Malcolm had served as a military bandsman, as well as playing in various military bands, Malcolm had shown an aptitude for repairing musical instruments, both woodwind, as well as brass and upon demob, had to set up his own business. Very quickly, he established a thriving enterprise; the word quickly spread around bands in the area that Malcolm did a good job in putting bent and dented instruments back together again.

Crumpled bells, twisted slides, broken valves all restored by Malcolm in his workshop at the bottom of his garden. The broken instruments of the brass band world entered Malcolm's shed. And following some skilful attention departed the shed ready to give many more years of banding service.

All around the workshop were the tools Malcolm used. On one of the shelves, he had a line of instrument mouthpieces ranging from the soprano right the way through to the BBb and all instruments in between. The bench and shelves were laden with instrument parts. From the ceiling beams instruments hung down, including some which were totally unrelated to either brass or woodwind. There was a double string bass suspended from the roof which Malcolm felt fairly certain was, "The home of a happy family of mice".

As you approached the shed, down the garden path, you could hear either the gentle tap of the hammer on metal or notes being blown through an instrument before finally being passed ready for use. It was into this world that Mark was going to enter.

"You married my daughter and one day all of this will be yours", said Malcolm spreading his arms and waving his hands around the shed. What a prospect thought Mark. Mark was going to be Malcolm's apprentice, or as Mark understood, he was going to be Malcolm's second. "Dad is anxious to pass the business onto you: he really does want to retire," said Lauren. "Does that mean I can become number one in the future?" ventured Mark.

Mark was a keen apprentice and quickly set about learning the business of repairing brass instruments, an occupation far removed from what his university degree indicated. Watching Malcolm and then working under his direction, Mark proved to be a very adept apprentice. Malcolm was delighted to see his progress.

Within the band, Mark got promotion away from the second cornet bench. Malcolm suddenly had need of a second horn player. The other members of the horn section said that in their view it most certainly was a promotion from that rabble on the cornet bench. This was not the promotion within the band that Mark anticipated but for the good of the band and to please his father-in-law Mark made a move. Second horn might in time lead to the solo horn.

Mark soon realised what a thriving business repairing instruments was. It seemed that brass band players were a very clumsy, careless lot. They did not look after their instruments. Once finished playing the instrument was quickly put away, very often with saliva still running through the tubes. Players would spend big money on buying their own instrument and then failed to properly look after it. The simple routine procedure would give added life to the instrument. It was nothing more than the basics. He often remarked that rarely would a violinist treat their instrument in the same way. Wiping down and loosening was all part of looking after a violin in a stored condition. It was not a surprise to Mark that so many brass instruments came into the work shop. Collapsed cornets, battered baritones, trampled trombones.

"When you finish playing and before you put your instrument away, just loosen the valves and loosen both the top and bottom valve caps, pull the slides out a little, and if you are going to mothball an instrument remove all the slides completely," advised Mark.

Much of Malcolm Dewhurst (Brass Band Repairs Ltd) was servicing instruments. Through lack of maintenance, into the shed came instruments very often with nothing more than an inability to get slides out or to undo valve caps. "This is bread and butter work Mark, not much to do but knowing how to do it is what matters." Malcolm was an excellent teacher, and Mark a willing learning pupil. Over the years there was pretty much nothing that hadn't come Malcolm's way in terms of instrument repair, and his knowledge he passed on to Mark.

Malcolm could identify the owner of an instrument just by looking at it. While a well-known euphonium player could play superbly he was a disaster in handling his instrument. "Freddy has just brought in his euphonium, he decided to put a chair through the bell", Mark reported to Malcolm. "Well it makes a change, the last time he decided to sit on it, euphoniums aren't designed to act as a cushion for 17 stone euphonium players" observed Malcolm. Malcolm's philosophy was "If you can push a dent in, I can push the dent out".

Mark learnt that there was very nearly 39 inches of tubing in a soprano cornet or in metric terms a metre. The Bb cornet had tubing length of 52 inches, the baritone and euphonium 102 inches and the BBb came in at 208 inches. All this information was essential in both the manufacturing and repairing of instruments.

Mark suggested that there was merit in having a tariff for most of the standard work. "Our customers would know how much the repair and MOT would cost," recommended Mark. "You mean like a take-away menu from the local Chinese. No 49 – One valve removed and serviced £15.00, No 55 – Two valves removed and serviced £23.00. No 57 – All three valves . . ." said Malcolm.

At the moment Malcolm decided what to charge job by job, very often trying to assess what the owner or band could pay. As likely as not he would not charge at all for the small jobs. Malcolm could see that now the business was providing for two, a fresh approach to charging was needed. Malcolm was convinced.

The Old Comrades Band continued giving programmes, attending fetes and regularly playing in the park bandstand. There was always movement within the band, players moving from one instrument to another. Indeed some players never seemed to be settled. Mark was to prove one of them. "I've got a problem with Angus who plays the second baritone", said Musical Director and father in law, "Angus has been playing the part for a good many years, and as you can see he is finding it increasingly difficult to get to all the rehearsals and engagements. Angus would like to retire, and for this reason, at the very least, I need to find a quick replacement". "Are you looking for volunteers, or are you asking me?", smiled Mark. "Well the former, but if not, I'll settle for the latter", said Malcolm. Mark was on his way to the third section he had played with. "It's just as well I can't play the trombone, or I've got a feeling I might be heading for the second trombone seat in the very near future", sighed Mark.

The band committee held one of their quarterly meetings. "I'm moving away", the deputy Musical Director announced, "I'm going to do what they call relocate, most unexpectedly the bank wants me to move to head office in London. It's a big opportunity. We do have mixed feelings about it, but as a family, we are convinced it's the right thing to do, I have to consider the future, not only or myself"

"It goes without saying that the band and myself in particular will be so sorry to see you go, you've been a great asset to the band, and I've been particularly grateful to you for the support you have given me as my deputy", said Malcolm.

"We are going to have to set about picking a replacement", noted the band secretary, "We need a new deputy Musical Director, although some bands have renamed the position Bandmaster". "Do you have anybody to recommend Malcolm, you know the players in the band, does anyone spring to mind?", the band treasurer enquired. Malcolm was not giving any reply; the other members of the committee could see he was reluctant to come forward with any suggestion.

"I think Malcolm's hesitancy is because he is thinking of Mark as the new deputy, but it's a bit within the family, so he is reluctant to put the nomination forward", suggested the band treasurer. "The fact is", said the current deputy, "we have nobody in the band who has any qualification, indeed neither do I. I don't think Mark is a risk and it will go down well with the rest of the band. Should you make the appointment, or at least ask him?".

The treasurer wanting to be helpful offered, "There is no question that Mark is well-liked, he's been to college, in my conversations with him, when we've been talking about music and the band he really is quite switched on. I don't think he would have a problem with the theory side of music, he knows the rudiments, a quaver from a crotchet and where middle C is. Working with you Malcolm, he must've picked up the mechanics and technology of banding. The question is, can he wave his arms around in the air and conduct the band. If he can, then he might be your man".

Malcolm put the idea to Mark, who reflected and accepted. "Does that mean as deputy I am the second in command?" asked Mark. "Don't worry Mark", said Malcolm, "I know you've got a thing about being a second and the deputy, Lauren told me. We might just be able to do something about that. About a week later Mark arrived at work, the name over the shed had changed; it now read, 'Malcolm Dewhurst & Son-in-Law (Brass Band Repairs Ltd)'.

Euphonium Eddie

(13)

DECORATING the bandroom walls were photographs taken of the band down through the years. The earliest one showed a collection of miscellaneous men dressed in an equally miscellaneous manner. Pill box hats, odd looking tunics, and a collection of weird and wonderful instruments, mixed in style and shape. The first picture of The Salvation Army band was taken on the Village Green, identifiable because of the public humiliation stocks that stood there then. It was years since anybody could accurately identify the men in the photo.

The next photo along showed the progress of the band, better dressed and more in number, a moustache with sideburns seemed to be the fashion in vogue. In the second photo, the backdrop was the parish church wall. Charlie Fenton, who should have retired from the band years ago, but still made every effort to blow a bass, would stand in front of the photo and gazing up extend the finger and say, "That was my grandad, he played bass as well. Times were hard in those days. He would come in from milking, have a quick bite to eat, give grandma a kiss and then he was off to band practice".

"One day, just for a bit of fun he went to band practice on the back of the farm horse, tied the reins to a post outside the Village Hall, and went in to band practice. Trouble was he hadn't secured the horse well enough and when he came out the horse was gone. Then the band had to go on a bit of a horse hunt. They found the old nag outside the pub enjoying a pint of beer. 'T'were an expensive ride that, grandad said, the horse should have made its way to the Mission Hall, tea is cheaper than beer! When the pub was refurbished, it was renamed the Nags Head".

Charlie Fenton had served during the Second World War, "I thought I'd give old Churchill a hand", he said, "The old Prime

Minister came to Salisbury Plain to see how the army was being trained. Usual thing, he had a little walk around, looked inside a tank, examined a machine gun and left giving us a two-finger salute".

On the band room wall were sepia photos of the band pre-war. The band ceremonially dressed in festival tunics and white-topped caps. At the back was the Band Colour Sergeant, with long, up to the elbow gloves, holding the band flag. In the centre of the photo, trying to look regal were the Corps Officers at the time, the Corps History Book records the names of Adjutant and Mrs Howard Piper. "You could take home a week's shopping in the size of her bonnet!" observed Charlie. "Did you notice that the photo was taken outside the hall, in those days it was almost impossible to have a band photo taken inside the hall".

Sitting between the officers was the Bandmaster, trying to emulate the pose of Lord Kitchener, a walrus moustache adding to the appearance. Across his chest was a wide, highly polished black leather belt around his chest. Part of the belt was a pouch which contained the chained Bandmaster's whistle, his authority on the march.

At the head of the march, three steps behind The Salvation Army flag, with polished, practiced movement, using first finger and thumb, he would release the whistle from the pouch. With a wide upward sweep of his arm, whistle and lips were joined. A blast on the policeman style whistle was the order for the bass drummer to 'double tap' followed by five single step beats. The Bandmaster was very strict; one band march played on the way to the Open Air, only hymn tunes to be played on the route back to the hall. Another whistle and 'double tap' to halt the march and then the bandsmen were drumbeated, in single file into the hall, of course, the Bandmaster leading the way.

Comparing a picture of the band after the Second World War showed graphically the impact that the conflict had made on the band and the wider Salvation Army. Bandsmen, who you might have expected to see in the band photographs, were now, sadly names on the Corps Memorial plaque. Bandsmen returned from the war, but not all returned to The Salvation Army.

The band recovered well following the war. In the loft of the old barn building of a hall stored music was found, although some music interested the mice, the euphonium part being favourite. The band secretary sorted the music through and with the aid of the 1930 invention, Sellotape, managed to repair most of the journals. Whilst the band had hobbled along during wartime conditions, now, early post-war was the time to get the band back into a more recognisable form.

In 1949 the band had their first postwar photograph taken. The band had accepted a weekend engagement to another neighbouring Corps. For quite a number in the band, it would be their first weekend 'away'. In later years most things were dated from that weekend, other weekends came and went, but for a couple of reasons, the first one remained in the memory.

The logistics of the weekend proved testing. Enquiries were made about using a char-à-banc, but the owner of the vehicle was terribly uncertain that the vehicle would make the 120-mile return journey. There were just three cars spread amongst the band, the principal trombone player had a split front screen Morris Minor, the Bandmaster a pre-war Riley Executive Car with full leather interior, and bulb lighting indicator arms which shot out of the car body announcing to other road users that they were going to turn either left or right.

The band sergeant had paid £129, from his demob settlement, for a Standard 8. For him Saturday afternoon was a car polishing time, a ritual he rarely broke. "Did I tell you that I spent a week of our holiday touring. We stayed at a lovely bed and breakfast in Bournemouth. We even had a little bedside carpet on either side of the bed; we paid a little extra so that our room was on the same floor as the bathroom." Most of the band had heard it once or twice before.

British Railways came to the rescue. The Great Western Railway, (God's Wonderful Railway), was ideal, being able to take the band from one station to another without changing. The band would travel as a 'job' lot, eight to a reserved second-class compartment, the band luggage travelling in the goods van. The band would travel in full Salvation Army uniform.

The plan was to travel down on the early Saturday afternoon train, arriving in time for a sit-down tea to be followed by an evening festival. Of course, the younger members of the band wanted to sit in the same compartment. The ticket inspector opened the compartment door, took one look at the younger generation, backed away, closed the door and moved on. It was not that they were unruly, rather simply high-spirited, dangling band caps through an open train window seemed rather good sport. The band sergeant was detailed by the Bandmaster to, "Go and break them up, separate them!".

Fortunately the outskirts of the town they were going to visit came into view, and within a few minutes the train pulled into the station. "You don't mind if we march to the hall, we've got plenty of time before tea, I know it's a bit uphill, but the march will give you an appetite", the home Corps Sergeant Major invited. That explained the greengrocers vegetable lorry parked close by. The home Corps Bandmaster arrived to lend support to the occasion, and asked, "Do we go the short route or a long way through the town?". The short route might have got the vote, but the long way won the day.

The Band Colour Sergeant had formerly served with the Coldstream Guards, "I did 18 years before the colours, signed on before the war, took the King's shilling. I know my way from Wellington Barracks to Buckingham Palace". In truth he had every reason to be proud of his military service, what he learnt then he remembered now. He could with a parade ground bark, suggest to the new entrants into the band, "Am I hurting you, 'cos I'm standing on your hair. Get your haircut, you charming lot, and put some polish on your shoes".

For the Band Colour Sergeant, there is nothing more pleasing than a parade, and the long way back to the hall suited him. With flag flying in the breeze, he was ready. The gentle slope out of the railway carpark gave way to a steeper incline. In the far distance could be seen the top of the church tower, the march was heading that way and it did appear to be quite a step.

Wanting to impress from the first note the Bandmaster shouted, "*'Victors Acclaimed'*. We will play the march all the way through as written, back to the beginning and finish at fine!", the number was quickly passed around the band, with shakes of heads. Second cornet asked his mate, "What's this back to the beginning and finish at fine nonsense?" and when the Bandmaster deemed that all were ready the opening bars of the march sounded forth.

Wisely Eddie, the euphonium player, opted to travel up to the hall in the greengrocer's lorry, perched in the back amongst the instrument cases, suitcases and all the other band paraphernalia. When the wartime restriction on clothing rationing ended, Eddie sent off his measurements for a new uniform to Salvationist Publishing & Supplies Ltd. Not believing what they read, they sent back a telegram seeking confirmation and indicated it would take a lot longer to complete the order because of his size. Eddie was 'well off' the tailor's measuring tape.

"What took you so long?", said Eddie, a cup of tea in hand, as he welcomed the band to the hall. Spirits were lifted with the pre-festival tea, allowing for postwar shortages the band tucked into a really fine feast. A good crowd turned up for the festival, in fact, there was hardly an empty seat. Eddie was to be the star of the night playing the in vogue euphonium solo *Ransomed* by Bandmaster George Marshall. The more the audience applauded, the more Eddie's face beamed.

Festival over, the matter where they were going to sleep was next on the itinerary. During the pre-planning for the weekend visit it was made clear there were not enough billets to go around. "Would some of the band be prepared to sleep in the Junior Hall?" Chairs and forms were converted into beds, blankets and pillows provided. There was a great deal of larking about, it was well past 12 o'clock before things finally quietened down.

Eddie was put in charge of the dormitory with instructions

from his wife not to put up with any nonsense. In the morning the sleepers were woken at eight o'clock sharp. A full English breakfast was on the menu.

The weekend was memorable. Going by train, the long march up the hill to the hall, the over-night and the sight of Eddie searching for his socks!

Next door to the Army Hall, Euphonium Eddie owned the fish and chip restaurant, the aroma of which, profusely, travelled with him. Eddie was both large and jovial, like the smell of fish and chips his belly laugh travelled, he had been recorded with a 98db decibel reading, just a touch over farmer David's tractor.

Eddie was the corps treasurer, and along with other local officers would assemble in the officer's room for prayer prior to the meetings. From the officer's room, adjacent to the platform, the small group could hear the band play the opening tune. Somehow the conclusion of prayer and the band tune ending coincided. Eddie had his music and euphonium already in place, tune book open and euphonium propped up against his chair, bell end on the floor. Closing the officer's room door behind him, Eddie would ascend the five steps onto the platform; his chair gave an alarming creak as he sat down. Euphonium cradled in his arms he would pick up the hymn tune.

Over the other side of the platform, the younger members of the cornet section followed this routine Sunday by Sunday evening. Roy, recently up from the junior band, had a vision in his mind's eye. He outlined what he thought would be a really good practical joke on Eddie. Although Eddie was a number of years older than them he was not quite in the 'old codger' bracket, Eddie could be a good laugh, Roy was sure Eddie would take it in the right way.

Most of the band were interested in football. Eddie was a keen supporter of Arsenal who won the League Title in the 1948 season for the sixth time in their history. It was free chips all round that day, with Eddie serving with an Arsenal scarf around his neck. Eddie liked to show his loyalty to Arsenal; his scarf was all year apparel. It didn't quite go with Salvation Army uniform, but free fish and chips didn't come free either! Wearing his scarf with uniform was the price Eddie charged. The embargo, which Eddie excepted, was the ban on wearing the Arsenal scarf on a Sunday at the Open Air. Flipping from shop to hall and hall to shop was okay.

Eagerly the cornet trio anticipated the Sunday evening arrival of Eddie. Eyes followed him as he went into the band room. Eddie emerged carrying his euphonium, music stand and music. Instrument, music and stand in place Eddie lumbered off the platform and headed for the officers' room. The game was on.

The opening tune was *Crown the Saviour*, the second note of just about every bar was a sharp 'accidental'. The Bandmaster looked across to the cornets, "Mind your fingering, you've got a few 'sharps' in there". It made little difference. Overheard by the congregation, the Bandmaster could be heard annunciating, "First, First and Second, Second and Third". The fact that the same four bars were repeated three times made did not occur to them. Clearly, the three youngsters were not concentrating, their mind was not on the music, he doubted if any of them were actually looking at the tune book, there was an air of expectation, he felt sure something was about to happen.

Halfway through the second time playing through the tune, with no improvement at all on the first, Eddie arrived on the platform. If Eddie could blow up a bit it might just cover some of the cornet errors.

Eddie picked up his euphonium; he knew the tune well enough, he would pick it up halfway through. Ready to play middle C, he took a deep breath and blew, he blew again, he didn't hear any notes coming out, in fact, the instrument was jolly hard to blow. Last four bars, nothing, he thought he detected a slightly muffled sound. The tune over, time to check his mouthpiece to see if there was a blockage. With all the valves depressed, Eddie continued just blowing through without trying to produce a note. Nothing. Blow, blow, blow, nothing to report. Giggling from the cornet players interrupted the Corps Sergeant Major as he was giving the announcements, he turned towards them with a disapproving look, the giggling now turned to raucous laughter.

In effect, the meeting had stopped. All eyes now turned towards Eddie, as resting his euphonium, he inserted an arm into the bell, his fingers felt something soft at the bend of the instrument, gripping the material, out came Eddie's red and white Arsenal scarf! Laughing and giggling can be very infectious.

By now more than half the band was in fits of laughter. Even the Home League Secretary, sitting in the songsters, never one given to humour could see the funny side of it.

The incensed Corps Sergeant Major, there and then, demanded a month's suspension from the band for each of the miscreants. The Bandmaster concurred. The Corps officer, a Senior Captain, a placid kind of fellow, wanting to sit on the fence, said, "Well I don't know . . .", and left it at that.

When Eddie finished howling with laughter, he announced that if they took any action against the youngsters it would be the end of free chips.

A wise and saintly retired Brigadier promptly stood up, sensing that the meeting was over before it had begun, pronounced the Benediction! "Praise God from whom all blessings flow - including free chips!"

Librarian Liability

(14)

In Appreciation of Librarian Terry Brittan

THE Town Market Charter stated. "The Title to the Town Market made by Elizabeth I with Letters Patent dated 27th June 1590. The market to be held on a Wednesday throughout the year between the hours of nine before noon and the second hour in the afternoon for any of our subjects whatever to buy or sell in that the market all manner of goods and chattels". The first holder of the Charter was the Lord of the Manor and subsequently his heirs.

However, towards the end of the 20th century, with the number of street markets dwindling and pressure from out-of-town supermarkets The Town Council, in 1990, announced plans to acquire the Market Charter from the holder of the title. It was also the 400th anniversary of the market's inception.

The Town Council decided Wednesday 27th June 1990, would be the date to celebrate such an important event. The celebrations would begin with a procession from the Town Council Civic Hall, including voluntary groups, to a church service at 11.00am when the full text of the town charter would be read.

A funfair was booked and would be held on the 'village green', a full programme of activities was planned, the day would conclude with a grand firework display. As part of the market, space would be given over for charity stalls.

Press releases were published prior to the celebration day. One resident wrote into the council, "It is good that the town has something to celebrate, let's ensure that we make it a day to truly remember".

When Terrance Smart moved to the town, he was

disappointed that the town did not have a brass band, he had always played in a band from a very early age. He missed his banding. Reading about the transfer of the Charter and the 400th anniversary of the market and the big celebrations, Terry felt that a brass band was the missing ingredient. There was so much the band could add to the celebrations, they could play in the church service, give a concert in the afternoon on the village green, and also perform just before the firework display.

The idea of a town band went around and around in his head; he just could not let the idea go away. Passing the Town Civic Office, he thought 'I'll go in and have a word with the Town Clerk you never know'. Mr Dale, the Town Clerk, greatly regretted the fact that the town did not have a band. He expressed the hope that Terry might be able to do something about it. "I am certain that the Town Council would be quite prepared to put some money towards the inauguration of a town band, the Mayor is very keen", said the clerk. "I'll send out a press release about forming a town band, let's see what sort of response we get, we could title the piece, 'Would you like to blow your own trumpet!'.

Both Mr Dale and Terry were in amazement at the response. Sixteen people turned up to the informal meeting, gentlemen who had formerly played in military bands, some youngsters who had been taught instruments at school, and other people, who like Terry, had banding experience. From the group, it seemed that one of the former military bandsmen was best placed to become the first Musical Director.

Brass instruments might be a problem, but it was surprising how most of the folk who turned up had their own instruments, including a chap who played tuba in a dance band. The embryonic band could look at leasing some instruments was suggested. Someone mentioned that they had heard of a band in another county which, sadly, was closing down. The Town Clerk would investigate.

During the intervening week, progress was made. The Town Clerk tracked down the band that was being disbanded and managed to secure several instruments and the entire library of band music. He was surprised when he went to pick up the purchases, that included in the overall price, was a set of jackets. The town now had a town band.

The Mayor came to the first rehearsal and had a go at banging the bass drum. The opinion was divided as to whether or not to invite him to be a band member. Someone suggested that he should play the gong seeing as he already had one around his neck!

Terry offered to be the band librarian which was readily accepted. Whilst the band's repertoire was limited the newly inaugurated town band not only accompanied some of the hymns in the church service, they also attracted a big crowd when they gave a concert during the afternoon on the village green. The last engagement of the day was playing at the firework display. Not only did they play well, but they also managed to attract folk who were interested in joining the band. Invitations to play at garden fetes and summer fayres came in.

From those early beginnings, the band developed musically and numerically; members came and went. Old instruments were replaced, and new jackets purchased to mark the beginning of the new century.

Terry recalled those days when, 20 years later, he was to retire as the band librarian. "Time I stood down and made way for a fresh face", said Terry. At his retiring dinner dance, Terry remarked, being the librarian was the one job that he'd wanted in the band. Not for him Musical Director or deputy, neither for him any of the 'end' chairs. Being a band librarian would be the height of his ambition. To other people, it was one of the most boring of jobs in the band, no glory in distributing music.

The MD thanked Terry for all the hard work he had put into serving the band and for suggesting that the town had a band in the first place and being a founder member. The Town Mayor, always keen on a photo opportunity, presented Terry with a Civic Award. "You can get in free to any of the town band concerts!", concluded the Mayor.

"Essentially, there are two elements to a band library. The

first is how the material is archived. The second is controlling concert music. Both need to have robust systems. Storage of music breaks down into two subdivisions. Both are primary, one repository by part and the other silo by title", said Terry in his retirement speech. Wanting to sound clever, he recited what he had read in a book, not knowing fully what it meant.

"At one time, there were just two methods of storing sheet music, both have merit, and both involved some sorting. One method is to store the music by the title, every part in the one docket envelope. The sorting involves getting sheet music into the full score list in order, beginning with soprano and moving down through to percussion."

"The second method favoured by many librarians is having a docket envelope for every band member in the band. In a very large band that could be over 40 players requiring file boxes to contain their music. Sorting through box file after box file putting the contents in order can be a very time-consuming exercise. The digital age has introduced a third way of storing music and keeping music. Increasingly we see the use of iPads, a complete music library on one tablet", concluded Terry.

Nobody was quite sure which method Terry used. "Probably a mixture of the two, but who can tell?", the band secretary offered.

The subject of Terry's replacement was on the agenda of the next meeting of the band committee. The executive members felt they ought to make the position open to applicants, and once the list had been whittled down, interviews should be held. "Is this really necessary?", enquired the band secretary. "Well, the big bands these days are advertising when they have an opening for a librarian. Often, they are seeking a non-playing person to do nothing more than looking after the music", countered the Bandmaster. "Is this going to be a paid position, or are we seeking someone who is prepared to do the job on a voluntary basis?", asked the secretary.

"Well, voluntary if we can, but if not we may have to pay a small honorarium, that is the practice in some bands", voiced the MD. The committee decided that they would advertise the position in the local press rather than The British Bandsman, they did not think that the band was quite in the top league.

The band secretary sat down to write a job spec. 'A band librarian', he wrote, 'is a person who administers matters pertaining to band music maintenance, cataloguing all the music of the band'. Not believing it himself he continued, 'band librarians tend to be artistic individuals, creative, sensitive and articulate. Some of them are also 'enterprising, extroverted, energetic, enthusiastic, expressive' he was now running out of 'E's, 'confident, and optimistic'. "If old Terry can 'crib' a bit, so can I", thought the band secretary thumbing his way through a job vacancy magazine looking for suitable text.

Three replies were forth-coming, worth following up. One from within the band, Di Roberts. One from a former member of the band, Jeff Tomlin and a Mr Arnold Agnew.

Di Roberts enjoyed greeting people with, "Llan-vire-pooll-guin-gill-go-ger-u-queern-drob-ooll-llandus-ilio-gogo-goch! I'm Welsh, you see". When Wales won at rugby, he was quite unbearable; he would raucously play the verse of *'Land of My Fathers'* on his trombone and then with great passion sing the chorus in Welsh, it was like being in the middle of a thunder storm.

When asked at his interview by the band secretary, "What would be your system to make sure that all the players had the music in their portfolio and was the order?" replied "Oh I would not check to make sure everybody had their music. I work on the 'hands up' principle. The Musical Director calls out the piece to be played, and then I wait for the hands to go up of those who can't find the music, like school children wanting to go to the toilet. Then I'd go off and hunt for the missing parts".

Jeff Tomlin had not been what you might call a committed bandsman. He seemed to enjoy an excessive amount of ill-health, which prevented him from attending rehearsals and engagements. "You don't want to come anywhere near me", he would say before rehearsal, "I've got the dreaded lurgy, I've been feeling poorly all day, I shall have to go and see the doctor in the morning, I'm certainly not fit enough to go to work, but I did manage to go to work one-day last week!"

The local health clinic had a team of ten doctors; Jeff had been in the consulting room of each of them so often that he addressed them by their Christian names. For the band mastermind quiz evening, Jeff's chosen subject was 'Ill Health', he scored a maximum number of points. He had retired from the band citing general permanent unwellness, stating the side drumsticks were proving to be a little heavy and could he be put on triangle. At the interview, he was asked, "Do you think you could cope with the amount of music photocopying there might be?" Jeff said he was very uncertain, pressing the start button might aggravate strain on his index finger, and lifting the photocopying lid would exasperate the problem with his wrist joint.

Mr Arnold Agnew was someone that nobody in the band could say that they knew. When Mr Agnew attended the interview, he was smartly dressed, his appearance was completed by a small pair of glasses, precariously set at the end of his nose giving the impression that any moment they would slip off.

Most of the committee thought that it was a complete waste of time bringing Mr Agnew in for an interview. His application form stated that he had been a private music teacher, mainly giving lessons to paying students. Mr Agnew had also been a supply teacher at various schools; he specialised in teaching brass. Mr Agnew was asked if he could play a brass instrument, in a cultured voice, he replied, "Un peu, un peu, orchestral, but never in a brass band." The band secretary thought the manner in which he uttered, 'brass band' was rather, "peu dédaigneux". The Musical Director said he wanted to ask the simplest of questions, "Why, Mr Agnew, have you applied to be the band librarian of the Town Band?"

What followed was Arnold Agnew giving a band committee six of the best, and both barrels. "I've been to a number of your band concerts, and observed what goes on, and while I make no comment on the music that was chosen and how it was performed, what was apparent is a problem with some players trying to manage their music. It is not uncommon to see bandsman looking around the platform trying to find the next piece of music, was it under the chair, was it already on the music stand, had somebody else got the music?"

"On one occasion, I witnessed a rather nasty altercation amongst the basses; they nearly came to blows over the music. Clearly, there was only one part and two basses. How that sheet of music wasn't torn in half I still cannot understand. How that music suffered. In the end, because the band had already commenced playing, they had to share a stand and the one sheet of music. They were continually moving the stand between them. I'm sorry to say things are in an absolute frightful state and need sorting out so that never again do we witness the traditional 'let's hunt the music game', played out on the platform in front of the embarrassed audience."

The committee was taken aback; the Musical Director had thought Terry had done a first-class job and said so at his retirement. It was true to say that there were occasional mishaps, not Terry's fault. One example being, like a bad game of Chinese Whispers, number 36, 'Ave Verum', was called out and passing from one player to another became number 32, 'The Hallelujah Chorus'. A minor mishap. Some in the band maintained that by the time the number got around to the soprano he was playing number 38, 'Excerpts from Samson'! The fact that both the Hallelujah Chorus and 'Ave Verum' were in 4/4 time and excerpts from the Samson minuet in 3/8 time didn't appear to make any difference to the soprano player. Fortunately, he didn't come in until the second bar and then only with a quaver which probably helped the situation.

"Perhaps", invited the band secretary, "you would explain how you propose to improve the situation. Looking after the band music has never been as good as it could have been I'll accept, but we've struggled along, with the system we have, why change something with which the band are comfortable? Second horn enjoys being last to find his music. It is just a big game used to make Terry cross. Sometimes he'd put his hand up indicating he didn't have the music, when all along he had. If the second horn had every piece of music ready at the drop of the Musical Director's baton, we would send him off to see the doctor".

"Give Mr Agnew time to explain, let's hear the good gentleman's plans to change and improve the system", said the Musical Director.

"Indeed, I can explain. I will bring science to the band librarian job", said Arnold. "Forgive me interrupting", said an irritated band secretary, "we are simply talking about sheets of music, so I don't know where science comes into it. And how does science sort the music, know which is the bass part and which is the cornet part, how does science know that Jonathan has his music upside down and left his mouthpiece at home?".

"Oh, but it does", said Arnold, not in the least bit offended. "There is much that science can offer to the library of instrumental music, be it orchestral, pop, folk or brass band. If appointed, I will offer the band a scientific course in sheet music appreciation. I want the band to value their band parts. Once they see the music in a more enlightened way, not having the correct music and not being in playing order will become a thing of the past. What really matters is values. Musical science can be a great enabler. Once Jonathan has completed the course, there will be no more upside-down music or mouthpieces left at home. Jonathan will be scientifically transported into a sheet music appreciation orbit".

As he approached the door on the way out, Arnold turned around, "I myself have a diploma, MSc in Library Science from the University of London, so you see I am well qualified to be a band librarian. Have you ever thought it might be a mistake to give bandsmen band music!".

The committee pleaded with Terry to come back out of retirement.

Tenor Horn Twins

(15)

JANICE and Susan were twins. "They couldn't get on in the womb, and it's been like that ever since", a tired and exasperated mother, Mrs Bateman would say when mention was made of the twins. Indeed it was so.

The twins knew when they had to behave themselves, were charming in public, and they loved people saying how alike they looked and how gorgeous they were and wasn't mother lucky to have two adorable daughters and not just one. They would smile and react to the crowd. "Don't they get on so well, isn't that nice to see in children?"

Away from the crowd, their true relationship came out. Sometimes it was little skirmishes, and other occasions it could develop into a total war. Making the other one's life a misery was the aim and object of each twin. When they were toddlers, Janice was the taker and hider, Susan's Teddy bear would mysteriously 'leave home'. Janice would deny all knowledge, she had no idea where the teddy bear was, she couldn't remember the last time she had seen it. "We all know that Susan is very careless, I bet she's lost it herself", asserted Janice, in a grown-up way. "You took it, I know you did, you're really horrible, I hate you!" bawled a tearful Susan.

Susan was never slow in getting even, and perhaps she was even more devious. Susan sought to blame everything that went wrong on Janice, a ploy which often worked because Susan could be so convincing. "I am the good one", she would say, with a demure look on her face.

What the twins' parents remembered most about school days, was being repeatedly asked to attend the school by the head teacher to, "Have a chat with the staff. What were they like at home? Had the parents considered counsellin?" "For us or the children?" Mr Bateman asked. Were they really that unruly and disruptive?

The school was just another battleground. Susan's maths book was found behind the caretaker's shed, with pages torn out. A broken school window was definitely broken by Janice, "I saw her, she had the hockey ball in her hand. She is a rotten thrower", explained a persuasive Susan during the inquest.

Family holidays could be difficult, inter twin tension was always close at hand. But that said they were a family who enjoyed doing things together. With their minds on other things and being distracted, upsetting the other twin did not seem quite as important and engaging. Long holiday walks helped disperse animosity amongst the twins; they just did not have the energy.

As the twins got older, so relationships improved, there was something of a truce. Indeed there were times when they could be particularly nice to each other. The word considerate was often being used. The bickering of previous years became but a memory.

The family had other shared interests. Amateur dramatics. Both twins were very put out when they were cast as two ugly sisters in the Christmas pantomime Cinderella. "He's behind you!" followed by "Oh, yes it is!" and "Oh, no, it isn't!" brought back sensitive feelings. One young wag was lucky to get away with a slight bump on his nose from Susan when, in a rather loud, penetrating voice he was heard to say, in the bar after the performance, addressing the twins, "I see you two were correctly typecast!".

Banding was another shared interest. Each family member could play a brass instrument and doing things together meant they enrolled in the local town band when they moved into the area. Four more players were a very welcome addition to the band. "It's good to have new members, I'm sure they will make a difference, fit in well, and will be a great asset", said the Musical Director. "Talking just between you and me, Steve on the soprano is a bit over the hill", said the MD to the band librarian, "I think this new chap can play soprano".

"You'll need to go carefully there", said the band librarian, "you know how abrasive Steve can be, you don't want to get on the wrong side of him, he can blow up. You won't be the first MD to have a cornet mute thrown at his head! Remember last Christmas when you pointed out in the rehearsal that he was making a 'pig's ear' of the sop part in *'Christmas Joy'*. We all thought you'd be the first Musical Director to be strangled in a band rehearsal, the way he grabbed you by the throat!" The MD paled. He's going to have another think thought the band librarian.

Mark Bateman slotted into the solo cornet bench, number four down the row, his was mainly a bumper-upper role. He didn't want to play soprano in any case, having seen the fearsome look on Steve's face. Evidently, word had got around the band that he was to be Steve's replacement. Just like the rest of the band, he could lie. "You're doing a grand job, Steve, the soprano is not an easy instrument to play, there you are all alone and totally exposed. Everybody can hear every wrong note, and of course the good ones. I really admire you, it takes courage and stamina", said Mark, patting Steve on the back, as they talked during the tea break in rehearsal.

Mrs Bateman was comfortable playing the second trombone part. The band had never had a female member in the trombone section, it was a novelty, and all were on their best behaviour. "Have you got the music? Is the stand at the right height? Do you want a drop of my trombone oil? Here, let me carry your trombone case". Mrs Bateman was overwhelmed by trombone kindness and consideration. "Give it a month", said cynical Brian. He knew trombone players.

A universal dilemma for musical directors is the players that own their instrument. They have the upper hand, by privately acquiring their 'kit' they determine what they are going to play. The MD loses control and player flexibility. "Why did Harry ever go and buy that cornet? It's not as if he can manage. It's not without good reason that he has the nickname Mr Wobbly", wailed the MD when raising the issue with his good friend, the band librarian. "Harry does drive the band coach", observed the band librarian, seeking to support Harry. "Yes, and he's a bit wobbly with that!" retorted the MD.

The Misses Bateman were given a Tenor Horn each for their eighteenth birthday by their over-generous grandfather. His first thought had been a pair of boxing gloves each, followed by fencing foils. Babysitting the twins had involved signing up for a boxing referee course and the purchase of body protection.

Both girls had asked for a Besson Sovereign Globe Round Stamp, at the time still available. When told of the new price grandpa Bateman suggested that perhaps one daughter would have been adequate, a fact confirmed by his bank balance. In fairness, the girls were pretty good players, they had played in the school band and also the town band where they previously lived.

Now the universal banding dilemma came into full focus. Already the tenor horn section had enough for a hand of whist, although one of them, retired Public Health Inspector Andrew had to ask to be excused more frequently, "Weak bladder, weak bladder!", he exclaimed as he hurried for the door signposted Gents". Nowadays Andrew was spending more time in the toilets than in the band room!

With two more horn players about to join the band, the MD had to prune the horn section, that was clear but who would go?" the MD pondered, then he pondered some more, and the more he pondered the less any solution presented itself.

The sticking point was The Brass Band Rules for contesting bands which stated: "The Contest is open to brass bands only, consisting of a maximum of 25 brass players plus percussionists, as required by the band". The band would now be over that number by one.

Cynical Brian suggested that the band have nonplaying players. They could sit in the band formation and simply go through the motions, give their instruments a good shake from time to time, letting out the non-water through the water key, forage about looking for the music. Cynical Brian pointed out that there were at least a couple of band members who were already part of that exclusive club. All blow but no sound. All wind but no aperture release.

The MD was compelled, in one rehearsal, to bring the band to a halt and to ask the question which one of the suspects had indeed offered a note. They looked at each other, shaking heads, "Not me Guv", was the expression on genial faces. Cynical Brian, ever wanting to stir the pot, said, "We could let the nonplaying players only pay half subs, or they could pay the band subscription on a note basis, with a discount for over fifty notes played". There was something not quite right about cynical Brian.

The Musical Director was not the brightest, polished baton at the rostrum. Best hand the problem over to the Band President.

"Let's sit down and have a chat about it. What are the options? You know me ever ready to help", said the President. They found a quiet corner in the smoking room of the British Legion Club, where the band held their rehearsals, surrounded by military plaques and photos. With clouds of cigar smoke being puffed towards the MD the corpulent, full suited President re-capped. "Too many horns, you say, sack a few. I did that at the factory. The factory has been closed for five weeks, they're all out on strike in sympathy for the ones I sacked; still, my golf is improving". The MD coughed, a cough which the President interpreted as, 'not the best idea'.

"You say you have a couple of new tenor horn players joining the band, as I understand it twin sisters. The horn section has always been a bit girly, all nail polish and hair lacquer. Temperamental is not the word for it. You say twin sisters, are they identical, you know look the same?"

Suddenly the wily old President had a germ of an idea. Nodding his head with the attitude of the wisdom of Solomon, he brushed his cigar ash off coated lapels. "I think I might just have it. You're round I think", said the President directing his brandy glass towards the MD.

The plan was simple enough; you could write it down on the

back of a fag packet. In fact the scheme was so elementary, that it wasn't even needed to be written down. Thinking that a 'belt and braces' job was prudent the MD proposed a Special Meeting of the Governing Committee to decide on the matter. The MD quoted the rulebook to the band secretary and stated, "Under article 10 of the Bands Rules and Regulations, Section 14, Paragraph 5. "A Special Meeting of the Band's Governing Committee can be held subject to Five Clear Working Days of Notification and Three Members Agreeing. That's me, you and the band librarian".

Brass bands are notoriously bad for keeping secrets, like passing the parcel with the music rarely stopping, the news of the convened special meeting flew around the band. Chinese Whispers added a garbled version of the Present's Plan and it was transmitted quicker than passing the number of the next band item. Cynical Brian, quick out of the block, and drawing on the Dad's Army character, Private Frazer boomed, "It's doomed, it's doomed, the man's a fool if he thinks it will work out!"

The band legal bits being satisfied, the Special Governing Committee Meeting was called. In the small television room at the British Legion Club, fortified by drinks from the bar, the committee members assembled. The president being absent, the band secretary was voted in to take the chair. Exercising his new elevated status as the chairman, in pompous tones, he detailed the problem and then unveiled the plan advocated by the president. "Get on with it!", said an irritated band librarian. "The whole town knows the plan. My missus called it daft", adding, "What more can you expect from a bunch of idiot men?"

All members were agreed that the tenor horn section needed 'lopping', if the membership could not be reduced, by natural wastage, retirement in the case of Andrew, then the President's stratagem would need to be considered, a vote was to be taken and if accepted the resolution would be implemented. The band must stay within contesting regulation numbers. The vote was unanimous. Recommendation accepted. Minutes of the meeting were taken and recorded in the Minute Book.

The 'Cigar and Brandy' scheme was predicated on the fact that the twins were identical. Telling them apart was nigh on impossible. The simple idea was that both Susan and Janice could join the band, equally they could attend band rehearsals together, but only one twin could play in competition, thereby keeping strictly to the rules. "Well that was nice and simple", said the band secretary now reduced to his former status, picking up his empty beer tankard. "Time I think for another swift one before I go home". It was agreed that the way to handle Andrew was through his wife. The committee felt that the good lady would be able to persuade Andrew to stay at home and use his own toilet! A suitable token of appreciation would be made to Andrew at the appropriate time.

Cynical Brian, who had placed his ear to the television room door, burst in. "Get Andy an engraved musical toilet holder, every sheet a different tune!"

The Musical Director did not foresee a problem with the twins; they would be understanding, they were reasonable young ladies, they knew how these things were, what's for the good of the band. In any case, it would only be a temporary measure until the tenor horn section was thinned out when both twins would be able to play. Methodically the MD rehearsed his argument; he could not envisage anything going wrong.

He had asked the twins to come into the weekly rehearsal the night following the special meeting a touch early. The band secretary was going to attend providing moral support. Susan and Janice already knew of the plan, and happy with it they were not. During the day both had been brewing for a fight. Neither was prepared to make way for the other.

The ladies arrived together, Susan banged on the door of the television room. That single treble forte knock on the door was like the first maroon set off before a gigantic firework display. Boom, the knock reverberated as far as the bar, causing Andrew to spill his drink.

"Right", said Janice, avoiding any pleasantries. "pin your ears back and listen. I'm not sharing my place in the band with anybody, and certainly not Susan". Stabbing a finger in the Musical Director's chest, she added, "I know I'm the best player, she is rubbish. So tell her to sling her hook".

Susan, not to be outdone, with nostrils flaring, shouted, "My sister is a pain, she is nothing but trouble, you'll regret the day you ever allowed her to join your crummy band. I hope she falls over a music stand and lands face down on the floor. Play the horn, she can't even play toilet paper over a comb!".

By now the bar customers were gathered around the door. "Ladies, ladies", pleaded the MD, "decorum, decorum please". As the punch came in from Susan, missing Janice by inches, the MD was exploding, "Let's not come to blows".

"Just a usual night at the club", the secretary noted. "The Legion should charge for the entertainment", said cynical Brian.

"Why did we ever let women into the band"? queried the Musical Director.

Band Secretary/ Administrator

(16)

HENRY Chapman, the brass band's secretary, was a bit of a disaster. Not that he intended it, but so often he got things wrong. Sometimes he was able to get away with it, on other occasions, the whole band knew that the band secretary had dropped another 'clanger'. He always apologised profusely afterwards. "Sorry about that, but you know what I'm like, sometimes it's just unfortunate that I get the details a little wrong", he would offer.

There was a catalogue of band secretary mishaps. The band recalled the occasion in December when the band was booked to give a carol concert to one of the local social clubs. There were only three things Henry needed to get right, the venue, the date, and the time. Henry got two out of three right, the one he got wrong was the date.

The band arrived in plenty of time to get set up and to commence the concert. The problem was the date. "I felt sure I'd got the date right, I wrote it down, we've been there before, I always thought it was a Wednesday afternoon that the band played to these good folk", said a contrite Henry. "Don't worry Henry", said Musical Director Maurice, "it's an easy mistake to make, one day can be very much like another. I know that some of the fellas travel the distance to get to the engagement and were a bit cross as you would expect. Just one of those things I suppose".

"The man is an imbecile; he's a liability to the band, you'd think he'd know what day it is", said a disgruntled second cornet player putting his cornet back in the case. "I'll get him to check the rest of the Christmas engagements. I'll probably do it myself as well to be sure, I don't want another clanger", said Maurice.

Band secretary Henry was responsible for organising the

band's engagements, not in itself a particularly arduous task, it was hardly more difficult than writing down a shopping list.

What Henry had failed to mention when Maurice had asked him to assume the vacant band secretary's job was that he, Henry, suffered from dyslexia!

Henry would receive a telephone call, "I wonder if the band could come along and give a programme like you did last year to our Friends Club, the club did so much enjoy your visit and members keep on asking, 'when is the band coming back again?'. Now the date I have in mind is Tuesday, 19th March and we begin at 2.30pm. We have a cup of tea and a biscuit beforehand, but of course, you know that", said the chairman of the Friends Club.

"Let me consult the band's engagement list". Wanting to please Henry said, "you say the 19th March, well according to the list that date is available and I'm sure the band would love to come again. Let's confirm on 19th March at 2.30pm". Writing the booking down in the band engagement book, Henry would put the date as the 18th, thinking he was writing the 19th!

The second cornet, Robin, was not going to let it rest, "I do not know why you put up with him, surely you can find somebody else who can take the job on and not make as many stupid mistakes as Henry", challenging the Musical Director. "You don't think Henry was my first choice do you", retaliated the Musical Director, "In fact, Henry was not even my second choice. Getting rid of Henry may be much harder than you think". "You're pussyfooting around, Henry has to go, a Musical Director's life is not just waving a stick around in the air and expecting people to take notice of you. Man management comes into it; now is the time to man manage Henry. You have got to be executioner as well as a conductor".

Robin could be very hard and unforgiving to the point that he could make an argument sound more aggressive than it need be. The inescapable truth was that Robin was correct, Henry must be terminated, at least as band secretary. But just how? I need some advice on this thought Maurice, I must have someone in the brass band circle I can email. And immediately, a name came to mind. Peter.

Maurice composed his email.

Peter - I have to sack our band secretary in the next week or two, and I'm dreading delivering the news. The idea of taking him to one side and giving Henry such news has me anxious and losing sleep. I've been 'released' myself once or twice over the years, and I well remember feeling shocked and upset. How can I sack Henry nicely? Is that even possible? He is such a nice chap and I think, allowing for his limitations, he has done the best he possibly could in the interest of the band. I don't know that the band has grounds to dismiss him. Kind regards – Maurice

Maurice - Sacked, dismissed, dropped, laid off, let go, terminated. There's a reason why there are so many euphemisms for losing your job, and it's because it's often too hard to find the right words. As most leaders know, having to fire is probably the hardest part of the job of being a leader. It's tough to deliver such news! Perhaps, first of all, you might try dropping one or two hints and see if Henry takes the hint and offers to resign. That way you've achieved what you wanted without having to be Mr Nasty. - Peter

Maurice decided to discuss the matter with his deputy. "Well I agree, Henry is an embarrassment, I know he was keen to be band secretary, and on that basis, we gave him the job, little knowing some of the problems that would follow on from that appointment", said the deputy Christopher. "Was it last year or the year before, when Henry accepted an engagement for the band to be one of the duty bands at a Royal Garden Party at Buckingham Palace. Did Henry not look at the date of the royal party, April 1st - April Fools' Day"!

"He'd only gone and booked a coach and was in contact with the Lord Chamberlain's Office to discuss suitable music. We had to cancel that order for new stand banners. We only just got to the printer in time to stop them printing new letter headings with the emblem of the Royal Warrant and underneath 'By Appointment to Her Majesty The Queen - Providers of Royal

Garden Party Music'. What did Henry say? The caller sounded very convincing! What did the police say? Don't be so stupid. We were lucky that didn't get into the national press".

"I sent an email to Peter to seek his advice, he's come back with the idea that we should try and get Henry simply to resign", said Maurice, "trouble is I haven't got any idea how we go about it". "We could try asking, 'is the job getting too much for you, perhaps you'd like an assistant to lighten the load, someone just dealing with engagements", suggested Christopher. "Yes, that's not a bad idea it might just do the trick, he could remain as band secretary but could relinquish the part of the job which is causing us the most problems", added Maurice.

Christopher, his face darkening, "I've just thought of another 'Henryism'. The band was booked to take part in the annual carnival, this time Henry got the day, the date, and the time absolutely spot-on. What he had agreed to, and it was part of the contract, was that the band would be performing in the procession. Now just look around the band, a retirement fellowship band, pretty well all are pensioners, bus passes in our pockets along with heart pills and incontinence tablets, most have a problem walking onto the platform to give a concert. Some have not marched for years. What was he thinking?".

"We all know what the problem is but what is the solution? Henry is a really nice chap, gets on well with all the other fellas. It would not be popular amongst the band if we set out to sack him. You know folk can get really funny over things like that", said the Musical Director seeking sympathy.

"Well you could try a scheme that time and motion experts brought in at the place where I work", Christopher hinted. "What the boffins suggested was, that we would work much better as a team if we had a better understanding of what other people did, their roles, the kind of problems that they had to face. The idea was it would lead to a good team spirit".

"So how would that work in the band?", asked Maurice, knowing and dreading the answer. "Well how it operated at the office, was that we each performed somebody else's job for a week. For example, I work in the accountants' office; I exchanged my job for somebody in dispatch. I spent a week going out on the van doing deliveries and the person I exchanged with came into the accounts department and took on my job, which was the purchase ledger." "How did that work out?", enquired Maurice. "Well he did order some pretty strange things. I have no idea what the company is going to do with 250 books 'BATS - an implement used to hit a ball', when he should have ordered 'BATS - a nocturnal flying mammal'. We are a company that specialises in supplying educational nature books, not sport books".

"I see", said Maurice, "by exchanging roles, Henry could see how his job should be done and would realise that in that respect, he had been failing, therefore would feel it right for him to step down making way for someone who could do the job of the band secretary".

"You will have to consult the other band officers, they will need to agree, and Henry will have to be present at that meeting, but we can work out beforehand the swaps. To make Henry feel just that bit more important, I think it would be a smart move for you and Henry to exchange roles", suggested Christopher.

"What!", exploded the Bandmaster, "you're suggesting that Henry takes over the training and conducting of the band". "Well if it's going to work, it's going to need something like that. Not much point in Henry exchanging his role for that of the treasurer", retorted Christopher. "He could exchange with you Christopher, deputy MD, pretty important, number two and all that", proposed the Musical Director.

"Well, of course, it is your decision. I rather think it would go down well with the band. At this stage you have to say the exchange is just between the band officers and that bandsmen shouldn't get it into their heads that there could be an exchange of instruments, you know what I mean, cornet players wanting to play the trombone and that kind of thing", Christopher advocated.

At the next rehearsal, Maurice began by introducing the scheme. "As part of team building within the band, for a couple of weeks, the officers are going to exchange their roles. I am going to exchange my role as Musical Director with Henry the band secretary". Everyone sat up, very alert, this came as a surprise to them, most were mystified. Had the folk in charge of the band gone mad? Robin on second cornet asked, "Who has come up with this crackpot idea, and more importantly why?"

"I shall be acting as the band secretary, and of course Henry will be the Musical Director". He hadn't finished the word Musical Director before the suggested exchange was greeted with howls of laughter and derision, some even took to pointing and gesturing at Henry, waving their arms in conducting motions. Entering into the spirit of the moment, the side drummer gave an extended roll on the drum. What was being announced was nothing new to Henry, he felt honoured that the MD had chosen that he should be the exchange partner.

With a sense of ceremony, Maurice welcomed Henry to the rostrum. "Gentlemen will you please welcome our temporary Musical Director, Henry. I know that you will support him as you have supported me, remember we are doing this for the good of the band. I want Henry to have an appreciation of what it's like to be in control of the band, having an idea of what I have had to put up with, you lot. As for myself, I shall be learning what is involved in being a band secretary". "Dropping clangers!", shouted Robin. By now an eager Henry had the baton in his hand.

'Band secretary' Maurice joined the cornet section, he thought it would be nice getting back to playing once again. He could relax, and if he felt he could be helpful to Henry, he was quite prepared to give him the full benefit of his banding knowledge. Henry would need some direction and guidance, as the actual Musical Director, he would be failing in his duty to ignore the lack of experience which Henry was bound to show. He could not allow the ship to sink for want of a rather silly idea!

Meanwhile 'Musical Director' Henry, with the voice of authority nobody knew he had, announced, "Would you all please turn in your folder to number 2156, 'Prélude on

Lavenham', I thought we'd start with a piece of music that is well known to you and doesn't have too many surprises. We have played it through on several occasions, so we are going to be familiar with the piece and the music geography". The band was taken aback, even Robin was utterly lost for words, he just found the music and popped it on the stand. Something strange is happening here beyond his understanding.

"The opening note for the solo cornets is set at a modest, middle of the stave B, entering at a subdued *mp*, that volume of sound being carried continuously to letter B. Flugel you seamlessly pick up the theme from the solo cornets, at letter A, let the only difference be a tonal one. We must avoid any fluctuation in volume. This is one of those pieces which demand full value notes, particularly where a note is carried across the bar line creating a semibreve, please read very carefully the musical notation. The music must be fluid".

"Before we start, two very elementary things, can you ensure that without movement of your head, you can see both me as the conductor and the music on your stand. If you can see me, then I certainly can see you, and that will help with our understanding and interpretation of the music we are to perform, working together".

"Gentlemen, please, on my downbeat, 'Andante, dolce e cantabile', moderately slow 'walking speed', 72 crotchets to the minute. My beat will give you the speed. My point of the beat will be when my upper arm and my lower arm are at 90°", and with that, the baton assumed the entry point.

The band remained in subdued shock. Here was a Henry nobody could recognise, this was not the Henry who dropped clangers. Before them stood a very confident Henry, assured of what he was doing, and perhaps the most surprisingly he appeared to be very musically aware.

"Thank you, gentlemen, that was an excellent practice, thank you for your concentration and your sensitive approach to the music. I am sure you will be aware that the band has an engagement this coming Friday afternoon. We have run through all the pieces, either this morning or previously, and I do not foresee any difficulties. We are giving a concert to the Tables Club in the town. We meet at the Community Hall. We begin playing at 2.30pm. It's a full band engagement, but not red jackets. For further details or problems contact our temporary band secretary Maurice".

The band rehearsal continued afterwards in the car park - only one topic of conversation, MD Henry. "Well, I have to say it was a jolly good practice, I never thought Henry knew anything more about banding other than putting his mouthpiece into his instrument, finding the mouthpiece when he could find the instrument", offered the euphonium player. Robin, now Henry's most prominent fan said, "That was a band tuition and training masterclass".

Privately Christopher thought that Maurice had a problem. That practice had gone far too well, rather than solving an issue the rehearsal had produced another one. Would Maurice be able to get the baton off Henry? In the court of public opinion, if it came down to a vote of the band members for director, the decision would be for Henry. Also, at the back of his mind was, it would be very unlikely that he would be asked to be MD should Maurice retire, the job will go to Henry. All the scheming was falling apart.

No sooner had Maurice stepped inside his front door then the telephone rang. "Maurice, what time does the job start on Friday afternoon?", and so commenced a procession of telephone calls. "Did Henry say red jacket or not, what's the car parking like at the Community Hall, do you think it will be finished by 3.45pm, can you organise a lift for me because my car is going in for an MOT?, better cross me off I've got a doctor's appointment".

Maurice concluded that perhaps Henry wasn't so bad a band secretary after all. His mistake had been to listen to unreliable Robin. He was still the Musical Director; if he wanted, he could stop the experiment. He needed to bring an end to this exchange exercise as soon as possible.

Every step of the way he had been badly advised, he realised that he had not made a decision himself, it'd been left to others.

Mrs Maurice living through this crisis she had watched, listened as, during the next few days, her husband tried to deal with the situation he had created. "Enough", said Mrs Maurice, finally, "Sit yourself down and listen, I'm going to tell you what to do. By what you say, it is not going to be possible for Henry to go back to being just band secretary, you are going to create a new position for Henry which involves some direct musical input".

From that moment the role of Musical Director moved from being an exchange to a job share. Maurice retained his position as Musical Director, in effect honorary MD and Henry was elevated to the position of Band Mentor, 'a trusted adviser and consultant to the MD on all matters pertaining to the band, including tuition and training'. With his new found secretarial responsibilities, Maurice became the new Band Administrator!

Badly Fitting
Polo Shirt
(17)

Colonel Bernard Adams OF (1947 - 1975)
International Staff Bandmaster

IT was announced, locally and advertised in Salvation Army papers, that the International Staff Band of The Salvation Army was to make a scheduled week-end visit. The local Salvation Army (Corps) centre was to play host for this occasion.

From the moment that young Michael got to learn of the visit, he was so excited; the Staff Band was going to spend a week-end at his Salvation Army Corps. His banding heroes would be spending two days in the city. The Staff Bandsmen would be sitting and playing on the same platform that he, on some Sunday mornings, sat and played the cornet in the Young People's Band.

Michael had listened to the Staff Band on many occasions. At home, they had an ancient gramophone player which Michael had been allowed to keep in his bedroom. He had a small collection of Salvation Army 78 records. The duration of 78 RPM recordings was between three to five minutes per side. Just long enough to fit a recorded march on.

Amongst his favourites was a Regal Zonophone record, the blue label with gold lettering. On one side was *'The Pilgrim's Prayer'*, a transcription by Sydney Rouse and on the reverse side the popular march *'Starlake'* by Eric Ball. Michael would prop the solo cornet copy on top of the chest of drawers and play along with the band; he would make believe that he was in the Staff Band. Modesty prevented him from taking the seat of the principal cornet; he was happy to sit the third or fourth man down on the cornet row. Of course, he always played the top part for the little cornet duet in *'Starlake'*.

He had a recording of the cornet duet - *'Deliverance'* featuring Dep/Bandmaster James Williams and Bandsman Deryck Diffey. He played that record over and over again, marvelling, with envy, at the skill of the two cornetists. With practice perhaps . . .

Sometimes he got ahead of himself, with one of mum's knitting needles in his hand, he would be the Staff Bandmaster, and as the Staff Bandmaster he would conduct the band and put the band through their paces. Of course the cornets were always perfect, although the basses and trombones came in for adverse comment. At the end of the recording, he would take on the attitude of the bandmaster and give the band his opinion on their performance. His dream was to be in the International Staff Band, he wanted to be a Staff Bandsman above all else. He cut black and white grainy photos from out of the Musician and kept them in a scrap book. He read and re-read reports of the band's visit to other places.

For non-Salvation Army Bands, sometimes referred to as Contesting Bands, the normal engagement is an evening concert, playing at a garden fete, accompanying the singing on Remembrance Sunday, leading the parade, taking part in the local carnival procession. One-off engagements.

Months and months of planning was required for the week-end visit by the Staff Band, the itinerary agreed, finding host families to look after the band members, transport, meals, all to ensure the success of the visit.

A full week-end for a visiting Salvation Army band is almost non-stop activity from the moment they arrive at the venue until they put their foot on the bottom step of the coach to go home. The Staff Band week-end engagement began at the Army's Headquarters in London, boarding themselves and their banding equipment plus personal luggage for the trip to the week-end engagement.

Michael's father came home from senior band practice; he now had as much information as was available on the week-end. Final arrangements where unveiled. The coach from London was expected to arrive on the Saturday at about 4.00pm. The evening band festival would commence at 7.00pm. The smaller of the two public rooms at the hall, known as the YP Hall, would be cleared for the exclusive use of the Staff Band, with orders for the YP band members to, 'stay out'. A welcome tea was being organised. Members of the senior band were invited to share the meal. Michael looked at his father expectantly; he made a face when his father indicated that he would not be included on the guest list.

On Saturday morning, Michael was up early, he wanted to get his paper round finished, tackle some of his Saturday homework, and still get down to the hall to see the Staff Band coach arrive. At ten minutes past four the coach entered the Corps car park. The boys of the Young People's Band were told to keep out of the way and let the bandsmen off the coach. With about half the bandsman having alighted the next person down the steps was the dignified, dapper, distinguished figure of the International Staff Bandmaster of the Salvation Army. No movie star could have received greater adulation. The boys knew they were in the presence of someone very special. Keeping out of the way was going to be difficult and challenging.

The Salvation Army Hall was rather large and had the benefit, when needing to accommodate a large audience, of having a horseshoe gallery. Well before the commencement of the evening festival, the boys scampered up the stairs to the balcony as it was called and made for the front seats which overlooked the trombones but directly faced the cornet section. Michael's father appeared, the Corps Bandmaster appeared, the hall caretaker appeared, old Mr Simons appeared, followed very closely by Mrs Simons, all with the same message, "You lot, behave yourselves!" The boys allowed Daniel to reply on their behalf. "Good as gold, trust us!". To ensure good conduct, the YP Band Leader elected to act as 'gallery guard' and sat in the row immediately behind the boys. In case of any trouble, Mrs YP Band Leader was there to assist in any arrest because of inappropriate conduct.

The hall was quickly filling up. The ISB always created interest and a big crowd was guaranteed. There was a happy mix amongst the audience, Salvationists and friends from other centres plus folk with contesting band links. If you had the chance to hear the Staff Band, you didn't want to miss it. Just before 7.00pm light applause broke out quickly gathering in volume as the Staff Bandsmen made their way to the platform. The boys were quick in identifying some of the members of the band. The band was dressed in their very distinctive red festival 'hook and eye' tunics, high stand up collars, white braiding cascading down the front of the tunic and at the rear two lion tamer stripes, white 'twirled' epaulettes, the tunic design completed by two half stripes on the sleeve.

The Staff Bandmaster made a ceremonial entrance, graciously acknowledged the continuing applause of the audience, turning around to face the band, he motioned the band to sit, the applause was exchanged with anticipatory silence, baton raised, a flick of the wrist and the Staff Band commenced the evening festival with the march 'Starlake'.

Next, the Corps Officer stood up, advanced to the microphone to make the introductions and expressions of welcome, the boys felt that both were overlong and overdone! "Your Worship – The Lord Mayor, Lady Mayoress and other dignitaries, ladies and gentlemen, Bandmaster and members of the International Staff Band of The Salvation Army, what a great honour it is today . . . and in conclusion may I invite His Worship the Lord Mayor to chair and guide us through this festival".

Michael pondered if this is the sort of rigmarole the Staff Band had to endure every week-end, clearly, being a member of the Staff Band has its trial sent inflictions. How do they remain awake, that must be what makes them superheroes? Introductions and welcomes, gentlemen with a gold chain around their neck, speech from men with gold chains. Different venues and characters, introduction and speeches with variations all saying the same thing, weekend after weekend.

The Lord Mayor stood up to announce the next band piece as if he was calling the next item on the council agenda. The only thing missing was the call, "Order, order!"

"The Staff Band will play an Air Varie entitled *'The Old Wells'* composed by a gentleman with the name of Mr Eric Ball". The Staff Bandmaster went to the mircophone to assist the Lord Mayor by elaborating on the piece of music, something he was called upon to do quite frequently. "The next item on the agenda – sorry programme", announced the Lord Mayor, "is a cornet solo to be played by the band's principal cornet player, a demanding solo entitled *'Jubilate'*". Michael listened intently. For his solo, the euphonium soloist chose to play *'Ransomed'*.

Halfway through the festival, the audience stood up to sing a Salvation Army song, and at the same time, a collection was taken. All too quickly, the festival was over. Lord Mayor was escorted from the building, waving to the audience as if he had just attended an election rally. Folks leaving the hall engaged in post-festival chatter and banter, old friendship renewed, amateur adjudicators ready with their opinions. That festival confirmed Michael's aspiration to be in the Staff Band.

Over supper, the family discussed the evening's events. That it had been an enormous success was without doubt. The hall was full to capacity, they were pleased to see some former members of the Corps band had come along, and while there were one or two new pieces in the programme, the Staff Band had played some of the music they had also played whilst in the Corps band.

The boys decided to go autograph hunting, with Sunday presenting many opportunities. Michael had his list prepared in his mind; if he was honest, there were some autographs he would much prefer to get than others. Soprano cornet, the front row of cornets, solo trombone and the euphonium soloist were high on the list. He thought to have the autograph of a gentleman called the Flag Officer would be interesting.

The big prize would be the autograph of the Staff Bandmaster. How did you approach a Staff Bandmaster? "I mean", argued Michael to Daniel, "you just can't march up to King George VI, book and pen in hand and say, 'Please Sir can I have your autograph'. It was just like that with the Staff

Bandmaster". Michael thought he might ask his father if he would approach the bandmaster with his autograph book. As his father rightly pointed out, "You just can't go around disturbing the Staff Bandmaster he's got lots of things to deal with, make do with the deputy bandmaster, I'm sure he'll be only too happy to sign your autograph book, just make sure your fountain pen doesn't leak!"

Over Sunday dinner Michael suggested it would be nice to have a photo of the band. Actually, what he wanted was a photo of himself with the principal cornet. Mum brought into the room her Box Brownie 127. The Staff Band had Sunday lunch and tea at the hall. Prior to the final meeting, some of the bandsmen were standing around chatting outside the hall as Michael and his mum approached. "Here is the young man who wants to replace me in the Staff Band", said the principal cornet player with a big smile, introducing Michael. Michael went as red as his Army jersey.

Michael's mum took the camera from out of her black Sunday bag. Surrounded by a number of the Staff Band, Michael in the centre, mum looked in the small viewfinder, clicked the camera. "Just another", requested the cornet principal. With that, he took off his Staff Band cap with the white brim edging and placed it on Michael's head. Click went the camera.

Michael and his pals were not allowed to sit up in the gallery for the final meeting. The view of the Staff Band was greatly restricted by Salvation Army bonnets with large bows! The meeting finished, the Staff Band packed away their banding items. A final cup of tea, lots of "Goodbyes", and they were away on their journey back to London.

On one occasion the family travelled down to London with the express purpose of calling in at the Salvation Army store in Judd Street. Outside was the name of the store, just over the door, 'Salvationist Publishing & Supplies', or as his father referred to the shop as, 'Salvationist Publishing & Surprises'. It was new uniform time for both parents.

Up the few steps and into the foyer, straight ahead into the men's department, where there was a wonderful text above one of the displays, "All The Promises Of God Are Sure If Only You Believe" – The Founder. Michael considered that if you did not believe the Founder then you could not be sure about the promises! To a young mind, it wasn't very clear.

Declared to be in the way in both the gents and ladies departments by parents, Michael wandered off to look at the books, Army memorabilia, the display of instruments and to peruse the records. For his forthcoming birthday Michael decided that a music stand would be ideal, and one was purchased. He did consider asking for a baton to go with the stand.

Lt.-Colonel Ray Bowes (1975 - 1990)
International Staff Bandmaster

The next 20 years were significant for Michael. He transferred from the junior band into the senior band, becoming a member of the cornet section. He was fortunate enough to obtain a university placement, rather a long way from home, at St Andrews in Scotland where he took biology and chemistry. Returning home, he became a chemist for a national drug store.

At a Salvation Army Youth camp he attended, he was introduced to Elizabeth, following a short courtship they were married, both becoming active members of the movement. Among the items his mother gave him when he finally left home was a box of photographs, including the small square black-and-white photograph of Michael wearing the Staff Band cap, with the photo came memories of the week-end.

A further opportunity to hear the Staff Band came when they attended major Salvation Army events like the annual Bandmasters' Councils Festival held at the Royal Albert Hall. The International Staff Band was always on duty supported by other Army sections. Michael booked early and managed to get seats in a box. The event was well-advertised beforehand, looking at the programme it was certainly going to be a memorable evening. Making a Albert Hall appearance was the Amsterdam Staff Band

and a contesting band, the Dereham Band from Norfolk. The local Corps representative band came from Hendon. To balance the brass input, the International Staff Songsters contributed, and a Festival Chorus was assembled. Choirmasters were Norman Bearcroft and Howard Evans.

Under the 'microscope', Michael observed how things were different; changes had taken place since his first Staff Band Festival some years previous. The Staff Band had undergone a make-over. Gone were stand-up collar festival tunics, the Staff Band now were wearing what was in effect Officers' red tunics. The white epaulettes had been retained, but the cascading white trimmings had been replaced by two button-down breast pockets, the open front jacket required a clean white shirt and a navy-blue tie, at least they still had two white stripes on the arms of their sleeves.

He fully expected that there would be retirements from the band. His 'corner' men had been replaced. To his mind the band looked more youthful, certainly the section leaders much younger. The current Staff Bandmaster was a goodly number of years junior to his predecessor. Michael thought he brought vigour and vitality to the position; he was jaunty and bubbly. Michael thought he could easily approach him for his autograph. You could sit down and have a cup of tea with this Staff Bandmaster.

Some of the changes Michael observed were cosmetic and personnel. The music the Staff Band now played was a tremendous leap forward. For the Bandmasters' Councils Festival, the band entertained the audience with a sizzling performance of 'Shall We Gather At The River?', an arrangement by Len Ballantine. It was a showstopper, Michael wanted to be in the Staff Band all over again. The tried and tested straitjacket music of the years just prior and immediately following the war was being replaced by more adventurous and indeed demanding music. Composers were being encouraged to express themselves, to move away from the old restrictive format. Michael acknowledged that their music was for a different time and a different generation. Part of the function of the Staff Band was to introduce new music, to set the musical pace.

Michael looked at the band as they were playing *'Shall We Gather At The River?'* he observed a bit of a swagger to match the swing. The Staff Band was evolving. Change of uniform. Change of bandmaster. Change of music – but he was pleased to comment no change in mission. What he had witnessed in the Royal Albert Hall that June evening was a significant shift. Next he pondered was the future not only the International Staff Band but Salvation Army music, where to in the next couple of decades? The Staff Band was still for him the band to be a member of.

Rather later than he should have done Michael, then a little over forty, opened his own pharmacy shop in a village in another part of the country, it was an upheaval for Elizabeth and their two children. Whilst Michael made up the prescriptions; his wife ran the shop. The pharmacy side of the business was complemented by the shop being the local post office and grocery store. They had moved home a couple of times during their marriage, however when the village shop became available (which they purchased), it was a move away, it also involved changing the Corps they attended.

Banding had always been important to Michael; he enjoyed playing, being part of a worldwide fraternity. Certainly, he took pleasure playing some of the more traditional music, particularly from the blue-covered Favourite No 3 book. "There is some really good stuff in there", was his opinion. If he had a pound for every time he had played through *'Starlake'*, Mr Ball would have made him a relatively rich man, considered Michael. He still recalled the Lord Mayor at his first Staff Band festival referring to Mr Eric Ball.

He followed the 'comings and goings' within the Staff Band. He deeply regretted the demise of the Musician, the bandsmen's newspaper of information and learning. In his 'den' was a box with copies of the newspaper which contained something of special interest for him, and his old scrap-book. Some of the papers were 'colouring', showing the signs of age, printed in black and white, with photos which were a series of dots and under the magnifying glass people were almost unidentifiable. The replaced title, Salvationist tried to be fully encompassing, but in Michael's opinion it was neither 'fish nor fowl'.

Colonel Robert Redhead (1990 - 1994)
International Staff Bandmaster

Concluding a winter motoring holiday in France, Michael and Elizabeth travelled on the ferry from Caen to Portsmouth. South Hampshire was not a part of the country he knew particularly well. They decided to spend a further three days holiday in the area: Chichester, Salisbury and Stonehenge were on the visiting list.

From announcements in the Army papers, a festival was to be given by the International Staff Band in Portsmouth Cathedral. The timing was just right, a day in Chichester and Arundel, stopping off at Portsmouth on the way back to their hotel. The festival was entitled *Celebration of Praise.*

They were in the cathedral early enough to watch as the Staff Band set up for the evening festival. As he expected, there had been a turnover of one or two bandsmen. It was still a band that had members with Officer rank, something which had been a feature since the early conception of the Staff Band.

The Staff Band entered the cathedral and took their places. Very little seemed to have changed. Someone had taken a pair of scissors to the festival jackets; you could no longer, in all honesty, call them festival tunics, and removed the pockets, and would later reduce the number of rings on the sleeve to one. Comforting to Michael was that the band were still using the same designed embroidered music stand banners.

The routine was still the same, the band entered, took their allotted places and awaited the arrival of the Staff Bandmaster. So that nobody could mistake the Staff Band Bandmaster, he did not wear a red jacket but Salvation Army dark serge.

The Staff Bandmaster commenced the festival without a great deal of ceremony. Michael's first thought was, that like policemen, Staff Bandmasters were getting younger! Tall, slim, topped off by a mop of hair. Here was a Staff Bandmaster breaking away from the previous style. The festival commenced with his composition, *'Fanfare of Praise'*. The principal cornet offered up *'Glorious Fountain'*. This was followed by a flugel feature, *'Sweet By And By'*. The programme notes had a touch of the Judd Street Founders about them. "A newly departed Saint (name of bandsman – flugel horn) . . ." Misread was the assertion that a member of the Staff Band was a saint and although departed was going to play a solo!

The Staff Band made a special tribute to Michael Kenyon, bringing together five of the former Southsea Bandmaster's musical contributions. The Staff Bandmaster had completed Michael Kenyon's unfinished last song setting; *'I Need Thee Every Hour'*. It was quite a poignant moment.

Michael recognised that it was not a usual Staff Band programme, difficult to draw meaningful conclusions. He considered that the Staff Bandmaster had consolidated the position of the Staff Band. Would he still like to be in the Staff Band? A rather silly question to ask.

Dr Stephen Cobb (1994 -)
International Staff Bandmaster

Michael had given up marching with the band, no longer coping with the cornet he had moved in semi-retirement to play baritone. He was now an elder statesman of the band. He had transferred the business over to his son as soon as he could accept the government pension. The tempo of his life changed.

His dream of being in the International Staff Band was capsulated in that small black and white photo. Years ago, he had taken the photo to the local camera shop, asked them to repair it and blow it up bigger. Every member of the band knew that Michael had a photo taken when a youngster, wearing a

Staff Band cap. "Is there anybody in the corps, and beyond, who has not seen a photo of Michael in his Staff Band cap?" Michael took in all in good part. For his 75th birthday, the band had a special birthday cake made, appropriately decorated; the centrepiece was a Salvation Army Band cap made of icing the brim trimmed in white.

Michael finally accepted that he was not going to get an invitation from the Staff Bandmaster to join the Staff Band; the cap on his head was as close as he would ever get. He consoled himself with the fact that no Staff Bandmaster had ever heard him play, had they done so things might have turned out differently. "When did you ever play the C scale without getting the fingering wrong?", queried his son, with mock humour. "I think I did it once before you were born, so you were not about to hear it!"

Michael received a letter from Daniel, his pal from all those years ago in the Young People's Band. The substance of the letter was that the International Staff Band was going to spend the week-end at the Corps. Daniel reminded Michael of the Staff Band's previous visit sixty-plus years ago. Could Michael manage the stairs up to the balcony? Michael wanted to go; 'you never know' he thought, 'it might be my last opportunity to be a Staff Bandsman'.

Sadly, it would be an occasion when Elizabeth could not accompany him; she was now far too frail. 'Well', thought Michael, 'if the wife agrees, I will make my final pilgrimage to hear the Staff Band'. With his son to support him, Michael journeyed back to his old Corps. Michael and Daniel had lunch together and spent the early part of the Saturday afternoon in the hotel lounge where Michael and his son were booked in for the night, inevitably revisiting memories. Out came the photo. Daniel just closed his eyes and gently shook his head. "I should have that photo buried with you", joked Daniel. "I expect I will", replied Michael.

A taxi took them to the hall. The gallery had gone, replaced by half mezzanine floor. The platform had disappeared. The old wooden benches had been superseded by padded chairs. The mercy seat no longer had an inscription written as part of the penitent form. They both remembered the wording, 'Boundless Salvation'. To Michael's thinking, it was all rather sterile and clinical, nice clean lines, devoid of character. Looking at the audience as they came in, they were smart, with sharp fashions, it was easy to see that the Salvation Army had a more affluent membership than sixty years ago. It was not a critical observation but merely a statement of the obvious.

The Staff Band made their entrance. It was summer and rather hot for comfort, so the band were dressed in short sleeved shirts, only the epaulettes denoting that it was the Staff Band.

During the festival Michael found himself musing on the changes that the Staff Band had undergone during his banding career, short sleeves sixty-five years ago, Michael doubted it. The band photograph on the programme brochure showed that the double white braiding on the sleeve had been replaced by a single piece of braiding. In sixty years, Michael estimated, all that remained now from as it was then, was the white epaulet twirls and Staff Band cap.

Both Michael and Daniel agreed the current Staff Bandmaster had style, presence, command of his musical forces. The band's playing was neat and crisp, technically brilliant. Perhaps, unkindly, Michael thought that sixty years ago the Staff Band was more amateur, this was now a professional set up, which owed much to the bandmaster, it had his stamp on it.

There was now no player in the band who was a Salvation Army officer. The Staff Bandmaster was no longer drawn from the officer ranks of The Salvation Army. A range of occupations and skills was represented within the band, folk with non-Army day jobs.

There was diversity, a female member of the band, certainly not in the Staff Band of over 60 years ago. But then many Salvation Army Bands would have difficulty in functioning were it not for the ladies in the band. Not only were ladies playing, but in some cases leading the band. Lady bandmasters, he could think of at least a couple, he struggled to recall their names, his memory was not as once it was. Then they came to him. Margaret Sherratt from Weymouth on the south coast, and Yvonne Ferguson at Bellshill near Glasgow, they looked much smarter than many of their male colleagues.

Different from his first festival was the interval, an opportunity for some banding retail therapy. Michael's 78 records had long been replaced by CDs, and there was any number of them to purchase from the stall in the foyer.

A collection of music by numerous composers, CDs devoted to Salvation Army marches, one could purchase CDs which featured the band soloists. Michael even noticed that the blue label with the gold writing had, as he discovered, been what was called, remastered. You could listen to the Staff Band in the lounge, in the kitchen, in the car, in the bath, even in the gym.

Michael could not recall 78 records being on sale at his first ISB festival. SP&S missed an opportunity there.

Both Michael and Daniel knew what to expect visually in the second half of the festival. It would be casual polo shirt time for the band. The traditional band seating formation being scrapped in favour of a rearrangement of instrument positioning. As anticipated the band emerged for the last section of the festival in blue polo shirts.

Michael closed his eyes. He had a mad thought. 'Why did the Staff Bandmaster not arrange to have the name of Staff Band players and their instrument displayed on the back of the polo shirts? Like football stars. Name Sop; Name BM; Name Trom; Name Bass; Name Euph; Name Bar; Name Cor; Michael Cornet'.

Daniel nudging Michael brought him back to reality, "I now know why you never made it into the Staff Band, you've got a terrible figure for a polo shirt!".

Foul Play
at the Bandstand

(18)

THE Lantern Acting Dramatic Society, one would have thought might have gone by the acronym LADS, but no, perhaps because they also had female members, collectively they were known as the 'Lanterns'. Amateur dramatics was a thriving society, with a strong membership of both stage players and support staff, all volunteers. For years they have been putting on shows, pantomime and workshops.

From their number came the stars and starlets of their productions. Members of the Lanterns fulfilled the roles of producers and directors, stagehands and lighting engineers.

Lanterna was situated on an old Roman road. One of the many roads which straddled Britain. The settlement, established during the early Roman period grew. Through the centuries the area had expanded, had become a town to the position that some residents considered that Lanterna deserved city status.

With progress The Old Town Hall was deemed to be in the way of a multi-mall retail complex development, coupled with a new route system servicing community. The developers, by way of compensation to the town, using developers' contributions, agreed to build a much-needed community theatre and arts centre.

When the scheme went out to consultation, displayed was a theatre with the capacity to seat more than 400 people, a full-size stage and ancillary rooms. Included was a basement restaurant and Arts Centre, an area which could be used for other community activities, like conferences. Space for the Town Council to be able to run their official business and hold council meetings was included.

The people of Lantern were enthusiastic and welcomed the proposed municipal asset. However, by the time the complex was completed, a number of 'building elements' had disappeared. The Arts Centre, half of the ancillary rooms, the Council Chamber and the overall size of the theatre. What was left was a Community Centre plus with an underground cafe.

The Lanterns committee gathered in one of the small rooms. It was a big evening for the dramatic society. Being decided was the choice of the next production, to be 'put on' during early June the following year.

The chairman was all for playing safe. Agatha Christie was always an acceptable bet. Against that proposal was the fact that the dramatic society had just about done Agatha to death! Perhaps a light comedy might fill the bill, a Whitehall farce, there were one or two nods of heads and a few suggestions.

The Lanterns secretary urged the committee to consider perhaps a non-Christie 'whodunit'. She had been reading a number of theatre magazines and one production appeared to be very popular. It was a 'whodunit', the plot and the location were interesting and different.

The stage set was simple and remained in place throughout. The cast called for a mixture of ages, both men and women. The play had two acts, allowing for an interval.

As it so happened, the secretary had a copy of the play in book form with her. She outlined a synopsis of the play.

The setting was a municipal bandstand, used by the local town band. Before the concert had even commenced, the dead body of the caretaker was discovered, clubbed to death by an instrument of the band, a cornet.

The play was entitled *'Foul Play at the Bandstand'*. The play took place in the fictitious town of Silver Dale.

The committee looked at the various characters: the victim, the committee members of Silver Dale Band and the investigating Police Inspector. The pre-production notes provided a degree of information about the main characters, assisting the actors for getting into their roles.

The Lantern Dramatic Society now considered the play. *'Foul Play in the Bandstand'* was an interesting departure, a different 'whodunit'. Lots of suspects, plausible motives, strong characters, all revealed in the play's dialogue. The victim was a thoroughly bad lot; sympathies lay with most of the suspects. As always there was at least one piece of vital evidence which would unmask the murderer, withheld until the very last moment.

The Victim
Ronald Williams
Background information on Ronald Williams
Aged 55   Bachelor.   No known interests.   Lived alone.
Ronald Williams was the caretaker of the Silver Dale Community Centre. A central building in the town which many clubs and associations used for their meetings. With the caretaker job went a small single bedroomed accommodation, on-site.

The Town Council advertised a seasonal caretaker vacancy for the town's bandstand. Ronald Williams got the job.

There was very little that happened in the Community Centre of which Williams was unaware. He sat in his 'cubby-hole' at the entrance to the centre, watching and listening, noting comings and goings. He had an ear for picking up any item of scandal or information, using such 'ear droppings' to his advantage. Members were less than discreet. Always dressed in his brown warehouse coat, he seemed to be just about everywhere.

Over years of service, he had acquired, by one means or another, a key to every single lock within the entire building. He had access to areas he should not, and his collection of filing cabinet keys enabled him to peruse the most confidential papers. He would always deny that he had one, but Williams had a master key to the individual lockers which members could hire. There was something very secretive about him. He was creepy.

The Silver Dale Town Band hired, weekly, one of the main halls in which to rehearse and had a smaller room for the band's use to store the larger instruments and the library of band music.

The Band Committee Suspects

The Silver Dale Town Band was typical of many local brass bands. A volunteer band organised by a committee.

To assist the actors in understanding their part the play the author had provided some background profile information including feasible motives for each member to commit murder. Each were possible suspects, they were all present at the bandstand and had a reason to be there early.

Daisy Picking   2nd Baritone   Band Librarian

Background information and motive

Aged 47.   Married.   No children.

Daisy has been a Band Librarian for nearly ten years, loves the job. Daisy is generally well-liked but can have her moments if upset. Daisy has had frequent 'run-ins' with Ronald Williams, perhaps only over minor matters, but Ronald Williams enjoyed making life harder than it need be for the Band Librarian. He was forever complaining about the amount of space that the band required for the storage of music, instruments and equipment. 'I'll swing for him', she often exploded to her husband, David.

Daisy was not born and bred in Silver Dale. She had just simply appeared in the town, with no family. Secured a job with the local authority in the civic administration section, settled in well. She met her husband who worked for the council and played in the town band, and as a result, she became a member of the band. When the role of Band Librarian became available, she was a natural choice.

Daisy appeared to have no past. It seemed that, for her, life began the moment she stepped foot in the town. Digging into her past, the Ronald Williams unearthed the secret fact that Daisy had a serious criminal past. A matter, which Daisy was at pains to keep a secret - even from her husband.

Going through Daisy's personal locker, Williams came across a letter, tucked away in an old handbag. Dated years previous, it was from the Home Office. It was a letter Daisy could not risk her husband finding, hence the locker hide-away, a letter she should have destroyed. The letter referred to her criminal history.

At one band rehearsal, Ronald Williams had taken Daisy to one side and whispered into her ear, "Have you heard from the Home Office recently?" Daisy went cold.

Daisy had arrived at the bandstand early to sort through the music.

Crystal Clear   Flügel Horn
Background information and motive
Aged 38.   Unmarried.   Numerous affairs.

Crystal Clear is very career-minded. A professional Vocal Specialist Tutor, a posh way of saying she is a private singing teacher. There have been men, but none managed to last long enough to go through to the final chord! Some had even failed to get past the first few bars introduction! Delights in informing people she has a Master of Arts, Music. She is the leader of the Silver Dale Town Choral Society. Her repertoire of choral music ranges from West End shows to Verdi. She would chirp, "My choral society has performed, under my direction, the three main Verdi operas, 'La Traviata', 'Aida' and 'Rigoletto'".

Crystal Clear was always distant to the point of being outright rude towards to just about everybody. Aloof and bad-tempered. She noted that Flügel horn was a cultured instrument to play, nothing barbaric or uncouth like a baritone.

Her name was a matter of some mirth. She was unconcerned that it was associated with a skin beauty product. Her birth certificate Christian name was Violet, a name she detested. The day following her sixteenth birthday, she legally became Crystal Clear by Deed Poll.

Considering her snobby behaviour joining a brass band appeared to be completely out of character. She felt it was very good for her image. It was also comparatively easy to persuade the Musical Director that she could become the band's vocal soloist as well as filling in on the Flügel horn part. Her presence in the band also assisted in increasing the number of tenors and basses in her choir. They were like bees around a honey pot!

Perhaps it might have been the hint of being additions to the 'CC Gentlemen List'.

Community centre members were aware that Williams had been the cause of a fatal road accident. Williams, driving along Silver Dale Sea Road, in the early hours of the morning, had driven into the path of an oncoming vehicle, the car veering off the highway, clipping safety bollards before bouncing high over the seawall into the sea. Although cleared, and not even prosecuted, many believed the inquest verdict was flawed. Williams is unaware that Crystal Clear is a relative of the deceased's immediate family. Crystal Clear is marking her man.

Crystal Clear was early at the bandstand to check on the PA system.

Philippa Horsecart   Tenor Horn   Band Press Officer
Background information and motive
Aged 43. Divorced. No children.

Philippa Horsecart, known by the nickname, 'Filly', has been the Band Press Officer for eight years.

Recently divorced, Philippa was compelled to go back and live with her elderly widowed mother, Elizabeth.

Philippa Horsecart was employed by Social Services and had acted for the service in a number of roles. She was now working in a school for maladjusted children, youngsters who had violent and disruptive backgrounds. Sadly the time came when Philippa could no longer manage to cope with the deteriorating ill health of her mother. Elizabeth needed more personal attention than Philippa could provide.

Connections with social services enabled Philippa to place her mother in a suitable nursing home, where she could regularly visit, spending happy times chatting to each other. Elizabeth still owned the family home in which 'Filly" lived.

Ronald Williams was often asked to call in at the nursing home to do a number of odd jobs, a bit of a handyman. He saw an opportunity to befriend the elderly Elizabeth with 'sob' stories, persuading the elderly woman to transfer her home over to him.

He argued that if he lost his job, he would be without accommodation, Philippa was likely to get remarried and would be, 'provided for'. The family solicitor telephoned Philippa enquiring if she was aware that her mother was proposing to make the house over to a gentleman named Ronald Williams, and he was required to draw up the papers. It was evident that if the daughter was unable to get her very strong-willed mother to change her mind, she would be homeless, should the transfer go through.

Philippa Horsecart was early to meet the local press photographer who was going to help her cover the concert.

Patrick (Pat) Elliott   Trombone   Band Secretary
Background information and motive
Aged 64.   *Married 40 years.*   *Grandfather.*
Elliott considers himself one of the 'old school' members of Silver Dale Town Band. Does not take easily or quickly to new and fresh ideas, finds it hard to adapt to changing times. Often refers to the good old days. Expects to retire next year, having been in the butchery trade all his life. Patrick Elliott is a Master Butcher, with his own butchery business, Silver Dale Butchers.

Elliott has reason to believe that Ronald Williams has been spreading untrue rumours about him and his butchery business. Someone has reported him to the Borough Council Environmental Health Department for selling underweight and rotten meat products. Could be prosecuted under The Food Standards Act 1999, and forced out of business. Financial and social ruin faced Elliott.

Elliott suspected that Williams, who had been lurking in the band room, had overheard the butcher confiding to another band member that he was having severe trouble with his cold storage units. They had utterly broken down. Getting them repaired was proving to be a significant problem and if he were unable to get the units up and running again the meat hanging in the cold storage would be unfit for human consumption and therefore unsellable. It was pay-back time for Williams. He and the butcher had, for many years, almost come to blows over Elliott parking his big butchers' van in the Community Centre car park and leaving it there all day. The fact that Elliott was a member and entitled to park meant little to Williams. It was always in the way. A letter was sent suggesting an unscheduled inspection of the butcher's shop, citing non-operating cold storage as justification.

Patrick Elliott was one of the first members of the committee to arrive. It was his usual practice to ensure that everything was in order for the concert.

Graham Carter   Musical Director
Background information and motive
Aged 25.   Single.   Shares a flat.

Graham Carter has been Silver Dale Town Band Musical Director for three years. Previously he had been the band's principal cornet player. As MD he has successfully developed the playing ability of the band, which currently has 33 members. In competition, they are moving up the ranks and are suggested to be a band of the future. By profession, the MD works as a senior laboratory technician in the local hospital mortuary department. He is hoping to gain a University place and thereby become a pathologist. As part of his career pathway, the MD had applied for a very important promotion within the hospital. The appointment was vital for two reasons. One was advancement plus the new job would also mean a substantial increase in salary, putting an end to the financial worries which currently beset the MD. He was in deep debt; the bailiffs were almost beating on the door. He just could not manage money. Using numerous credit cards, both bank and stores had created the situation. Arriving at work on Monday morning, a letter was awaiting him informing him that he had not been successful in his job application. Indeed his current position was now under review, and termination of the post was a strong probability. An administration colleague told Graham that a letter from Ronald Williams to the selection board was 'quite appalling' in its content giving the appointments board little option. The Musical Director was seething with anger. Facing an uncertain future, he vowed to get even. "That Ronald Williams needs a smash over the head", he roared. Williams had decided, whilst the band was rehearsing, and knowing that the MD would be occupied for at least an hour, to go through Carter's things. Using his master key, Williams opened Graham Carter's locker. The exercise proved very fruitful. Inside the MD's jacket pocket were two or three letters from collection agencies. Court action and possible bankruptcy proceedings were hinted. It did not take very long for Williams to know where that information should be sent.

Graham Carter was always one of the first to arrive, he saw it as the Musical Director's responsibility.

Oliver Jones   Bass Trombone   Treasurer
Background information and motive
Aged 36.   Married.   Three Children.
Band Treasurer Oliver Jones has a banking background and is ideally suited for the job he does for the band. He has been in the position for about five years. At the bank, he is the assistant manager, with responsibility for large and corporate accounts held at the branch. His hobby is a strange one; it is the study of the cases of Sherlock Holmes. He is a member of the Silver Dale Sherlock Holmes Appreciation Society and holds the office of President Spyglass. He is also the honorary treasurer of the community centre.

Ronald Williams had observed the developing relationship between the treasurer and the community centre manager, Julie Barnes. Williams became increasingly convinced that something was going on between the two of them. Jones would hang around the centre manager's office for no obvious reason, joking and laughing, just like two teenagers. Barnes would be on the telephone to Jones on some minor pretext asking him to call into the centre. The times the two of them spent together was increasing and with it the familiarity. There was no doubt what passed between them was flirtatious. Frumpy Julie became glamorous Miss Barnes, time spent in the cosmetic department was evident. The bank manager's image was being replaced by more casual attire.Oliver was to be seen in the more fashionable gents outfitters.

Williams knew he was on to something. If he was correct, he could certainly profit from the relationship if it existed. Evidence and confirmation Williams needed. Sooner than expected, it came his way.

Late one evening searching through the secretary's filing cabinet he came across a new file marked 'Forward Planning - Private'. Inside was nothing more than confirmation of a hotel booking and details of a conference. Julie Barnes had booked to attend a Community Centre Administration Conference to be

Delegates were expected to arrive Friday afternoon in time for the opening evening session, Saturday there was a full conference programme with delegates leaving on the Sunday morning after breakfast. It would be two nights away, paid for by the Silver Dale Community Centre, authorised by the treasurer. The booking was for two people. The hotel booked was not in Brighton but along the coast in Worthing.

The conference dates were entered in the centre diary. There was no indication that a second person would accompany Julie Barnes. The conference was being held on the same weekend that the band had an engagement. Jones offered his apologies. He needed to attend a Bank 'Bonding' Staff Seminar.

Williams admitted all he had was conjecture, solid evidence was required.

Following the weekend away, Williams went searching. If there was evidence to be found, he would find it. The file marked 'Forward Planning - Private' was now much thicker, no longer a single hotel confirmation sheet and conference information. 'Oh dear', thought the caretaker, 'they have been naughty'. Julie Barnes had printed off quite a few 'conference' snaps taken in the hotel bedroom. Switching on the photocopier Williams soon had his collection of private weekend photos and the evidence.

Both Barnes and Jones were married. Now, just what was this portfolio of photos worth? Which one of them to tell first he had the compromising photos, and quite a number of them? He now had to consider what did he want? Ronald Williams knew he had a strong hand.

The morning post arrived and the caretaker collected the post from the postman. Williams added one A4 plain brown envelope containing just one photo of the couple. Inserting his envelope into the postal bundle, he knocked on the door of the Community Centre Manager and handed over the post.

Williams sat and waited in his caretaker's cubbyhole. The verbal explosion from Mrs Barnes ended with, "What do you want?"

Oliver Jones knew there was personal trouble about to break, he had heard from Mrs Barnes. He planned to try and reason with Williams prior to the concert, perhaps buy him off. At the moment it was only the three of them aware of the situation.

Police Officer   Inspector Jack Swansea

In his investigation report, the Police Inspector noted the following. He was called to the bandstand at 7:15pm on a Saturday evening. At the bandstand, preparing for the evening's concert were six members of the band committee. They were: Daisy Picking; Crystal Clear; Philippa Horsecart; Patrick (Pat) Elliott; Graham Carter and Oliver Jones.

In one of the below stage dressing rooms, the body of the deceased Ronald Williams was found. It was clear that Mr Williams had been attacked from behind. Adjacent to the body was a mangled brass instrument, a cornet, which was without question the murder weapon. On the floor, adjacent to the body was a music book. The door had been locked and was broken down to gain access. A member of the band had observed the prone body of the caretaker on the floor through the door window and raised the alarm.

It was indeed foul play at the bandstand. The Inspector sealed and secured the crime scene. The officer was able to establish that Ronald Williams was known to each of the suspects. The Police Inspector undertook a systematic investigation of the incident. He wanted to know everybody's movements on arriving at the bandstand. He informed the band committee that he would be doing background checks on all of them. Formal interviews will take place over the following few days. Each would need to attend the police station to go through the procedure. With that, he allowed the people to leave the bandstand and to go home.

The Inspector called in the fingerprint boys: he and his sergeant made a thorough inspection of the room. Apart from the body, the murder weapon and the book, the room revealed precious little else.

Back at the station, the Inspector went through the background information on all the suspects which had been collated. He also conducted a search of the deceased caretaker's cubbyhole and his flat, removing a number of vital bits of evidence. He now felt he was in a position to reveal the murderer.

Swansea instructed his sergeant to assemble those members of the band under suspicion to meet at the dressing room of the bandstand. The room was as they recalled, only absent was the body of the caretaker. The cornet and the book lay in the same position as they had been found. The Inspector announced that all of them had a reason to kill the community centre caretaker. The motive was evident in all cases.

Graham Carter, the Inspector revealed, was very deep in debt, facing bankruptcy and the loss of his job. Copies of letters from collection agencies were found in the cubbyhole of the caretaker, also a copy of the letter sent to Carter's employers. Reason enough argued the Inspector for Carter to want to kill the caretaker. It was Graham Carter who was seen going to the dressing room with the cornet case. Graham explained that the cornet was a 'spare', sometimes used by visiting bandsmen wanting 'a blow'.

It was also a letter, a copy of which was found in Mr William's cubbyhole, sent to the Borough Council Environmental Health Department, by Mr Williams accusing Mr Elliott of selling underweight and rotten meat products. The letter was rather damning. That letter was a convincing motive. Mr Elliott admitted that the letter had ruined him. He went to the dressing room seeking Mr Williams, "I wanted to confront him, to find out the truth, but he was not in the room".

Being swindled out of her family home by a deceitful, devious, scheming man, was more than Philippa Horsecart could contemplate. The man deserved to die. She was protecting the public; it was a public service. Philippa conceded every time she saw Williams she wanted to 'throttle him'! Yes, she had gone down to the dressing room, she wanted somewhere quiet to commence putting together her press report on the concert. She knew Williams was in the room; she had heard him jangling his keys from outside the door. Philippa entered, and Williams left.

Revenge had been on the heart and mind of Crystal Clear for years. Thought and planning her revenge was never far from the mind of Crystal Clear. She would provide the justice where justice had failed her family. If the motive was needed, the accident provided it. Crystal Clear had gone to the dressing room, with a couple of gowns which she was planning to wear during the concert and wanted to hang them up. Mr Williams was in the room doing what she described as 'tidying up'. He was alive when she left.

Passion was the 'spark-plug' which ignited a plan to kill the caretaker. The murder was one way of concealing the affair between Oliver Jones and Julie Barnes. Murdering Williams might have been a way of retrieving and destroying the photos. Oliver Jones said the only reason he had to enter the dressing room, which he did, was to leave his instrument case. He observed that the cornet case was strangely open. There was no sign of Mr Williams.

The Central Police Criminal Records quickly revealed the trouble Daisy Picking had with the authorities. Perhaps not a strong murder motive, but one nevertheless. It was Daisy Picking who discovered the body. On my way to the toilet, I looked in on the dressing room. Williams was on the floor. She had nothing further to add.

All the accused appeared to be able to provide an alibi for some of the time in which the murder took place — frequently backing each other. There were gaps which the Inspector accepted.

The one item which might have assisted them in their police enquiries and indicate to the Police who was the murderer, was the cornet. No fingerprints of any use were to be found. The pathologist report indicated that Williams had not died instantly. The high loss of blood from the head wound hastened the death. The Inspector suggested that Williams had turned his back on his assailant, providing instant opportunity. The weapon was readily available. Williams had been struck twice. Once while standing and the second blow administered as he collapsed. The bell end of the cornet had acted like a butcher's slice. The murderer could not leave the room with the cornet in his or her hand. It had to be dropped at the scene.

The Police were pretty certain that Ronald Williams knew his attacker. The Police were convinced that Williams was alone when the murderer entered the room. For some reason unknown, Williams probably locked the door behind his assailant, so the meeting could be private. There was no evidence of a struggle, neither found were the caretaker's bunch of keys.

So who was the killer? Swansea suggested that when Ronald Williams dropped to the floor, a paper-book, with his name inscribed inside, had slipped from his pocket and lay on the floor just by his fingertips. The book was entitled 'An Introduction to the Orchestra'. Williams, still conscious, had wiped some blood from his head wound and with his blooded forefinger had high-lighted the word Orchestra on the book cover. Turning to Philippa the Inspector said. "When we searched through your house Mrs Horsecart, we found the caretaker's bunch of keys in your Tenor Horn case. Very careless that, but then you had no reason to think you were a suspect. You locked the door to delay anyone finding the body, giving you more time to conceal your action. However Williams told us who his killer was. He almost indicated the name in blood. The anagram of Orchestra is Horsecart".

The Training Band

(19)

A tribute to the many
Band Training Leaders
and
Young People's Band Leaders in The Salvation Army

Press Bereavement Notice

WIGGINS Arthur (Tailor) MBE
Passed away suddenly on 1st August aged 78 years.
He heard the last trumpet call.

Arthur was a well known and respected businessman of Oakbridge and a member of the Oakbridge Town Band. For over forty years Arthur was the Training Band Leader. Arthur will be greatly missed by his family, friends and colleagues. A Funeral Service is to be held at Oakbridge Parish Church on Thursday 11th August at 1.30pm. Family flowers only thank you, but donations if desired for Oakbridge Town Training Band. Donations may be sent to Oakbridge Funeral Services, 19 Brickyard Road, Oakbridge, West Sussex.

ARTHUR was remembered for two particular things. He was the town's tailor, 'making clothes for all occasions', both men and women. "I've had my arm around more ladies' waists than Fred Astaire", he would joke. While not as famous as shirtmaker Thomas Pink, those who wore a 'Pink' shirt were, 'in the pink', people in Oakbridge and further afield could be 'Wiggins', wearing outfits that had the 'Wiggins' label.

Many people would recall that they had been introduced to music and taught a brass instrument by Arthur. Arthur was a member of that very special brass band club, people in charge of the Training Band. Like all members of the 'Training Club' they put in hours and hours with their students. Reward was the satisfaction in seeing and hearing the progress, from playing the C scale, simple and undemanding tunes, tackling traditional brass band marches and enjoying playing themes from West End shows. It all began in the classroom with Arthur, as teacher. It was the Bandmaster or Musical Director of the senior band who capitalised on Arthur's musical industry. Arthur trained them, his apprentices, having reached senior band standard were transferred, leaving Arthur to start all over again with a fresh class of trainees.

Arthur played in the senior band, changing band instrument about every ten years or so. His first instrument upon joining the band was the cornet. A few years later he was moved to the horn section, followed by a short period by a transfer to the baritone section. There he remained until a vacancy in the bass section found him on the back row, tackling the smaller of the two basses. Arthur often expressed the view that it seemed to him strange that as he got older, the weight of the instrument he played got heavier! Indeed, it should have been the other way around!

He, and his wife Mabel, had lived in the same house since their wedding. The three bedroomed semi-detached property in Albany Terrace had cost them £2,500.00 in Coronation Year, 1952. The Wiggins' semi was next door to the corner shop, separated only by an unmade track which serviced the back of the Albany Terrace. The shop was typical of so many similar shops, open from first thing in the morning for the sale of newspapers and milk, and closing late into the evening. It was a shop which sold, as the owner was eager to say, 'essentials'. Albany Stores opened Christmas Day morning from 8.00am until noon. The owner proudly claimed, "Like the Windmill Theatre in London, we never close".

The occupants of the shop and No 1 Albany Terrace were the best of neighbours. Arthur made some of his purchases at the store, his morning newspaper and his weakness for a bar of chocolate. Mrs Wiggins sometimes helped out in the shop.

In Coronation Year, just a few months following his marriage, Arthur commenced his own tailoring business. He had learnt his trade from a national gents' outfitters. He had gone to the firm directly from school. He showed an aptitude and skill, he found that some of the more difficult tailoring jobs were passed over to him. Mabel encouraged him to think about the future, she suggested that he should branch out on his own. She convinced him that he could make a 'go of it'. He was more than good at what he did. Convinced he handed in his notice.

Arthur placed a small advertisement in the local paper, not the more expensive display box advertisements, where the newspaper charged by the column inch and had a premium rate for right-hand pages. Arthur choose the Classified section of the paper, at the back. There was a section heading of Dressmaking It was there that Arthur placed his advert:

Need a Suit?
Dislike shopping?
Can't find the time?
Made to Measure tailoring
Ladies and Gent suits and separates
chosen in the comfort of your own home.
Anytime - Day or Evening
~ Alterations ~
• Choose from over 700 cloth samples
• Styles to suit all tastes
• Personally delivered
• Prices to suit all pockets
Telephone Arthur Wiggins

The same evening as the paper came out, Arthur had his first enquiry. Not a three-piece suit, but altering trousers where the length was too long. From that moment, the dressmaking and tailoring business was a success. Whilst Arthur cut and sewed, Mabel attended to the books and accounts, the dining room table serving as an office desk. Work was steady, and the business flourished. A combination of advert and word of mouth ensuring business success.

Needing a name for the business, the couple decided on Arthur Wiggins (Tailor). It was not long before the surname dropped off. People knocking on the door would ask for Mr Tailor. About the town, he was Mr Tailor. As far as Arthur was concerned the name was good for business. Arthur set up his tailoring workshop in the upstairs second double bedroom. He nailed a small sign to the garden gate: Arthur Wiggins (Tailor).

Arthur was a neat dapper man. The manner of his sober attire had to reflect his business. Even when casually dressed, Arthur looked 'dressed up'. Arthur might have left the house in just his shirt sleeves, but nobody could remember for sure that he had. Suit or jacket was always part of Arthur's dress ensemble. There was some relaxation of the dress code for Mabel. Mabel was his dress model. Most of her clothes were made by Arthur. Mabel was the best advert for his work, slim and attractive.

With the help of the advertisement and word of mouth, Arthur's reputation grew. Even his previous employers would put work Arthur's way. The newly installed Town Mayor commissioned a new double breasted suit with shoulder loops on which to attach the mayoral chain. To commemorate fifty years of service to the town, the congregation of the Parish Church decided to purchase new vestments for the Vicar and turned to Arthur to make them.

Less auspicious was the request, in about 1970, by the Secretary of the town band to alter a couple of band jackets. One evening following the band rehearsal, the Secretary called round at Albany Terrace with the jackets to be adjusted. The pair got chatting about the band, Arthur was interested to learn of the band's history and how the band was doing now. "Why don't you pop into a band rehearsal?, I'm sure you will find it interesting", said the band secretary.

There didn't seem to be very much point. Music was not one of Arthur's interests, and he could neither read music, nor play an instrument. Arthur recalled the standard, very old, Christmas cracker joke and retorted, "When I was very young, I used to play on the linoleum!"

Following the end of the war, the former, now redundant, Oakbridge Military Camp had been sold off lot by lot. Most buildings were acquired as premises for smaller industrial usage, such as, light engineering, garage workshops and small jobbing printers. Others were refurbished for retail use.

Included in the sale was a large military dormitory, not ideally located on the site. The band committee considered that the hut would make an ideal band room. Pleading poverty, the band secured the hut for a knock-down price.

With band jackets over his arm, Arthur made his way to the Oakbridge Town Band building, from a distance he could hear the music of the band. Arthur pushed open the hut door, the volume of sound of the band suddenly increased. Unknown to him the band was running through *The Floral Dance*, it was a tune that Arthur failed to recognise.

Not to disturb the rehearsal Arthur took a seat alongside the back wall and commenced observing the proceedings. He recalled one summer holiday in Eastbourne sitting in the sunshine and listening to a band playing in the bandstand, but that was about his only connection with a brass band.

Arthur was surprised at how much there was to take in. Little did he know he was about to learn a whole new language and also observe things which he had never questioned. There was a lot more to this brass band malarkey he concluded. Concentrating on the conductor, Arthur was introduced to the peculiar language of the brass band world. "From the top", "Don't forget the second time bar", "Basses you are not following my beat", "What are dynamics for?", "Give the notes their full value". "There is a rit at the end of letter C". "Pianissimo, pianissimo!", "Euphoniums you are overblowing!", "2nd trombone you need to listen to your tuning". The band seemed to understand the conductor even if Arthur did not.

Arthur took in his surroundings. The band was sitting on

three sides of a square, in two rows. The fourth side of the square was occupied solely by the conductor. Arthur had little idea why the band seating was in that formation. From his observation instrument bells either pointed straight out in front, cornets and trombones or, the rest of the brass players were aiming at the ceiling, he glanced up, not a stain on the ceiling.

Arthur considered that perhaps the layout of the band was determined by cosmetics, it looked pretty that way. To his ear, it appeared that where players sat had little at all to do with the music. Would you notice, musically, he questioned, if the players decided to sit just where they wanted? Mix them up a bit. It might make for improved instrumental relationships, they could get on a bit better. A tenor horn sandwiched between a bass and a trombone, he mused. Arthur thought the current seating arrangement was a touch 'clicky'; all the cornets sat together, they being the largest group looked formidable. The basses gave the impression of being a tough lot, and the trombone section were closer than a troop of monkeys. Breaking them up might be a good for band discipline.

Arthur had seen music before; mainly pianoforte. His mother played the organ at the little Chapel in their home village. Mother had a hymnal with the words of the hymn separating the two lines of music. In one corner of the living room stood an old 'pump' organ which Mother had to pedal. On the organ stand was the music hymnal, always open.

He glanced over the shoulder at the music of the cornet player behind where he was seated. He could see it was a single line of music. Noticing that Arthur was interested the soprano cornet player moved his chair allowing space for Arthur to pull up his chair and sit next to him. Arthur explained that he had no knowledge of music, to him, it was all dots, open dots and lines with a funny squiggle at the beginning of the line of music.

Arthur had his first music lesson as the instrumentalist played, using his index finger, he pointed to the notes of the music, tracing the music line, Arthur was able to follow. At that moment Arthur was 'hooked'.

"I've just joined Oakbridge Town Band", was not what Mabel expected to hear when they had their late-night cup of Cocoa that evening. Mabel shook her head; it was so out of character. She had nothing against brass bands and enjoyed a good carol sing-along with the town band whilst out Christmas shopping.

She needed to know what was involved in 'banding', a new word which suddenly entered the Wiggins' conversation. Into her mind flashed the expression, 'golf widow', was there such a thing as a band widow? Mabel feared there might be. Joining the band just to play was one thing, but what went with it?. There would be other bandsmen and bandswomen and their loved ones to meet. It was akin to going to a family wedding and acquiring a mixed collection of unknown relatives. The prospect was daunting.

Wisely Mrs Wiggins decided to accompany her husband as he joined the Oakbridge Town Training Band. The band commenced the training sessions in September to coincide with the school term. Both Mabel and Arthur were a little surprised when they entered the room, not an instrument to be seen. The beginners class was a very mixed assortment of ages, although divided equally between female and male. The band's Training Officer welcomed everybody and explained they would need to learn music first. The necessary personal details forms were completed. Arthur was a little bemused when Mabel stretched out her hand and took a form and filled it in.

On the wall was a large green chalkboard, with musical images which Arthur recognised as notes with numbers underneath. The instructor explained the five-line stave. "Simple really a note is either between the line or on the line. All the notes have a letter name, from A to G, they are always in the same position on the stave. Once you get to G you start all over again from A. On the stave the four notes between the lines spell F – A – C – E, and crossing the line, five notes, before F comes E; thus E - G - B - D – F or to help you remember, every good boy deserves fudge, or whatever you like beginning with F". From the notes on the stave discussion the lesson moved to the value of notes, explaining in mathematical terms how notes related to each other. Up on the chalkboard was a graph which visually detailed, brieve down to semi-quaver, the notes most used in brass band music.

On the usual Saturday morning trip to town, they called in at the library and took out a music tuition book and another which explained the theory of music. From WH Smiths they ordered the *Oxford Companion to Music* by Percy Scholes. The local second-hand book shop offered a slim volume by Frank Wright entitled *Brass Today*. Percy Scholes and Frank Wright proved valuable, the one for information and research the other as Sir Adrian Boult noted in the foreword, 'Wright has collected the wisdom of experts'.

At the next Training Band session, the Training Officer circulated a simple test paper to see how much they had retained from the previous lesson. Top marks with 100% from the Wiggins. Both Arthur and Mabel had no problem with the 'school-room' work. In front of the trainer, arranged on a table was a selection of mouthpieces. A bit like a Russian doll paraded from the smallest to the largest, and all sizes in between. The trainer went on to explain how what seemed just a small part of the instrument was quite complicated and technical, essential to the instrument and the producing of a musical sound. To illustrate the point, he highlighted six cornet mouthpieces. All had significant differences. A shallow cup aided producing high register notes, whilst a deeper cup produced a sweeter, warmer sound. Mouthpieces came in different sizes, and whilst the outside of the mouthpiece could sometimes be quite ornamental, the business was done in the cup or, as some people called it, the bowl.

Training Band members were invited to select a mouthpiece. The Training Officer then explained the process of producing a note through the mechanism of the mouthpiece. On the chalkboard there was a cut-away diagram of a trombone showing a column of air, vibrated by the lips and tongue of the player, commencing in the mouthpiece then passing on through the tubing of the instrument to the bell end. Time for the students to try just using a mouthpiece. Many peculiar sounds were heard, some of them could just not get the hang of it, whilst others it was clear, would very quickly be able to play a note on an instrument.

The next session would involve trying to get some sound out of the instrument. The band trainer went around the band asking what instrument the embryonic players would like to start playing. All instruments were in the pitch B-flat. E-flat could be explained and introduced later. In the very early stages of training having all the instruments in the same pitch made a great deal of sense. Cornet, euphonium and trombone were popular choices. Arthur and Mabel stood to one side, letting the youngsters have first pick.

Left on the table, a bit like Hobson's choice, were a cornet and a monster BBb bass, the bass about eighteen feet of tubing and perhaps over twenty pounds in weight! It was expected that Arthur would pick up the bass. Not so. Clearly, Mabel supported and practiced equality. "I don't mind trying the bass provided we can call it a tuba", exclaimed Mabel, "I don't like the word bass". Arthur thought they might have a flugel horn or baritone tucked away somewhere, which he felt would better suit his wife. Mabel was adamant, name and instrument decided.

Feeling a bit limp Arthur picked up the remaining cornet. Already he knew it was going to be a case of Arthur carries tuba and Mabel manages the cornet. Why did he not stick to tailoring? Home practice was quickly organised. Mabel in the conservatory, and Arthur in his upstairs work room. Mabel listened at the bottom of the stairs, when the sewing machine stopped, a few moments later Arthur was doing all he could to blow a note. 'If that is the very best he can do', Mabel thought, 'there really is no competition in this household'. Mabel was determined to be the better Wiggins player.

In no time at all Mabel was playing the C scale with no problem whatsoever, she felt a sense of achievement the first time she went up and down the scale without an error. Within the first week Arthur had made steady progress, he was now able to pitch an individual note and was capable of sustaining it without a wobble. With the aid of the tutor they had borrowed from the library, and the practice they put in, the couple were way ahead of the other trainees.

Just before Christmas, the couple who owned the corner shop took the decision to retire and in the process offered Arthur the opportunity to purchase the unit. It seemed too good an opportunity to pass over and so Arthur moved his workshop from the house to the shop.

Into the shop windows went tailor's dummies dressed with examples of Arthur's tailoring skill. With Mabel's assistance the new premises were quickly fitted out. A bright new name board was placed over the entrance, Arthur Wiggins (Tailor). Accompanying the sewing machine move from home to shop was Arthur's cornet and his newly purchased music stand.

It was December and seasonal music could be heard. There was a great sense of achievement when Arthur mastered a verse and chorus of *Ding Dong Merrily on High* all in one go. Mrs Wiggins was ushered into the shop, instructed to sit down in one of the customers' armchairs and listen while Arthur ran through the Christmas Carol again just for Mabel's benefit.

Mabel was far from impressed. "It doesn't take much effort to play the melody, almost everybody can whistle *God Rest You Merry Gentlemen!*" asserted Mrs Wiggins. "Now just look at the bass part, sometimes it goes all over the place. We have to count our time. You, cornet players, rely on the basses to give the music a solid foundation". Arthur was in no mood for an argument.

At the suggestion of the Musical Director, Arthur and Mabel attended senior band rehearsals in November with a view to playing out with the band during the carolling season. The MD suggested that Arthur slot onto the second cornet bench. He now found himself in the same position as his wife, having to play a part rather than the lead melody. He conceded it was all part of his brass band development. Mabel was positioned amongst the male row of basses. "Do you want a hand up with that bass luv?" asked a jovial bass colleague, winking to his mate. Women in the bass section might take a bit of getting used to. Never the best behaved section, and often guilty of personal antisocial behaviour, the result of which drifted around the band room, the male members of the section had to quickly change their ways.

The band secretary equipped both of them with the blue band jacket and band bow tie. The issued blue jacket was never going to do for either of them. *'Off the peg'* was blasphemy for Arthur. In the interim, before Arthur could order a bolt of blue band cloth to tailor make jackets for himself and Mabel, a bit of alteration was necessary. Both bow ties had been badly treated by a number of previous owners. From some surplus black cloth, Arthur made new ties.

Mabel and Arthur wanted to keep the link and association they had established with the Training Band. Trainees often required one-to-one tuition, Arthur and Mabel felt they could be mentors, particularly to the youngsters. They could see the value of the Training Band. They recognised the Training Band Leader's hard work. They wanted to support him in his efforts. Indeed, the leader of the Training Band was grateful for any help he could get from the senior members of the band, he welcomed the couple into the sessions.

On reflection in a matter of months, the Wiggins had part taught themselves to read music, been instructed on how to play a brass instrument, they were now members of the town band, they had in effect joined a completely new, to them, social community and were enjoying every single moment of it. It was an association which was to last for many years.

The band committee, at one of the band reviews, acknowledged the contribution which the Wiggins had made to the Training Band. Committee members considered that the couple should have a more formal position within the Training Band. Mabel and Arthur were officially made members of the Training Band team. Later Arthur had an opportunity to exchange the sewing needle for the conductor's baton. Mabel became the unofficial matron and 'mother' of the Training Band.

Not all youngsters came from stable family backgrounds. 'Aunty' Mabel had to wipe away many a tear, try and mend a broken heart, listen patiently, share their anxieties, be the band's care and welfare worker, take time to spend with parents who came to the sessions with their children. If it was only teaching a child to play a brass instrument then it would have been comparatively easy. A Training Band was very demanding, so much occurred within the framework of a Training Band. Even the Musical Director and playing members of the senior band had literally little idea at all as to what it entailed. Mabel convinced the band committee of the need to set up the Amenity Fund for the Training Band, a better title than Welfare Fund.

After a couple of years Arthur was approached to take over the leadership of the Training Band. The committee were convinced that there was nobody more suitable in every respect to be the leader. Arthur never hesitated for a moment. In fact, Mabel was standing alongside Arthur when the approach was made by the Musical Director. "Yes", was the only word Mabel uttered, a word which sealed the couples commitment to the band. With the appointment Mabel became a part time player in the senior band, having quickly moved from tuba to baritone, one time sharing the stand with her husband. She still maintained she was by far the better player. And on the occasions when the composer required only one baritone player to play, Arthur simply dropped his instrument onto his lap. "I just let her get on with it – it makes for peace within the band and at home".

Mabel and Arthur were the Training Band leaders for many years. Arthur developed the training programme, each session well planned and structured. Arthur maintained two training terms, Autumn and Spring, with spare dates should it be necessary for additional tuition.

Between them Arthur and Mabel wrote a Band Training Manual. Not only did the manual deal with the rudiments of music and how to play a note, but also advice on the care of instruments. Just like stripping down a Bren gun, there was clear instruction on dismantling a musical instrument, how to clean it and prepare it for playing. Arthur felt that youngsters also needed social guidance and so part of the manual contained the Band Code of Conduct, to which he often referred. Not a book of only do's and do nots, but of sound advice.

Mabel kept the register. They both felt it was crucial that there should be a record of the trainees' progress. Important milestones were noted, even the first time a trainee completed the C scale. Exam papers were retained and filed in the student's folder. Award Certificates were presented to the students in front of the senior band thus making something special of the occasion.

Then came the day which Mabel called their Graduation day, which indeed it was. The Musical Director introduced the student to the senior band, helped them on with their blue band jackets, escorted them to their place in the band and presented to them the senior band instrument they were now to play. For Arthur and Mabel, it was always a very proud moment. As part of their graduation, the individual folders which Mabel had been adding to were passed over to the trainee, a record of their time within the training band.

There came a time when nobody could remember when Arthur and Mabel did not run with the Training Band. They were thrilled to receive a letter from a Military Director of Music. In the regimental band, two 'Wiggins' boys were members of the band, the letter thanked the couple for exemplary, dedicated service in commencing the two on the road they had taken to be professional musicians. The letter seemed to confirm their decision to organise the Training Band was well justified and had a purpose.

To their personal delight, and the congratulations of many, it was the announcement that they had each been made Members of the British Empire in recognition of the years they had given to encouraging the development of music in young people. During the month arrangements were made for the band to hold a Celebratory Festival in honour of the couple. For Arthur, it was an opportunity to tailor 'his and her' investiture suits for Mabel and himself. He questioned whether he could get away with distributing some of his business cards at the Palace? It was such a proud day to be at Buckingham Palace to receive their MBEs.

With the passing of the years the time arrived very reluctantly when Arthur and Mabel felt the time had come to retire. They could not recall how many students of the Training Band had come under their tuition, people they had influenced. The current Musical Director of the town band had been a 'Wiggins' as with a goodly number of other players who were 'Wiggins'. Arthur and Mabel still popped along to the training band sessions, not as often as they would've liked, but there was great joy in sitting in, listening and just being there. The room was more than a home to them.

During one Training Band practice there was a commotion in the band room, people heard and saw Arthur dropping to the floor from his seat, in sliding downward Arthur grabbed Mabel's hand and in doing so pulled her onto the floor with him. Arthur was dead.

Arthur and Mabel never had any children of their own. At his funeral Mabel noted in her tribute, "Arthur was never an exceptional player, but he was an exceptional band trainer. The Training Band was his children and his family".

The Sleeping Bass

(20)

In memory of Oswald Ford
The Salvation Army - Trowbridge Corps

OSWALD was a meticulous man. Everything in order and everything in its place. Oswald's life was governed by calm and good order. The routine of the day rarely varied. Up at seven, into the bathroom to ablute, other people might have a wash, but not Oswald, Oswald abluted. As Oswald closed the bathroom door, Mrs Oswald dropped the two eggs into the pan of water. It was always boiled eggs for breakfast, Mrs Oswald had tried to encourage Oswald to extend his breakfast menu. "I always went to school on a boiled egg, it was good enough then, and it is most certainly good enough now", the firm voice of Oswald declared. As a little demonstration of affection Mrs Oswald would neatly take the top off the eggs. Placing the eggs in front of Oswald, each egg in its own egg cup, Mrs Oswald awaited the gentle nod of approval and 'Thank You' which always followed.

Each day they shared breakfast together, Mrs Oswald only leaving the table to go to the kitchen and return with the toast and marmalade and to bring in the woolly covered teapot, a tea cosy which Mrs Oswald had made herself, to a pattern she had found in Woman's Own.

Orderliness meant matching crockery. Their wedding list included tableware, requesting the Minton china Haddon Hall pattern. It was flowery and colourful. Mrs Oswald said it brightened up the dining room table, to accentuate the pattern she always insisted on a plain white starched tablecloth. If guests came, she had a special tablecloth made of Honiton lace with frilly edging. Neither Oswald nor his wife would think of using anything other than breakfast size cup and saucer.

When he sensed the breakfast was over, he would lean back in his chair, pat his tummy and look at his watch. He wasn't bothered about the time; it was the signal that he was going to go to work. A final visit to the bathroom and then he was ready, waiting for him at the front door was Mrs Oswald. She watched as her husband took his overcoat from the coat stand in the hallway and bend down for his attaché case. Coat buttoned, he leaned towards Mrs Oswald and kissed her on her cheek. "Have a nice day dear." Mrs Oswald watched her husband walk down the short tarmac footpath of the small two bedroomed terraced house. Opening the gate he would turn around and wave, then he began his journey to work.

At school, Oswald excelled at maths. He loved mental arithmetic, "What is 9×7+5+2 divided by 10?" asked the teacher. As quick as a flash Oswald's hand shot into the air and back came the reply, 7. As always Oswald was correct. Two years running he won the maths cup. In his head, he could also count money. It was more difficult because you had to contend with, pounds, shillings and pence. Twenty shillings to a pound, four half-crowns to ten bob, 240 pennies to a pound it was all at his fingertips. "It's a banking life for you", was the parting words to Oswald by his headmaster on his final day at school.

National Service loomed. Oswald reported for duty. One look at the slight, diminutive figure of Oswald and the Army Sergeant knew there was not much the army could do with the new entrant standing before him.

Oswald completed his basic training, but only just. He was a smart soldier. Indeed he always passed his kit inspection. Making a bed meticulously was easy; often he would make the bed of his barrack-room colleagues. "I suppose he could make a Batman", suggested a corporal; "you could shave with the crease in his trousers". His ability in maths had not gone unnoticed. When the postings were listed, Oswald found himself as a member of the Army Pay Corps. Oswald would always be happier with figures rather than bullets, a biro rather than a rifle. His two years national service past agreeably, and whilst others went to 'trouble spots', Oswald remained at home never once hearing the burst of gunfire but rather the burst of typewriter keys. Leaving the Pay Corps Oswald returned to live with his parents and his younger sister.

It was not long after demob that Oswald met the future Mrs Oswald. Firing Cupid's arrow was his sister who worked in the office at Woolworths. Sharing the office with her was Violet. The two girls became the best of friends. Both were members of the tennis club and had also joined the local ramblers. Oswald's sister announced that she and her friend Violet were going to go on a ramble next Saturday and would the family mind if Violet came back to the house for tea following the walk.

Bashful Oswald sat at the tea table, to his left his sister and immediately opposite him Violet. He was captivated at first sight and although a little tongue-tied, he did manage to make some conversation. It was very clear that Violet knew more about him than he did of her. He should have been cross with his sister for giving out so much information, but he was not. He reasoned that if she was still interested in him after all the things his sister had said about him, then that might be to his advantage.

"I bet you did not know that Violet sang in the songsters at The Salvation Army?', his sister volunteered. Violet went a little red at this; she didn't mind him knowing but would rather that she had told him.

Oswald constructed a plan to just accidentally 'bump' into Violet one lunchtime. Standing concealed in a doorway, but able to see the staff door of the Woolworths, Oswald awaited his opportunity. Not this time though because when the door opened, both his sister and Violet stepped out. The next time luck, or better planning, was on his side. He would wait for Violet the day his sister had a day off. It worked perfectly. The restaurant in the British Home Stores was the venue for their first meeting.

Oswald knew a bit about The Salvation Army because, on his military camp there was a Red Shield canteen. Not for him the pub with the other squaddies, many an evening was spent at the Sally Ann canteen. For want of nothing better to do Oswald would sit in on some of the Sunday night meetings. Violet was impressed, she might convert him yet. Stepping out with Violet meant stepping into The Salvation Army.

Romance blossomed, he was compelled to attend The Salvation Army if he was to make any progress with Violet. Going through the process Oswald became a Salvationist and was enrolled as a member of the movement. He was taught a brass instrument. Music, he quickly learnt was a matter of numbers, four crotchets to a semi-breve, eight notes to a scale, counting resting bars, he was back at school. He thought the bass would be his preferred brass band instrument. The basses sat right at the back, the size of instrument meant you could easily hide behind the bass, ideal for somebody who is rather shy.

And so Oswald found himself back in uniform, khaki exchanged for Salvation Army blue. The peaked cap was a step up from his service beret. On the piano in the front room of the two bedroomed terraced house was a framed photograph of the wedding, it had been hand-coloured. They had been married in full Salvation Army uniform. Violet, with a new uniform specially made for the wedding, with a stylish, slightly flattened collar. Fixed at the shoulder and draped crossways to hip, was a white wedding cord. Oswald was meticulously uniformed, trousers pressed to military precision, shoes highly polished and wearing a double cuffed white shirt from Montague Burton.

One child was born to them, named Margaret Rose after the King and Queen's second daughter.

Now nearly fifty years old Oswald enjoyed his job as a post office counter clerk. For him, the world of postage stamps, postal orders, childcare benefit and pension payments. He knew why most people were coming into the post office. Mrs Nelson, four children and another one on the way, when she came to the grill, he knew how much her child benefit amounted to. "Has your Trevor got over his cough?" He knew the names of all her children and their ages. "You'll soon be getting an increase," smiled Oswald, "Yes, and with a bit of luck, it will be twins," laughed

Mrs Nelson, finally producing her child benefit book.

Being close to the end of the month Oswald would have slipped under his grill confirmation of a valid MOT, insurance certificate and applications to renew the Road Fund Licence, commonly known as the Road Tax. Oswald found this a tedious part of the job, so often people were not as meticulous as himself, the MOT was out of date, the insurance document was for a different vehicle. Why did people not check things before they came in? In most cases, there was a delay in proceedings whilst they searched around for a cheque-book. "How much did you say it was for six months?", Oswald repeated the amount, "What did you say, didn't quite catch that?". Oswald had a supply of scrap paper at his elbow; he would write down the amount and push the information underneath the grill. Finally, all in order Oswald would thump the Post Office Hand Date Seal onto the tax disc.

Pension day was always busy, from the moment the post office opened, a queue formed. Organised pensioners had their pension books open, across went the book and coming the other way the pension money. Shopping trolleys indicated the next port of call. From Post Office to supermarket, the pensioners made their predictable pilgrimage. Sometimes in with the pension book was the shopping list and Oswald could glance down and see what they planned to purchase. Could Mrs Appleby really get through a dozen tins of baked beans?

Top of the list for Alf Freeborn was tobacco; he was a 'roll your own' smoker, his fingertips stained by years of misuse. Oswald recalled that Alf started smoking at school, having been invited to join Alf and a few other school chums in a 'smoking club' behind the cricket club pavilion. "How do, Oswald, are you still playing that trumpet thing in the Sally Army?". It was always the same question, visit after visit never varied. Now Oswald's reply was nothing more than a cursory nod of his head. That trumpet thing was a bass, not the big gigantic bass but the next size down.

In quieter moments, Oswald reflected on how much he knew about his customers, you picked up quite a bit of information as a post office clerk. Just about everybody who lived within the town came to the post office. It was not a place for secrets. People chatted, folk gossiped, humanity could whisper in a very loud voice! Oswald had heard it all. He thought the post office was a bit like a confessional. He, 'Father Post Office Counters' sat behind a grill; the other side the voices of confession, omission and contrition. The 'Father' administered GPO indulgences, receiving the confessor's money, and in exchange they the 'Father's blessing, and permission to legally drive their car for another year! "Did he really say 'Go in Peace' to Mr Lambert?"

Members of The Salvation Army were divided into two groups when they came to the post office. The ones who avoided Oswald and the others who made a beeline for his counter position. The Home League Treasurer, Mrs Piper, always looked for Oswald, coming directly from the Home League meeting she would pass over money collected that day for the members' Thrift Club. "We had a lady come to talk to us about flower arranging today, she was very arresting, and arranged the flowers for Sunday". Mrs Piper often got her words mixed up. "I shall look forward to seeing them myself at the morning meeting", said Oswald politely. "Did you know Mrs James is not at all well at the moment?", whispered the treasurer as she left the counter. Oswald tried to place Mrs James; he'd ask Mrs Oswald when he got home.

Once a week the Corps Officer came in, dressed in full uniform, stand-up collar, tunic and cap. Tucked under his arm was a large brown envelope containing his weekly report back to Divisional Headquarters, for some strange reason called, 'The Budget'. "Look out, here is your boss, the General has arrived", his counter companion informed Oswald, although he knew already. "Will it be the usual Major?", enquired Oswald, "Yes please and two books of stamps". Knowing the officer would want a receipt Oswald produced one.

At the close of business for the day, counter staff balanced the books. Oswald could be a pain, he was never prepared to leave the post office until his books balanced. Indeed there were occasions when it might be only a penny out, but he still needed to find it, his meticulous side would not allow him to leave his place of employment until the books were correct and the last penny accounted for.

Mislaying just one penny of the post office revenue could not be allowed, Oswald would find it, he would go over the transactions of the day until that penny misplacement was found. Whilst others allowed for a margin of error, not Oswald; the penny was all the more important if it was on the deficit side for the post office. Neither could Oswald take a penny from his pocket to make up the balance. Every transaction was reviewed meticulously searching for the error.

There was very little over which Oswald could not be meticulous or sometimes as Margaret Rose said, "ridiculous". His Austin A30 saloon car proved the point. He and Violet had been able to purchase the car absolutely brand-new, with just delivery mileage on the clock. They had a small garage at the back of the house accessed by a service lane. With the car in its new home for the first time, and Violet thrilled with the bouquet of flowers sent by the garage, Oswald sat in his fire-side armchair and read cover to cover the Austin A30 handbook.

The next day Oswald came home with a large exercise book, sitting down at the table, he wrote on the cover 'Austin A30 Expenses Book'. With a ruler he created a column on the left hand side of the page and ruled it off, he did the same on the right hand side of the page. One was headed 'Date' and the other, far-right, 'Expenditure'. The much larger centre section was headed 'Detail'.

In the following years for the whole period of time that Oswald owned the car, he kept his own personal service history, recording every single penny he spent on the vehicle. The date when he filled it up with petrol, how many gallons and how much they cost. When he purchased his first top-up oil, that also went into the A30 Expenses Book; Road Fund licence and insurance were regular annual entries. The book revealed the increases in insurance costs which Oswald had to meet. On a little trip down to The New Forest, he picked up a nail, punctured the tyre. New tyre - fresh entry. The main headlight bulb went, cost of replacement meant Oswald was getting the book out again. In the early days of A30 ownership, there were very few entries recording car parking charges. He recorded in capital letters the first time he found himself compelled to pay for car parking.

Violet wanted a tartan rug for the car, "I can wrap it around my legs it will help keep me warm", there ensued a family debate. Was the rug a legitimate car expense? Oswald argued not, the rug was not a permanent car fixture, it was not even listed as an accessory, and he had been conned into paying for it. Violet, supported by Margaret Rose, maintained that its main purpose was for the benefit of car passengers, and was used for car picnics, therefore it should go in the book. Reluctantly Oswald conceded, though in the detail column he wrote 'Miscellaneous'.

Sunday by Sunday Oswald and Violet attended their Salvation Army centre in which they were both active, Violet more so than Oswald. Violet sang in the Songsters and attended the weekly Home League. When the vacancy arose, they invited Oswald to be the corps treasurer. Oswald declined, he was happy sitting on the back row, in the band, hidden by his bass.

Oswald could not explain his action. That he was going to get a good 'telling off' from Violet was absolutely certain. Margaret Rose would chip in; he feared his daughter more than his wife. He knew it was an impulsive action, he was certain he would never do it at the post office, and colleagues at the inner sanctum of the Army Pay Corps would have been aghast. How would he explain things to the officer, but he had no idea what he was going to say?

Of course, it caused a commotion, particularly as what Oswald did, he did during the Sunday evening Salvation Meeting. He heard someone shout, "Shall I call an ambulance?" Concerned wife and daughter quickly attended. "Is Oswald alright", asked Mrs Piper. "You just wait till I get you back home", said Mrs Oswald, "Just you wait". "It just came over me"; sounded very weak, from Oswald.

What happened was very straight forward. During the Major's

sermon, Oswald had come over very tired and sleepy. It might have been the heaters or the curry he had the night before. He was tired and dreary; the most natural thing to do was to get up and lie down and have a snooze. Just what he would have done at home, became what he did in the hall. He rose up from his chair and picking his spot on the platform, lay down and rested. He just lay there, his eyes closed, and his head cradled in his arm.

Quickly it became a habit. Most Sunday nights Oswald could be seen laid out prone on the platform floor, nobody now took any notice. "I see he's off again", said Mrs Piper. Even the officer accepted it. At some point in his sermon, the officer would say, "Time for your nap Oswald", and even referred to Oswald as an illustration when preaching on the occasion the disciples fell asleep. That proved to be a mistake, Oswald now had his bible reference for his action. "Just following in the disciples' tradition".

At the next welcome meeting for the new officers, the Corps Sergeant Major felt it only wise and prudent in his welcome speech to add, "Don't get upset if during your sermon Oswald gets up and takes a lie down on the platform! Someone will give him a kick to wake him up for the final song".

The Deanery Band

(21)

A NEW Dean was appointed to the Cathedral City of Vale. The process of selecting the Dean had proved long and difficult. Usually, it was expected there would be a good number of applicants entering the selection procedure; on this occasion, the number of applicants was disappointing. The thinking was that there were two possible reasons for so few folks coming forward. One was the Cathedral, which had to be acknowledged as a minor Cathedral. The other possible problem was the Bishop. He was not an easy man to get on with and had a reputation as such.

The procedure in appointing the Dean had been followed scrupulously; every aspect of the process had been very carefully observed to ensure that nothing irregular took place. The post had been advertised, and lines of communication opened between all parties interested in the appointment. From the applicants, there was very little weeding out to be done. For one or another good reason applicants were discarded, and only a handful made it through to the final selection. The Appointments Panel even extended the time period hoping to attract further applicants. Some names the panel thought might have applied did not. When one of them was approached asking why he had not submitted his name he replied with all honesty, 'Vale Cathedral is not quite up there'.

Vale was a small city, as was often remarked, rather too far north of 'nowhere'. It often tried to be bigger and put on weight but never quite seemed to get there. The surrounding area of the city was described as desolate and featureless. In a bad winter, it could be a plateau of snow. To balance the negative, a pleasing feature of the city was the River Vale, which swept around three sides of the city. In its time it had powered the flour mill, now its use was mainly recreational. The city made an effort to try and capitalise on the river by holding an annual Vale River Regatta.

It was a city which was well served by the arts and culture. There was the Vale Choral Society, the City Preservation Society, a functioning orchestra, the Vale City Band, cinema and bingo hall combined, a soccer team named the Vale City Rangers, the Rugby Vale City Cheetahs, and a sprinkling of national stores complementing boutique and speciality shops.

The City of Vale had successfully retained much of its history and heritage. The locals won the fight to retain the cobbles; they had successfully resisted the release of land for cramped and unsympathetic dwellings. A plan for a large out of city shopping retail park was thwarted by a resident led campaign.

For the tourist to Vale, the Cathedral was undoubtedly an immense disappointment. Inferior original building had meant a rebuild, subsidence in later years forced the almost total demolition of the Cathedral to be replaced by what the locals called the 'Factory Church'. Travel books often failed to mention the Cathedral as a place of interest, and even the local Guide to Vale City had little to say about the structure.

The Reverend Matthew Justin's wife, Amelia, had drawn her husband's attention to the advertisement for the vacant post, Dean of Vale Cathedral. She was always keen on supporting Rev. Justin's advancement. They both knew that the time was right for them to move on, for Amelia, it was upwards and not sideways. Of course, she would have much preferred that her husband became the Dean of Salisbury or Winchester but in the absence of any Deanery vacancies in those two diocese Vale would have to do.

The pre-appointment meeting with the Bishop, a must in the procedure, had required some planning and careful thought. Mrs Justin advised that perhaps it would be best to simply allow the Bishop to dominate the conversation. One never wants to make a comment which develops into an argument. "It's nice to chat time", advised Mrs Justin.

As things worked out, the prospective Dean had far less time in the personal interview with the Bishop then was scheduled. Rev. Justin waited and waited and still waited in the outer reception room. "I'm so sorry the Bishop is running a little behind time", said the Chaplain who arrived finally to lead the way into the presence of the Bishop.

Matthew knew the form and what was expected of him. He was happy to ingratiate himself. He was introduced by the Chaplain before moving forward to greet the Bishop, his potential new boss. The Bishop extended his hand, Matthew lips brushing the Bishop's ringed finger.

"Good morning Reverend Justin". Immediately two things were made clear in the greeting. One, the Bishop was not one to say sorry for making the applicant wait, Matthew doubted that the word apology was ever used. He thought the relationship was going to be terribly formal. Matthew reasoned, quite rightly that the Bishop was not fond of using Christian names.

Matthew did not expect His Excellency to be much interested in him or his family. Matthew was somewhat taken aback when the Bishop wanted to know if Matthew had any knowledge at all about parrots, poorly ones. The Bishop suspected his much-loved parrot might be sickening; he might be suffering from Psittacosis, parrot fever.

The Bishop said it was quite worrying. Matthew extended his sympathy and agreed it must be quite worrying for the Bishop, if not perhaps terminal for Pope, the name of the sickly bird, he thought. A discrete knock on the door and after a polite pause, the Chaplain, entered. "Your Excellency. Mr Franklin, the veterinary surgeon, can call around later, during the afternoon". The Bishop repeated, "Psittacosis", shaking his head, and walking over to have yet another look at his motionless parrot.

The Rev. Justin considered that the Bishop had far more important things to deal with than trying to get to know him, the new potential Dean. Without the Bishop really noticing, Matthew withdrew. "That went really well", encouraged the Chaplain, "I get the feeling he likes you, perhaps you have a shared interest in all things winged, particularly parrots? Lunch for you and Mrs

Justin has been organised in the dining room. Your interview is scheduled for 3.30pm in the Lord Smithson room, Lord Smithson was a great benefactor to the Cathedral".

"Short and to the point, don't be an old windbag", was the instruction issued by Mrs Justin for the afternoon interview with the mai panel. The Bishop's Chaplain, in the role of a cinema usherette, rather than a Bishop's Chaplain came to the dining room to escort Rev Justin to the Lord Smithson room to meet the Appointments Panel.

A portrait of Lord Smithson dominated the room. It was a fraction short of the size of a billiard table. On the way to the room the Chaplain had imparted the knowledge that Smithson was not a cleric, but was an industrialist. "The thought is that the noble Lord thought he could buy his way into heaven by underwriting the significant repairs to the Cathedral at the turn of the century".

The painting had imagery which depicted the interests of the generous peer. He supported the building of the local almshouses, the cottage hospital; he funded a cultural centre for the arts, including the performing arts. Looking a little out of place, in the corner of the painting, was a pair of trombones set in the figure of a voting cross.

The interview presented no surprises for Rev Justin. He was able to report afterwards to his wife that he had obeyed her instruction to the letter and on no account could he be called an 'old windbag'. Both he and Mrs Justin were delighted when confirmation was received of his appointment to be the Dean of Vale Cathedral. The official announcement was made, and the usual letters of congratulations came to the Dean elect and his wife.

There followed a period, in the Justin household, of farewell parties, final sermons, a great deal of packing and trips to the municipal tip. Before taking up the appointment the couple enjoyed a break on the Isles of Scilly. At his formal welcoming reception, Amelia reminded Matthew to enquire of the Bishop, "How was his parrot?" Matthew had been told that the parrot had recovered fully, so there was no danger of him asking an awkward question.

From his first day at work, Dean Justin went about things in a structured manner. Always eager to advise, Amelia Justin had advocated a policy of "Listen, listen and listen again". The Dean had to work alongside so many people, both colleague clerics and the numerous staff who worked and supported the Cathedral. He was in effect the CEO of the Cathedral; there seemed to be very little for which he was not ultimately responsible.

'There is more politics in a Cathedral than in the Palace of Westminster', thought the Dean. 'Who can you trust? Who do you need to be circumspect with? What if the Bishop's Chaplain was also the Bishop's spy? Where would allegiance to the Dean come from?' Perhaps he reasoned his powerbase might be amongst the laypeople, the people who served the Cathedral, good folk in the cafeteria, the army of cleaners, the administration staff, the volunteer guides'. These were the people that the Dean should court; they could be his friends and allies.

His wife questioned why he was thinking in this way. He had only been in the job a matter of weeks and it seemed already he was scheming as if he anticipated a Cathedral battle ahead. The Dean knew there would be days of struggle looking forward. Old ways and methods dominated the life of the Cathedral. He was dismayed to find that the Cathedral still used bench pews. There was very little you could do with the restriction of pews. Many churches and cathedrals had already replaced pews with comfortable upholstered chairs, chairs which could be removed, opening up a vast space which could be utilised for so many things. Stackable pews were also now available. That could be high on his list.

The gift shop had a limited range of souvenir items. The Dean noted the fridge magnets of the building, biros, postcards, a selection of religious books. One, he noticed, written by the Bishop, did not seem to be moving off the shelf. In one corner the cathedral shop appeared to be selling jumble, or secondhand clothing. There was no facility to take payment by debit or credit card. The refectory, hardly more than a drinks bar, offering, on the first day he inspected, a bacon butty roll, a slice of lemon drizzle cake, and assortment of crisps and small packets of biscuits. Within a week, the Dean pondered the challenge that lay ahead of him. Change and innovation must be his motto.

A military general once said. "Sometimes you have to be prepared to lose a battle that does not matter, then to win the battles that do". It was a ploy which he had used before and knew it could be very effective.

A letter arrived, welcoming him to his position as the Dean of Vale Cathedral. The substance of the letter was informative. There appeared to be; what the Musical Director of the city band called a covenant, the implication was that the Vale City Band were required to perform a concert in the Cathedral near or on the anniversary of the death of their benefactor, Lord Smithson.

From the letter it would seem that this covenant had been ignored, no concert had ever been held. The Musical Director was seeking clarification of the new Dean's view on the matter. The Musical Director would be very happy to call on the Dean at his convenience.

The Dean secretary verified the facts, although it was more of a request from Lord Smithson rather than a binding covenant. The concert had been viewed as a request, which need not be honoured. The opposition had come from the Bishop in residence at the time of the first anniversary death. His view was very simple, "Any person who called themselves a Christian and enjoyed and loved brass bands should go and join The Salvation Army". This view was handed down Bishop to Bishop. There were arguments to be made against the statement, but nobody had dared to challenge it.

The Dean decided to consult the resident Organist and Master of the Choristers. The occupant of the office was a middle-aged gentleman, very well qualified and respected. All acknowledged he had done wonders with the choristers. He was a slim man and somewhat gangly, he liked to be thought of as flamboyant, as this fitted his status. When engaged in conversation, he would close his eyes and tilt his head upwards as if giving counselling guidance to the Almighty, rather than receiving it. He had been in post for a decade and considered himself 'well seasoned'.

"Well, of course, the bishops were absolutely correct, brass bands do not sit well in the Cathedral set-up, they lack the majestic majesty of the organ. Absent is the gentle finesse of the stringed instruments, as also is the mellowness of the woodwind. If you want a brass band as part of your worship then as the Bishop recited, 'Go and join The Salvation Army'". With that, he walked, with some purpose to the choir stalls, head still tilted heavenward.

"The matter of a brass band concert in the cathedral hasn't been debated for a goodly number of years, in fact I am unable to say when the last time it came before the Bishop for discussion" - informed the Bishop's Chaplain. "I'll mention it to the Bishop that you brought the issue up".

Here the Dean felt was his battle. He would urge and support for a brass band concert within the Cathedral, knowing it was opposed. He was very capable of making a solid case, honouring the memory of the man who had been such a tremendous benefactor to not only the Cathedral but the city. The Lord Smithson Memorial Concert had a certain ring about it. He was already planning it in his mind. Perhaps he should invite the Lord Mayor of the City?

The Dean welcomed the Musical Director of the city band into his office. Rev Justin wanted as many people as possible to know that he was meeting with the Musical Director of the city band. Eyes and ears would soon observe who he was meeting and being escorted around the Cathedral by the Dean, and speculation about the meeting would spread throughout the Cathedral. "Let's have a stroll around the Cathedral and chat as we are going along", said the Dean. "Tell me about Vale City Band", prompted the Dean. The Musical Director responded "Well the band began as a temperance band in the dim and distant past. At some point in the band's history, the temperance bit was dropped and we simply became Vale City Band. Our main band numbers about 26 players, both men and women, which is known as contesting size. We are very lucky to have a training band, primarily made up of youngsters. The band does most of the things that other bands do".

"I believe one of our cornet players is also one of your Cathedral guides. He tells me that he sounds Last Post and Reveille at the Remembrance Day service held in the Cathedral. He has often said how good it would be for the band to be able to play in the building," added the Musical Director.

"It was our band archivist who came across a document detailing the bequest from Lord Smithson. The good Lord had been very generous to the band. When he was alive, which is many years ago now, the band would go and play carols at Vale Hall where he lived. The Vale Hall has a superb ballroom where the band gave the concert. Lord Smithson loved to conduct the band, and even though it was Christmas, he would request that the band had the music for 'I Vow to Thee My Country', which he insisted on conducting".

"Are you telling me", said the Dean, that the band has never played in the Cathedral for any occasion?" "Indeed, as far as I am aware, that is the case", said the Musical Director. Dean stopped and turned to the musical director to emphasise the point he was about to make. "I would like the Vale City Band with the training band to give a concert in this Cathedral. It's long overdue. I am sure that, even in this imperfect building, the band would sound great. Let me work on an invitation".

Mrs Justin was appalled. A woman of strong advice and opinion she expressed dismay, verging on horror, over the manner in which the Dean was planning to misuse the city band for his own purpose. A battle he was happy to lose. It was disgraceful and underhand and he had better go away and think about it, because if he thought at the moment it was a two against one, the Bishop and the choirmaster, it was soon going to become three against one, the Bishop the choirmaster and Mrs Justin.

The Dean sat in his library and contemplated. He could never get his wife to change her mind; therefore he had no alternative but to change his position. The battle he didn't mind losing had suddenly become a battle he had to win. He even considered that perhaps the only way out might be for him to go and join The Salvation Army! Suddenly chairs for pews, card payment in place of cash and a well-stocked gift shop all seemed less important. Perhaps Mrs Justin might have the answer.

Clearly, the Dean had to win over the Bishop. If the Bishop agreed then all other members of the cathedral faculty would simply raise no objection. They might moan and object privately or even to each other, but the Bishop's word was law.

"I think now might be a good time to adopt a parrot", suggested Mrs Justin. "Oh no", wailed the Dean. "I dislike parrots; I really don't think I could live with a parrot. I may have to run away and join The Salvation Army!" "Well, of course, you could do a lot worse, but before you pack your bag and get out your trombone, I think I know where I can find a parrot. You clearly have forgotten, my sister Charlotte has a parrot. I'll give her a call later".

Wisely Matthew decided to leave whatever scheming Amelia had in mind to her. Charlotte, a widow, was very happy to allow her parrot to go on holiday to Vale. The following weekend the parrot arrived, the sister suggesting that it would be really nice for her to spend a few days with Amelia. 'Even the parrot comes at a price' thought Matthew.

Amelia and Charlotte planned a little soirée. Formal invitations were sent out to selected guests to join the Dean and Mrs Justin at the Deanery. The Bishop had planned to finish his paper on parrot training which he had agreed to pen for 'Pretty Polly', a newish parrot dedicated magazine. He felt he could not decline and so instructed his Chaplain to accept the invitation. Other senior Cathedral figures were invited, bringing a gathering to a very sociable number. He would spend the evening looking at the ceiling, before deciding whether it was diplomatic to invite the organist to the soirée.

The day arrived. The Bishop walked from his Palace to the Deanery, dressed in purple Bishop. The Bishop was greeted at the door by the Dean and his wife. Immediately, over their shoulders, he could see, strategically placed, the parrot. It was to the parrot cage that the Bishop flew. Charlotte was introduced to the bachelor Bishop. There then commenced a conversation in parrot parlance, understood only by Charlotte and the Bishop.

"Might the parrot join us for dinner, but not as dinner"? joked the Bishop. A table was already in place upon which to place the cage. Between courses, talking about parrots and pets in general, somebody asked if people knew of Vale Pet Services, the shop in St George's Parade. "It's a really good pet store, a plentiful stock of accessories and various pet foods. A number of tanks containing fish, small mammals and of course birds, including parrots. The owner is that nice man who conducts the Vale City Band".

Mellowed by a bottle of good wine and enjoying the close company of Charlotte, the Bishop said, "You say he keeps parrots as well as conducting the band, perhaps he's teaching a parrot to give the band instructions", a jovial Bishop suggested. "You might like to meet the pet shop owner, Mr Lawton, the Musical Director of the city band", suggested Charlotte to the Bishop.

"I rather think I know where this is heading", said the Bishop, "this little soirée is all about Lord Smithson and his jolly request for a band concert to be held in the Cathedral, which could turn out to be a meeting of the Parrot Appreciation Society".

"Putting things right is one of the reasons for the church. Dean, proceed with organising the concert, contact Mr Lawton. Perhaps the band could play the Parrot Song", said the Bishop. "And yes I do have my spy, although as you might think, not my Chaplain. I wanted you to be my Dean, to look at this ecclesiastical pile, inside and out, and affect changes. If you want to take my book off the gift shop shelf, then please do and replace it with something that sells". The choirmaster was about to interrupt but thought better of it and simply looked at the ceiling.

"I don't know where the rumour started that I was difficult to get on with, perhaps it was my parrot, Pope, who was speaking out of turn. I'm a gentle pussy cat, all I do is purr. No claws at all! Now a piece of that raspberry roulade please Mrs Justin, and coffee to follow, perhaps in your library Dean which can seat us all".

At the end of the evening, and while taking his leave and thanking Mrs Justin for an absolutely perfect evening, she must be sure to invite him again, the Bishop turned to the Dean. "Matthew, please don't go off and join The Salvation Army, they are far too selective anyway!"

Carol Playing

(22)

IT was the usual rehearsal night in November. The Salvation Army Bandmaster looked around the band and to his surprise had a full complement in front of him. "No absentees tonight which is a nice and rare thing. As you know we have one other practice before we break for the Christmas period. But before that, in your folder, turn to the second series march *Alderney* by Dean Goffin. It's a good pacey march. The bass melody a few of you will not be familiar with. It's the old tune *Pull for the Shore, Brother, Pull for the Shore*. This is a march that the timbrels like to play to. A good tune to warm up on", said the Bandmaster.

March ended. "Thank you for that, it's so easy for a 6/8 march to drift, that march was written in the days when 6/8 marches were more popular than today. Remember it's a second series march and not a festival march but it's got festival qualities".

The deputy Bandmaster observed, "They have a Salvation Army Corps on the island of Alderney. Actually, when you measure the size of the Army Church by the population numbers, Alderney is one of the largest in the UK Territory. About 2,000 people live on the rather large rock, folks attending the Corps number more that 10% of population. Not a lot of people know that!"

"Thank you, deputy, for the information message issued on behalf of the Alderney Tourist Information Bureau. Now ladies and gentlemen, can I call you back to order. I need to talk to you about carolling". The statement was greeted by laboured groans. "This year it is cancelled", came a cry from the baritone section. "I vote for that, it's no fun logging this monster about", echoed the BBb player. "Thank you all for your outburst of enthusiasm, you all moan about it beforehand, but say how much you enjoy it when we are actually playing carols. You love it, some of you even ask for more". Over the top of the Bandmaster speaking, second cornet was midway through the refrain of *Ding Dong Merrily On High*. "Making a point are we Brian", joked the Bandmaster.

Most bandsmen have a Christmas carolling story to tell. Bandsmen catching their toe on the pavement, falling over, taking the trombone down with them onto the footpath, severely bending the slide and making the instrument totally unplayable, the fall injuring both parties. Which is only marginally worse than the sound of a euphonium clattering to the floor from the hands of a careless player. As the treasurer noted, "Carol playing can make a dent, not only into an instrument but also the band's repair budget".

The Bandmaster reflected that every band had players who wanted to improvise the carols embellishing the part by adding a little twiddly bit. You knew it was going to happen, for one carol it would be the basses messing about on the last bottom note, on another the trombones would have their own special quirk to add to the carol, making full use of the extended to closed slide position. Baritones and horns were normally better behaved, they did not appear to have the urge to 'go off page' when playing carols. Very reliable were horns and baritones when it came to Christmas music.

Cornet players are far from responsible when it comes to the yuletide season. With cornet players so many of them want to try and play another instrument. Solo cornet will sidle up to the euphonium player offering a swap, cornets don't want to play the second baritone part, it's beneath them, and not for them lugging basses about. Essentially cornet players see themselves as the principal stars of the show, only conceding that euphonium players are a touch prima donna; therefore, a swap is a bit like for like. All this was going on in the Bandmaster's mind as Lionel Sharpe, just about the oldest bandsmen stood up to speak.

Every year, nearly retired Lionel Sharpe repeated the same stories, "I recall way back in the 60s, before the days of decimalisation. As you know I lived then near the seaside and the band that I was playing with at that time always had a standing Christmas Eve engagement with the local holiday camp complex, you know, a bit Billy Butlins. Accommodation was called chalets, rather basic, some of the rooms still had iron bedsteads, a bit of a rug on the floor, single ceiling lightbulb in the middle of the room, shared facilities and communal eating, and Izal toilet tracing paper".

"Anyway, the band would turn up to play carols in the camp ballroom, we used to go about in the greengrocers van. The greengrocer played first horn. You knew what was the 'offer of the week' as soon as he opened the rear doors to let you get in".

"By the time we arrived most of the campers were full of high Christmas spirit. I don't recall them singing the carols much, but I do remember that they danced a great deal. In fact, they danced to each and every carol, waltzing to *Away in a Manager*, dancing the quickstep to *Ding Dong Merrily On High*, and performing the Gay Gordons to *God Rest You Merry Gentlemen.*

Refreshments provided in the communal food hall were great. The entertainments manager was a queer odd fish. He would stroll around the ballroom counting the number of carols we played. He had a set fee, he paid us £3.00 a carol and not a penny more".

Overhearing the story, Gerald, who had been listening carefully offered the opinion that Lionel had changed the fee per carol from last year's £4.00 to this year's £3.00, "I wait for next year listening to Lionel repeat the story!"

The band librarian gave out the Christmas music. Some tried to give him the music back. The Christmas Praise carol book with over 100 carols and the seasonal Sounds of Christmas, a book of 36 brass band arranged Yuletide Music. The band arrangements were such that the pieces could be played by a limited number of players, some of the pieces being cut down version of pieces scored for larger band sizes. Equipped with the two carol books the band was ready for the season.

"I doubt very much that we need to run through any of the

traditional carols, most of you will have been playing them over a number of years, and no amount of practice is going to make them sound any better now", commented the despairing Bandmaster.

Going down memory lane Lionel recalled, "I remember when we had just three cards with the carols printed on, I think there was just about thirty or so carols to choose from. That was just after the war, of course those were the days when we used to play carols around the streets, carrying a Tilley lamp, by which to read the music. It seemed to be colder than now".

"Coming back to today and this century, I've got the carolling list", said the band secretary, waving sheets of paper in the air. "The list is very much the same as previous years, with one or two 'ins' and one or two 'outs'. The three Saturdays before Christmas we will be playing in the morning, the first Saturday in the town centre outside Civic Square, supporting the town's switching on of the Christmas lights, the following Saturday we will be inside the Old Railway Shopping Mall. The management will again be supplying chairs for the comfort of the band. The final Saturday we will have our usual stand in the foyer of the supermarket. Any questions?". By this time most of the band had lost interest and were flicking through the pages of the Sounds of Christmas book.

"Are we still going around the hospital wards on Christmas morning, bringing a bit of Christmas cheer?" enquired Jonathan. "Yes, we are", said the Bandmaster, "and you can leave that sprig of mistletoe you smuggled into hospital last year at home, it was just as well the deputy Bandmaster spotted it and confiscated the twig before any real and sustained damage was done". It looked very much that Lionel was about to go down memory lane once more, interrupting him before he had even started, the Bandmaster asked the band to turn to the old favourite *Christmas Joy*, number five in the *Sounds of Christmas*. "Hands up anybody who has never played it, I should add properly, well now is your opportunity to do so".

The band played through *Christmas Joy*, but the Bandmaster

was well aware players were not concentrating, the piece was far too familiar for that. *Christmas Joy* was another good march for the timbrel brigade, best now have a coffee break.

During the half-time refreshment break, Lionel was back walking down memory lane. He had gathered enough around him to justify relating another story. "Playing the march *Alderney* just now, I remember sailing from Guernsey to Alderney in an old rust bucket of a ship. It was one Christmas. We were going to sail there and back in a day. We left early on the Saturday morning to arrive in Alderney at about lunchtime. In the afternoon we were to give a Christmas service combined concert in the Island Hall. Tea would be provided, and then, using the only coach on the island they would transport us down to Braye Harbour for the return journey. All that seemed fine at the time. I was looking forward to it".

The full story was told bit by bit, when reassembled it appeared that . . . For December the weather couldn't have been better, the sea was unusually calm and the boat made good progress, the band, about eighteen in number, were on the island of Alderney well before noon. The capital of Alderney is St Anne. Victoria Street, a cobbled street is the only shopping street, the locals call it 'town', it had just about the usual one of everything and considerably more in terms of liquid refreshment. The street and the shops were decorated with Christmas lights and Christmas trees dominated the theme.

After lunch at the Salvation Army Hall it was sardine time in the Island Hall. The audience had very little room to move, and the younger and fitter members readily gave up their seats to the more elderly Alderney residents. The hall had been prepared for Christmas with an impressive Christmas tree fully decorated erected outside the hall entrance.

It was suggested that the islanders attending the concert should wear Christmas hats, which only encouraged Lionel to fish out his flashing Father Christmas hat.

The President of the Island of Alderney said how pleased he was to welcome the band, and it was good to see so many island folk present, and remarked on the seasonal headgear. The Vicar said he was delighted to be leading the service and to have the support of such a magnificent band to help with the singing and the band would be playing a few numbers. The local Salvation Army Captain simply said, 'Welcome Comrades', much to the confusion of quite a few in the room.

The opening carol was *Hark The Herald Angels Sing*. One of the schoolchildren next read a lesson from the Christmas story, which was followed by another carol, the band played a piece and waited for a carol chosen by the audience. Cheers and wolf whistles went up when it was announced that the popular bar maid from one of the local hostelries was going to sing a Christmas song. She came on dressed as a very revealing Christmas fairy.

About halfway through the concert a gentleman, somewhat out of breath, emerged through the front doors, waving a piece of paper in his hand, he pushed his way from the back of the hall to the front with a great deal of, "Excuse me. So sorry, hope I didn't tread on your toes. I don't mean to be a nuisance", as he headed towards the President handing him a note. The President read the note, screwed up his face, and passed the note to the Vicar. The Vicar glanced at the note, shrugged his shoulders and out of courtesy, passed it to The Salvation Army Captain. The Captain looked perplexed.

The enthusiasm for singing *Once In Royal David City* had lapsed, what happened in Royal David's City was not, at that moment, as interesting as the contents of the note was to the audience. The Salvation Army officer felt Bandmaster should also be made aware of the message and showed him. The reaction of the Bandmaster was, "Well what can I do about it?" What followed next was the party game of 'excuse me' or 'after you'. The President gestured to the Vicar, the Vicar returned the gesture, the President looked pleadingly at the Captain who held out his hand in dejection and picked up the carol sheet instead.

Up jumped Lionel from his place in the band. "'Ere give me the note, if you lot can't read I can!" The outburst was greeted with applause from the audience. Speaking into the microphone to ensure that he could be heard, Lionel adjusted his glasses, held the note in front of him for all to see so there was no doubt that he was reading the original message. Lionel remembered, just-in-time that all important messages commenced with a cough, very important messages warranted two coughs, this could be a three-cough message.

"Cough, cough. Ladies and gentlemen the message says. 'Ship's engine in need of repair. Unable to sail today. More information to follow". Cries were raised from the audience, "Oh dear, what a pity". "What are we going to do?", "The elastic band has broken again". The Vicar now taking command of the situation said something to the effect, "I am sure we are terribly sorry that the ship is in need of repair. I think the message applies to the band, who might be on Alderney longer than they anticipated. I suggest we don't let a little thing like a broken engine spoil our carol service. Let's get on with the next carol, which is, *I saw three ships come sailing in on Christmas Day in the morning*".

There really was no alternative but to press on with the concert. Afterward everyone agreed it had been a really super carol concert, and that the band made such a difference. Folk hoped that the band would soon be able to get back to Guernsey. One helpful islander remarked that it was not unknown for people to be stranded on the island for a couple of days or more. "I've only got the shirt and socks I came over with, my mum is very particular about a clean pair of socks every day", wailed a very young Graham.

A twice divorced Alderney blonde 'bombshell', who went by the local nickname of 'Grenade', attached herself to the Captain, "I would be very happy, indeed delighted, to put up a couple of bandsmen, two nice young bandsmen will do fine", she purred.

It was getting back to Guernsey which was the topic of conversation at the tea table. They now had a full assessment of the repair needed to the ship's engine. They listened with dismay to the report. The ship's engineer said he was fairly certain that it was a problem with a piston rod which was giving trouble. With a bit of luck, they might get the ship going in a couple of days, provided some of the bits needed could be flown in by aircraft. They all sat down to tea feeling they were about to become marooned.

The Captain felt responsible for the band. The band had travelled to Alderney at his invitation. Putting them up overnight was not part of the plan. The matter was discussed over a ham salad, cake and trifle. The Captain said he felt it would not be a problem to find host families on the island who would be prepared to 'stable' the band overnight, thoughts of the blonde lingered. The band were not keen on that idea. They were of the mind that if there were other options that should be explored first. They didn't want to put local families to any trouble.

The local police officer offered, that at the moment they had nobody in the cells and whilst they couldn't accommodate all 18 there was certainly room for a few of them, provided the police had no unscheduled 'guests'. The officer assured them that if they did spend the night in the cells, he could rustle up a pretty good breakfast. "What crime do I have to commit on the island of Alderney to get an overnight stay in the cells?" asked one of the bandsmen. "Just blast away on your trombone outside the police station, that should get you locked up!"

The band and guests continued with their evening meal whilst around them discussions took place as to how the band was to be accommodated. The Captain thought, if not staying overnight with Alderney families, he could get his hands on some pillows and blankets and proposed that the band bed down in the Salvation Army Hall in the High Street, the heating was already on, and it could be nice and cosy just for the one night. He would arrange for breakfast at one of the local pubs, indeed there was one immediately opposite the hall. The Bandmaster thought that was a very good idea as he was anxious to keep the band together.

They were getting around to the second cup of tea, when the shipping company agent walked in. Everyone looked at the agent waiting for the next announcement. "I have excellent news. Without getting too technical what the ship's engineer thought the problem was, a piston rod, it was not. It was not the piston rod but a loosening connection. Anyway, the ship's engineer got out his Swiss Army knife, twiddled it about, gave something a thump with a hammer, found a suitable spanner", "and a stronger elastic band", interrupted the euphonium player, "and now everything is fine", concluded the agent. "The ship's master is confident that he can make the return journey back to Guernsey".

Outside the Island Hall, a coach belonging to Riduna Buses, awaited the band. The band quickly loaded their kit and themselves. "Thanks for coming, perhaps we might see you next year", shouted the Captain as the coach pulled away. The Riduna Bus bumped along the cobbled streets, into High Street, and headed for Braye Road heading downhill all the way for the harbour.

Somehow the Christmas lights looked different in the dark. It was beginning to dawn on the bandsmen that they would be sailing in the dark, on a boat in which they had very little confidence. One of the bandsmen was all in favour of spending the night on Alderney, even if it meant bunking down in the hall. "I would sooner fly out, than risk my life on the Channel Islands answer to the Titanic!"

The captain of the vessel greeted them warmly on the quayside. "Good evening gentlemen, welcome aboard. So sorry about the confusion, the engineer is a bit new to this ship, and he got a bit muddled. I suggest you make your way to the saloon, settle yourselves down and we will be underway very shortly. Once we've turned the corner at the end of the break water and we have a few nautical miles on the clock I'll pop down and see you".

Altogether there are just over 50 passengers making the sailing from Alderney to Guernsey. Somebody suggested that perhaps the band could play a tune or two, 'For those in Peril on the Sea' was quoted, "I think we can do a little bit better than that", said the Bandmaster, "we can have our own private, personal carol service, six of you will be enough to form a balance", instructed the Bandmaster. The other passengers were delighted, and readily accepted carol sheets. The sound of the lone television in the saloon which was showing a French television station was switched off.

The ship's master came down to the saloon just as the band was about to give an impromptu carol concert. The Bandmaster acted as compere. He encouraged other passengers and members of the band to form into an unofficial ship's choir, and they made a pretty good job of *Ding, Dong Merrily On High.* He invented a new twist to pass the parcel, perhaps having been inspired by the President, the Vicar, and the SA Captain. "this is all very simple, a variation on pass the parcel. However, we are short of a parcel, therefore we will use this trombone mute. While the band is playing you pass the mute on to each other, when the music stops the person who is holding the mute, gets to choose the next carol".

The captain thought he'd like to be in this, so he found a seat so that he could be included. A couple of deckhands sauntered in. Next through the door was the first officer, followed by the cabin steward. On with the carols, and round and round went the trombone mute. The captain absolutely delighted, chuckled like a young boy, his face beaming, when the Bandmaster orchestrated the music to stop the mute was in the captain's hand. Just what was to be the carol choice of the ship's master. "I know it's not a carol, but I love to see the faces of the children when they sing *Away in a Manger,* do you have the music?"

Four or five young children came forward to sing *Away in a Manger.* "I think your singing would be much improved if you didn't have the band making a mess of things", observed Bandmaster, and promptly got the choir to sing unaccompanied, to the delight of parents and passengers.

"I've been waving my arms all afternoon", said the Bandmaster, "and quite a bit this evening. I think it's time I had a rest and we found some honorary bandmasters. With a bit of persuasion and quite a bit of arm pulling a number of the passengers and crew were cajoled into conducting the band in various carols. First in front of the band to conduct was the ship's captain. Baton in hand the Captain attempted to conduct the carol *Little Donkey*.

From the corner of his eye the Captain saw another member of the crew coming to the saloon. He was wearing a white boiler suit and had in his hand an oily rag.

In a matter of fact manner the voice of the ship's engineer uttered, "I just looked out of a porthole, and on starboard side the lights of St Peter Port are twinkling away brightly. In fact, if you don't wander up to the bridge and pull on the handbrake pretty soon, you will dent the boat and make a hole in the jetty – Oh and I think the piston is playing up".

"I think it's time to play, *We Wish You A Merry Christmas*', said the Bandmaster.

Oom-pah Band

(23)

BOTTOM Valley stretched for about ten miles. Either side of the Valley were sloping hills. Bottom Valley was approached from Bottom Wood running through to Bottom-by-Sea. Along the Valley was Upper Bottom and Lower Bottom, both were small hamlets, with a handful of dwellings. The two main towns in the Valley were Bottom Wood and Bottom-by-Sea, the larger of the towns was Bottom-by-Sea. Midway along the main road between the two Bottom towns was the Bottom Crossroads, with a small minor road leading to North Bottom towards Upper Bottom.

In the Middle English period, the Valley was called Botme, 'the lowest part'. During the Middle Ages, the Valley was part of a much larger estate in the former Kingdom of Wessex. Over several centuries large areas of land were progressively broken down into smaller units, and one of those segments was the length of the Valley, still called Botme Valley. The Valley had very little value; it was only suitable for hill farming, sheep country. Botme evolved into Bottom.

Spring was sheep shearing, a period of celebration, a time when the first fleece was paraded through the Valley. A sheep farm about a couple of miles from Bottom-by-Sea provided the sheep. The valley community would gather at the farm, to greet the first fleece and then make their way to Bottom-by-Sea for a blessing and celebration.

Fiddle and drum, for centuries past leading the procession had given way in more recent years to the Bottom Valley Brass Band. Villagers of the Valley, as their forebears had done for centuries, eagerly wanted to touch and have a strand of the fleece, using a piece of wool perhaps as a bookmark. At the Parish Church of Bottom-by-Sea, the Rector invited all into the church, accepted the fleece on behalf of the community and laid it on the altar. The hymn *The King of Love my Shepherd Is* was sung. Children from the Valley recited the 23rd Psalm and the Rector gave his blessing. The brief service over, it was time for refreshment in the Valley Bottom Pub. Over the years a tradition was established that the band played outside the church, and then gave a concert in Bottom Valley Municipal Park bandstand.

For centuries Bottom Valley had attracted little attention. You only went to the area if you had a very good reason, it was certainly not on the tourist map. But all that was to change. The reason was the growth of recreation. Gone was the traditional fortnight holiday, usually spent at the larger seaside resorts, people now had more time on their hands, holidays were longer. The holidays by train were superseded by cars, containing families wanting to explore every nook and cranny of the British Isles, looking for out of the way places.

Bottom-by-Sea suddenly had a sprinkling of bed and breakfast establishments. One sheep farmer with a suitable field put in a planning application to open a caravan and camping site. A proliferation of cafés opened, offering light lunches and afternoon cream teas. One garage became three. Soon Bottom-by-Sea had a supermarket. There was even mention of a Premier Inn being built in the seaside town.

Bottom Valley was now proving to be very popular with the recent phenomena of recreational walking. Walkers were discovering footpaths on both sides of the Valley. Up one side and then down the other, the Bottom Towns and Hamlets created an ideal walker's circuit; walkers could tackle the complete circle or some of the smaller circulatory routes. Uniformed walkers invaded the Valley. Natty bobble hats, sturdy walking boots, thick walking socks, weatherproof map pouches, miniature binoculars, customised drinks bottles, haversack, backpack and rucksack of varying size and design, walking knee breaches, plus fours, expensive outdoor jackets. No walking attire was complete without the mandatory walking stick or trekking pole.

In the year 2000, to celebrate the millennium, a proposal was made under the heading of the 'Bottom Valley Challenge'.

Walkers were invited to visit the Valley and to walk the long circuit beginning at Bottom-by-Sea walking to Lower Bottom then making their way to Bottom Wood before heading for Upper Bottom, concluding at Bottom-by-Sea. At each of the various stopping points, village stewards would be ready to stamp the walk card, pre-purchased for £5.00. Refreshments and toilet facilities were available. For health and safety reasons, the challenge had to be undertaken clockwise. It was emphasised that the challenge was not a race, no prizes for coming first. The second weekend in July was designated 'Bottom Valley Challenge'.

The popularity of the Bottom Valley Challenge weekends grew and grew. One of the national walking magazines decided to come down to Bottom Valley and write a feature on the event interviewing both villagers and walkers. Details of the Bottom Valley Walks began to appear in walking guidebooks, complete with photographs, diagrams and maps of the various walks, each walk graded and the suggested time given to complete the walk.

There was no doubting that the challenge was very important to the economy of the Valley. While tourists came throughout the season the big payday was the challenge weekend. Even when the weather was inclement, it seemed to make no difference, folk still flocked to the Valley.

Bottom Valley Challenge merchandise soon began to appear, T-shirts with 'I'm up for the challenge' emblazoned across the front. One or two cheeky and saucy illustrations appeared on mugs and polo shirts, a rotund red bottom, on one cheek, in a crescent 'bottom' on the other 'challenge' and in between, horizontally, the word 'valley'. Bottom Valley Challenge postcards were soon dropping through people's letter-boxes. Some people didn't even bother to write a message, just added who the postcard was from and the address of the receiver, and that was that. The front of the postcard said it all.

For the weekend the Bottom towns created a festive carnival atmosphere. A committee was inaugurated to organise the weekend. Themed weekends were introduced. The first one was

'Novelty Headdress'. Walkers were encouraged to decorate their hats and caps. One villager commented that it was like ladies' day at Ascot. Another weekend was themed as 'Crazy Trousers'. Most of the walkers entered into the theme. One walker renamed it 'Somewhere to put your bottom!'. One villager suggested to the committee perhaps another theme could be a beer festival.

One of the bandsmen in the Bottom Valley Brass Band returned from an extended walking holiday on the continent and had stayed in an area much the same as Bottom Valley, an area popular with walkers. Another comparison was that the town in which he stayed had a band, which he had listened to during his holiday. In this case, an Oom-pah Band, providing music at the local beer festival.

At the following Bottom Valley Band rehearsal, Neil the bandsman who had recently returned from his walking holiday in Germany suggested, "What we need is an Oom-pah section in our band".

Neil suggested the expansion of the Bottom Valley Challenge to, not only include the walk, but also to hold a beer festival in Bottom-by-Sea. "You know the sort of thing, Lederhosen, buxom wenches carrying multiple Beer Steins and an Oom-pah Band thumping raucous music out. There must be enough players within the band to form a German-like band. Malcolm has got that strange four valve, left-handed tuba, so he can Oom-pah, Richard plays the piano accordion, and I'm sure we will have no trouble filling other brass parts."

The Bottom Valley Challenge committee accepted the suggestion; they were running out of ideas. It had been brought up before that there is very little for walkers to do in the evening, some kind of entertainment was needed. "We don't want to call it a beer festival that would confuse the two events", said the chairman, "we could call it an Evening Soirée".

The timetable proposed was walking morning and afternoon followed by the evening soirée, beer in Steins listening to an Oom-pah Band. The venue for the entertainment would be the Bottom Valley Municipal Park, set by the sea, complete with paddling pool, bowling green, children's play area and bandstand. A very large marquee tent would be erected, incorporating the bandstand: trestle tables and chairs for the audience and an area from which to serve refreshments. Job done!

Bottom Valley Brass Band set about organising the musical side. There was plenty of Oom-pah music around, the old favourites, *Roll out the Barrel, Sweet Caroline, Que Será, Será,* members of the band were coming up with their suggestions. It was not long before a comprehensive list of Oom-pah melodies had been assembled.

The Musical Director considered that this engagement was not going to be the stroll that some of the band had suggested. This was very different from the usual programme of concert music. For a band concert, there was a comperé who would introduce the various band items, crack a joke or two, giving the band a bit of a break. In a band of nearly 30 players most would often have a little bit of a rest, with four front line cornets it was possible to take a sneaky little break.

An Oom-pah Band was 'full on' for just about the entire evening, perhaps just one or two trumpets, the tuba player having to pump out every other note. The stress of bashing away for three hours or more, would deem it to be a very demanding evening for the players. Getting the chaps to wear Lederhosen would probably be the easiest part of the exercise.

The band was keen and very eager. The Musical Director's advice was to, "Keep blowing as loud as you like, there is no call for musical finesse". At the next rehearsal, the players who would make up the Oom-pah Band were ready to have a go at *"Roll out the Barrel"*.

The other bandsmen complained that the rehearsal lacked realism. "To get into the atmosphere we need two things, giant tankards of beer and some buxom wenches", declared the solo horn player, looking at the fuller figure of the female second baritone player. "Just you wait till the soirée night, I might just have a surprise for you. They have been asking around the town for drinking waitresses. Evidently, I quite fit what they require!"

Following a good deal of debate and discussion, it was decided that two Oom-pah Bands would be formed, swapping players as necessary. The only slight drawback was that the band only had one person who could play the accordion. "I shall want double money for double work", said Brian, the nimble-fingered accordion player.

Fortunately, the music wasn't taxing, really quite straightforward, and that kind of playing allowed for a great deal of liberty and improvisation on the part of the players. Belting out pub melodies meant that you did not need to be precisely note-perfect. A wrong note here or there wouldn't really matter most people wouldn't realise. Obviously, the expectation was that the drinkers and revellers would join in and sing. The evening was not going to be like a regional or national brass band competition, full of tension, where everything needed to be absolutely spot-on and note-perfect. The band could have a bit of fun.

A fortnight before the Bottom Valley Challenge and Evening Soirée the committee convened to check over the event to ensure that nothing had been overlooked in the planning. Bookings for the weekend were markedly up, there was hardly any accommodation left in the B&Bs, and the Premier Inn now up and running declared they were full. The farmer who owned the campsite was forced to open up a second field; such was the number of bookings he had received. There was a feeling of quiet calm assurance amongst committee members.

The committee had agreed that there would be a charge for the soirée evening, they hoped to make a significant profit on the event. The concession to supply beer within the marquee had brought in a decent fee, which included paying for the bevvy of buxom waitresses. The required Temporary Event Notice had been obtained. The event was covered by public liability insurance. The local police inspector attending the committee meeting, 'sniffed' a bit about such a large gathering of people drinking copious amounts of beer. "I myself will attend the evening, and I have roistered a sergeant and at least ten constables and specials to be on duty. We will have a police transporter, Black Maria or Paddy Wagon to you, standing by, and cells will be cleared for occupants use at the police station". "Will you be in police riot gear, batons and shields?" queried the chairman.

Trestle tables and chairs had been hired along with ladies and gentlemen's temporary toilets. The marquee was going to be erected a couple of days before. The Bottom Valley Public Address Company confirmed they had all the correct and adequate equipment for the event. The Oom-pah Band representative made his report. As far as he was concerned the band was 'Good to go'. "That's what I'd like", said the chairman looking at the Police Inspector, "Short reports". Large posters advertising the soirée had been appearing in suitable locations up and down Bottom Valley.

The Bottom Valley Gazette printed a feature on the walking challenge and evening soirée. The Chairman of the Council was asked did he feel that holding the beer festival gave the town the right sort of image? The chairman replied that he had received reports that everything was going to be done in a proper, tasteful manner there would be no embarrassment to the town. These sort of events where a regular feature on the continent. Bottom-by-Sea was not the first town in the UK to emulate beer festivals from countries like Germany and Belgium. Indeed, he would be there himself and expected to enjoy a thoroughly good evening.

Interviewed for the newspaper the Musical Director was quoted as saying, "Of course, this is not a normal band concert as you well know. For years Bottom Valley Brass Band has been providing music at a number of events within the town. The Rector knows whenever he needs us all he needs do is ask. The band is proud of the fact that it gives musical service to the community. The Oom-pah Band is derived from the main band, you can be assured, we will not let the town down, my players are very versatile and can play any kind of music From *All In An April Evening* to *Roll out the Barrel*, and just about every melody in between."

There seemed to be more people than ever in the town for the Bottom Valley Challenge weekend. You could hardly move in the towns without being assaulted by rucksacks, or stabbed by a trekking pole. Every year the same question would crop up, "If this is Bottom-by-Sea and up the road is Bottom Wood, and you have a Upper Bottom and Lower Bottom where is Bottom?". "You're sitting on it", was the usual native reply.

Tickets for the Oom-pah Band soirée were soaring away. The excellent summer weather meant the people who were unable to get tickets into the marquee would still be able to hear the Oom-pah Band sitting in the evening sunshine outside the marquee.

The tent flaps opened at 7.00pm with the band scheduled to begin playing at 7.30pm, by which time the tent was just about full to capacity. People had come to enjoy themselves, with hooters and streamers, revellers dressed for the occasion. To sustained applause, the crowd observed the Oom-pah Band about to start playing. The band commenced with *Roll out the Barrel* and then moved to *Sweet Caroline*. From then on, there was no stopping. The Musical Director lost count of the number of times they played *Roll out the Barrel*. Other favourites included *Blaydon Races, She'll Be Coming Round The Mountain When She Comes,* with a number of unauthorised verses. While the band played, the revellers imbibed.

Amongst the audience were a number of aspiring brass band conductors, who stood before the band waving their arms all over the place. As the evening wore on it became a fun thing to snatch a beer tray and use it as a drum. Half a dozen young ladies who had consumed a little more beer than was good for them insisted on forming an impromptu choir to sing *Sweet Caroline*. All this the Oom-pah Band took in good part. One young lady braver than her companions or perhaps who'd had a little more to drink elected to kiss every member of the band.

At the beginning of the evening the bandsmen and women were very well disciplined and refused all entreaties to have a drink. Their resolve began to weaken. "Just the one half pint won't do us any harm", offered Adrian on percussion. "All brass players need a little bit of lubrication". An appreciative soirée crowd ensured that the half pints kept coming. Most of the players had to suddenly stop playing to burp, something they caught from the audience. Regrettably an inter-band competition developed. Who could belch the longest and loudest.

There were one or two very minor incidents for the Police Inspector to get excited about. Beer tipping over heads suddenly became popular. Who could walk the furthest with a Beer Stein upon their head was introduced to the entertainment. A start point was marked out on the grass and the furthest point suitably marked. Arguments developed, deciding the winner was utterly impossible.

When the evening came to a conclusion everybody agreed it had been an absolutely superb soirée, There would certainly be a number of sore heads in the morning as a result of the previous night.

At the next band rehearsal of the Bottom Valley Band an inquest was held. Under interrogation was Trevor, who played the cornet.

Trevor had wisely decided that he would leave his car at home. He lived quite close to the municipal park and he would cycle over with cornet case attached to the cycle rack, something he often did on rehearsal night. "I must admit, I did have a drop too much to drink, it's difficult to say 'no' when a buxom wench approaches you, gives you a big bright smile and offers you a drink. Truth to tell, I don't remember how many times she came over to me, drink in hand. What I do know is I never refused her once".

The final piece the Oom-pah band played was *Irene Goodnight, Goodnight Irene, I'll see you in my Dreams.* Cornet packed away, a little uncertain on his feet, Trevor had made for his bicycle. He mounted the bike, cornet case strapped to the carrier and he pedaled and wobbled towards the park gates.

At the gates, the raised hand of the Police Inspector stopped him, he had observed the erratic cycling. Indeed he had had to jump out of the way to avoid the front wheel of Trevor's bike. "Do you admit to riding a cycle in this park without complete control over the said cycle? Have you been drinking tonight sir? I have reason to believe you may be over the limit. I must ask you to blow into this bag".

On Monday morning a sober Trevor appeared in the magistrates' court the indictment cited, "Drunk in charge of a trombone while cycling in a public place". The magistrate, still feeling the effects of Saturday night himself, peered down at the charge sheet. "Case dismissed", roared the magistrate, "The fella plays a cornet, saw him myself. Get your facts right!"

The Royal Hotel

(24)

THE Annual Dinner & Dance was the next item on the agenda for the Twelve Boys Band committee meeting. The Musical Director as chairman of the committee opened up the discussion on the band dinner. "I don't suppose there's very much to say, we've held an annual dinner and dance as long as most of the band can remember, the date has always been the third Friday in January and the venue The Wayside Inn Hotel. The arrangements are left in the very capable hands of our excellent band secretary", said the MD, Martin, looking across the table at Frank.

Frank Austin leaned forward and was just about to agree when he was interrupted by a new member of the committee. "Some of the chaps have been having a little discussion and feel that perhaps we could introduce one or two changes, not only for the dinner dance but in other areas". The speaker was young Daniel, who had been voted onto the committee as the band representative at the last AGM. Daniel was a spirited young man. "He's got ideas", noted one of the bandsmen, "he's had education!".

"I assume you're talking for the younger members of the band", said a rather 'put out' Frank. You could always tell when Frank was a little 'put out', he would stroke his moustache, not that there was much to groom. "What do they want a disco and Go-Go dancers? If that's the case, then don't expect me to arrange it. I've never been to a disco, and I don't know how to go about hiring Go-Go dancers".

The Twelve Boys Band had been using the Wayside Inn Hotel for a considerable period of time. For Frank, it was a repeat of previous years booking. The only thing that changed was the price per head. One of the downsides to the hotel was the inadequate parking, never enough to meet the requirements of the band. Being a town centre hotel, it was in the midst of traffic-controlled zones, which even operated in the evening. Members of the band always complained about parking, no bus service and a reluctance to use a taxi, they moaned and put up with it.

Four months before the event, Frank would call into the hotel. When he saw Frank coming through the hotel front door, the general manager knew what it was all about. "Good morning Frank, nice to see you, you're looking well, I assume you've come to make arrangements for the band's dinner dance". "Absolutely correct", said Frank, "you did us proud last year, and the year before and I am confident we can expect the same again this year I'm sure". A beaming general manager consulted the hotel diary, "There you are, Frank, it's in the book. When we commence the new booking diary, yours is the first one to go in, the third Friday in January".

The Wayside Inn Hotel sounded far more attractive than in truth it was. It might have had three stars rating, but there was evidence that the three stars were well over-stated and had lost much of their glitter. 'Wearing a bit thin' was the summing up many people who visited the hotel had commented. 'Seen better days – it wants a whole load of money spending on it'. The function room was adequate; the décor reflected the last time the place was decorated; it was certainly a bit 60s. The primary function room had a double purpose. A ballroom with a parquet floor, now warped in one or two places. Overhead a couple of ballroom mirror light reflecting revolving balls. There was a small one step platform set into one of the corners. Installed on the platform was the equipment for the DJ.

The room also served as the dining room, either a sit down table setting or buffet style. The ballroom had a long bar, with a foot rail. It was a buffet meal that the band always booked, a cold meat platter, cherry tomatoes, cubes of cheese, breadsticks, crisps, crackers, salad, an assortment of fruit and a black forest gateau cut into small slices. "It gives plenty of room for people to dance, people are able to circulate, move around the room, a buffet is so informal", said Frank. "You can relax more with a buffet, and of course you don't have to dress up in a 'penguin suit', you can almost come as you are". And many did thought Daniel.

Daniel was a lot smarter and more intelligent than Frank, and they both knew it. "Give the fella a chance; let's hear what he has to say. It's always good to have another opinion on how we have done things in the past and to see how there might be changes, improvements going forward", said the Musical Director Martin, realising that he sounded rather pompous and unconvincing in his own argument.

Seeking to smooth things over a little bit, a diplomatic approach by Daniel was, "Frank, I wonder if you'd like to come with me and have a look at another possible venue for the band's shindig. See if we can do a bit better. For example let's look at the best, rather than settling for what is probably the worst. The Royal Hotel on the seafront", suggested Daniel.

The Royal Hotel was one of the best in the north Devon town, five stars and a well-merited five star. When the promenade hotel first opened in 1932, it was named the Bandstand Hotel, a modest unpretentious hostelry, almost part of the town's bandstand. During the Second World War it was requisitioned and during that conflict used as a recuperation hospital, lots of sunshine and sea breezes.

On one occasion, the wounded were visited by a member of the royal family who asked a patient, "Are they treating you well, are they treating you royally?" "Indeed, Ma'am, very royally", was the reply. The brief exchange was reported in the national newspapers. After the war, The promenade hotel was vastly extended and renamed The Royal Hotel, because, as the sub-heading noted, 'We treat you royally".

The treasurer, Jethro Armstrong, began shaking his head, his face in a deep foreboding frown and started counting on his fingers. At the thought of The Royal Hotel, a dazed Martin dropped his pen on the agenda papers and allowed it to roll onto the floor. Frank merely repeated, putting his face in his hands, resting his elbows on the desk, "The Royal Hotel, The Royal Hotel". This was proving to be a seismic committee meeting.

Daniel took control of the meeting while the other members could do nothing else but listen. "At the moment the annual dinner, or rather buffet is dress as you like, jeans, T-shirts or if we are lucky open-neck shirts and trainers, even flip-flops and that is the better-dressed bandsmen and guests. We all know the pattern for the evening. Find a coffee table surrounded by chairs, head for the buffet table, frequent the bar, back to the coffee table. The only change in route is . . . coffee table, gents or ladies toilet, buffet table, drinks bar, coffee table. That is what passes for a good band night out". "Fortunately, it's a few years since we witnessed the usual punch-up between the brothers Slater or should that be Slaughter", remarked Frank.

"Some of the lads have been discussing elevating the dinner dance, making it more of a gala occasion", explained Daniel, "Let's replace the tired old buffet with silver service, napkins, table linen and more than a knife and fork each. Three-course dinner served on warm plates, full place setting, make it black tie or lounge suit. Let's give the ladies a function for which they can dress up, best party frock and hairdo to match. A really entertaining top table after dinner speaker."

Butting in, "I can see a whole load of problems", said the treasurer. "I struggle to get the players to pay £18.00 for a buffet meal. You must be looking at least double that amount for your sit-down job", said the treasurer. In response Daniel said, "Of course you are right, it will cost more, but then you are getting better value for your money. It is also a well-known fact that you spend less money at the bar with a waitress served meal then you do with a buffet. However, I think we could take this Gala Dinner a step further. Currently the meal is open to band members and their nearest and dearest. With a 'posh' do we can make the dinner open to people who do not have a direct connection to the band".

Hoping to convince the treasurer Daniel continued. "The Gala Dinner would be an excellent opportunity to network, perhaps pulling in a few sponsors, increase the number of engagements we receive. It would give the band a much higher profile in the community, a higher profile would almost certainly lead to an enlarged band bank account".

"Well it is an idea, a Gala Dinner; I suppose it is one that we should have a serious look at. It would be a departure from the norm for the band, all we can do is put it to them. I'm sure Daniel will be able to do a first-class sales job", said Martin hoping that the idea would simply drain away. "Moving on to the next item on the agenda, oh I see it's Any Other Business. I'll go around the room".

"Frank, anything to bring to the meeting, I think you said you wanted to mention the subject of how sloppy the band is becoming, standards in deportment have fallen". "Indeed so", said Frank, "I noticed the other day that Jack on flugel horn, was not wearing the official band tie and the sleeves on his jacket were rolled up. I did have a word with him, but all I got was a shrug of the shoulders". Martin responded with, "Yes I had noticed, I think I'll send out a general newsletter to every member of the band to remind them that when on duty, they are representing the band, and they need to look as smart as possible". There was a nod of approval from the other members of the committee.

"Jethro, your turn next", said Martin. "Not much to report, all the members' subs have been paid, one or two stragglers as usual. The band supporters club is showing an increase in contributions, we are meeting the bills. Oh, I received a grant from Deep Quarry Inc., they have been sending us an annual donation, which is always very welcome, and they want to book us again for their Public Open Day. People do enjoy a big explosion".

Looking at his watch, Martin said, "I think we've just about time to have the band representative's report or complaints sheet". Knowing that it was going to wound, perhaps even kill. Daniel immediately aimed for the heart! "As far as I and a number of us can see, little has changed in this band for years.

The truth is we are a static band, slowly sliding backwards". Frank exploded, "I want to tell you, young man, that I take great exception to the insult you have made in respect of this band. I and many others have worked continually and hard to keep the band going in the very difficult circumstances. It's not been easy and for you to come along here, your first meeting, and to suggest that we are sliding backwards is an affront, as I say an insult".

Following that not unexpected outburst Daniel was fully geared up for the announcement that Frank would resign on the spot, not that he wanted his job. But Frank was a bit cannier than Daniel had predicted. Frank waited to hear what Martin was going to say. "Daniel does have a fair point. I was looking through some of the programmes that we performed fifteen years ago, and I realised we were still playing the same pieces today. We may have introduced one or two new ones, but fifteen/twenty years ago we were playing a selection of melodies from Gilbert and Sullivan, and even then, they were pretty ancient. I was thinking how uninteresting some of the programmes looked and I have to acknowledge that it's pretty well all my fault".

Daniel wanting to stick a first-aid plaster on the initial stab wound said. "There is no doubt the people love brass bands, every time we give a concert, we have pretty good audiences, and when we play in the bandstand the public are there in appreciative numbers. But do you not think that what we are currently doing is, 'playing at them rather than playing for them'? What we play, we assume the people who listen, want to hear, but I don't recall us ever asking them", said a confident Daniel, "we get the occasional requests but that is not exactly the same thing".

Martin, picking up the thread of the argument, "I think Daniel is saying that we need to be more connected to our audience, you could say more tuned in! Audience participation". Suddenly, from nowhere, Frank was 'on side', no longer smarting from an insult, Frank was no longer affronted. "Perhaps we could find out if it's anybody's birthday on the day or around that time. The band could be ready to play Happy Birthday, dear Mavis or

Marvin, people would like that, we could give them a band birthday card", offered a perky Frank.

"We could print up some song sheets and have a sing-along session in the programme. People will sing if they have the words in front of them", was Martin's idea. "Try and dress a little bit more appropriately", chipped in the treasurer, "last night of the Proms concert, the band could wear red, white and blue bowler hats. Give the evening some colour, a bit of flag-waving. I am sure we could find some youngsters who could jitterbug to the music". "Not those Go-Go Dancers again", said Frank, "and Martin could wear a Union Jack waist-coat". The committee was now on a roll. "For some engagements, in the bigger halls and certainly churches, cornets and trombones could make an entrance", added the treasurer. By now the band secretary was feeling a little bit out of it and felt it was time he made a revolutionary suggestion. "We could change the formation of the band after the interval, I've seen a number of bands do that. It's very popular with The Salvation Army's top band, they even take off their red and white epaulette tunics and are very casual in marine blue T-shirts".

The next occasion the band met was the Friday evening rehearsal before the Sunday afternoon concert in the promenade bandstand. The band librarian passed out the programme sheets around the band. "What has happened to Gilbert and Sullivan, has HMS Pinafore sunk with all hands?", enquired Jack. Also missing was excerpts from the Grand Operas. "Jack! What is this piece of music on the programme?" demanded Adrian, first baritone. "I don't recall playing it. 'Barcarolle from The Tales of Hoffmann'. It's billed as a duet for euphonium and baritone. I've never played a duet, let alone with a euphonium. I think that bit is going a bit too far."

"Ladies and gentlemen, please can I have your attention. One or two new pieces I'd like to add to our repertoire, nothing too stressful. You'll also find coming round a compilation of hit songs from the Beatles. That should bring back some memories for some of you, time we tried some new music", announced Martin.

At the same rehearsal, band secretary passed around the band newsletter. Jack read it and realised that some of the comments were clearly aimed at him. Martin concluded the rehearsal half an hour earlier, that was suspicious for a number of the players, fresh music, a 'pulling your socks up' newsletter, and now drawing 'stumps' half an hour before going home time and that was not going to be extra time in the pub. Not crisis time but very nearly.

"Ladies and gentlemen, banding colleagues", said Daniel standing before the band on the podium. "This is a significant day in the history of the 'Twelve Boys Band'. Ours is a band of commemoration, a band of remembrance. On the town's War Memorial is an inscription, "They Served – They Gave" and a list of twelve names of those lads from this town who made, perhaps as we too often glibly say, 'the ultimate sacrifice'. The significance is that on this day, eleven became twelve. Six of the town's lads played in the battalion band, inspiring the founding of this band after the war. I ask myself is the band of today worthy of their memory? This band could and must do better. You have elected me as the band representative, I can see the potential in this band. I have a vision going forward. Some of you may have heard that I was less than charitable in the comments I made at the first committee meeting I attended. Sometimes to take a step forward, we need to make a purposeful break with the past, maybe nothing more than a symbolic break, enabling us to make that move forward".

Daniel explained that the old dinner dance was symptomatic of the malaise which ran through the band. With a new approach and fresh endeavour, the band could become a musical force, able to challenge and compete in brass band contests, perhaps even making their way to the Royal Albert Hall. Now that would be honouring the Twelve Boys.

The band unanimously supported the move of the dinner dance to The Royal Hotel, to be re-styled as a Gala Dinner. Daniel and Frank met with the Functions Manager, a charming young lady. "Indeed, the third Friday in January the Royal Assembly room was available. The room could comfortably seat 160 guests. I look forward to welcoming the Twelve Boys Band and their guests". Martin took Daniel to one side. Daniel had seen what Martin had failed to see, the band now would be a different band, an even better band if Daniel would accept the post of assistant Musical Director.

It was Frank who spotted an outline planning application in the local newspaper for the Wayside Inn Hotel. It was proposed to demolish the hotel, clear the ground and build a block of flats for elderly retired people on the former hotel footprint. It was going to be called Happy Wayside.

The Final Drum Beat

(25)

WHILE the final Sunday evening service concluded in the Clifton Hall, the home of The Salvation Army in St Peter Port, Guernsey, the Second World War was about to descend on the congregation. Overhead they could hear the drone of German aircraft. Expected for days, it had now become a reality. In the early summer months of 1940, there had been time to evacuate, leave the island of Guernsey, but on 30th June 1940, the 'gate' firmly shut.

"Did you hear those German planes, they didn't half make the windows rattle", said Bandmaster Tony Robilliard speaking to Gerald Ogier, the deputy Bandmaster. Gerald looked at Tony, everybody on the island must have heard the aircraft noise, he thought. No one wanted to remain in the Salvation Army building a moment longer, no social chat.

Edith and May Le Cornu, sisters, joined their other sister on the steps outside the hall. Almost to the point of rudeness, they wanted to get home as quickly as possible. Why had they not left the island when they had the opportunity? "What is to become of us?" they queried amongst themselves.

There was a strange atmosphere in the town; other folks were hurrying to seek the safety of their own homes, to be with family. May remembered saying, "It will be fine; I am sure we can get through this together". Uncertainty entered their minds, for them, and others, it would be a sleepless night.

In the coming days, the cobbled streets of St Peter Port would ring out to the sound of German jackboots. Troops were rich in occupation Marks, and quickly brought many of the holiday trinkets which previously visitors from the mainland of England would've taken away with them. Gifts to send back home. The soldiers were young and fit, proud of the fact that they had conquered a piece of the British Empire, albeit just a small island in the English Channel. So began what was known as the 'occupation'.

Very quickly German Orders were issued, printed on the front page of the local press. A dusk to dawn curfew was imposed. The sale of alcohol was forbidden. Children would be taught German in schools. All vehicles would drive on the right-hand side of the road. Disobedience would be heavily punished. Church services could continue.

The German Order did at least allow The Salvation Army to hold their meetings. The local Corps (Church) advertised Sunday meetings as if everything was completely normal. They wore their uniforms but considered it prudent not to march or hold open-air services. The curfew meant a re-scheduling of meeting times. Strange was an invitation to the band, by the Germans, to play to soldiers in the German hospital, an invitation which was repeated!

It wasn't long before the German garrison brought over their military band, entertainment for the troops and the islanders. They gave concerts all over the place, including the bandstand in Candie Gardens. From a discreet and respectful distance, islanders stood and listened. Bands will always gather a crowd, whether enemy bands or not. Standing by the statue of Victor Hugo, Tony and Gerald discussed the merits of the German military band. "I can't get used to bands with woodwind; frankly I don't think they add a great deal, they were more than a bit 'reedy' in the William Tell overture", commented Tony. "I was reading", interrupted Gerald, "about their Bandmaster in the Guernsey Evening Press. Obermusikmeister Anders is young, genial; has bright eyes that flash with the genius of music when training his accomplished military band of thirty musicians. Tony, you see that's your problem, you haven't got bright flashing eyes, if you had our band might have played better!"

It seemed just about everywhere you went in St Peter Port there was Anders and his grey uniformed military band. Opposite the French Halls in the Market Place, pumping out a selection of

German Folk Tunes, down by the Weighbridge the music of Wagner could be heard. Meeting up again with Gerald, Tony nostalgically said, "Do you recall when we used to hold our Saturday night open-air in precisely the same spot? We played until it was dark and almost impossible to see the music". "Indeed", observed Gerald, "that was a lot of playing *The Day Thou Gavest Lord is Ended*' over the years. A good roll on both band drums and then into the Doxology, home for a Horlicks before bed. Do you think those days will ever come back?" "We have to believe", said Tony, as they sauntered off before the band played the German National Anthem, bringing the concert to a close.

"Did you hear the SP&S band on the radio the other night? They played the march Torchbearers at a cracking pace. I thought they would give old Anders and his woodwind mob a run for their money", asserted Gerald." "It occurred to me", said Tony thoughtfully, "I wonder if they have any former German Salvation Army bandsmen amongst the thirty of Anders' men?"

The Pettits were the hall caretakers of The Salvation Army hall and lived immediately opposite Clifton Hall. Occupation or not, a house proud Mrs Pettit, insisted on scouring and scrubbing her front doorstep and cleaning the downstairs windows, a job she did on Tuesday mornings. Earlier in their marriage, Daniel Pettit had learnt to 'step jump', very necessary for a happy marriage. "Just you mind where you're putting your clumsy feet, I've just cleaned that step", scolded Mrs Pettit.

Looking up from her weekly cleaning chore Mrs Pettit glanced across the road towards the hall. A German soldier was taking an interest in the building, looking at it from various angles. He moved to read the noticeboards still attached to the wall by the double front doors, seemingly satisfied he turned the corner of the hall and went down Clifton Steps leading to the town centre.

"I saw a German soldier earlier today having a good look at the outside of the hall. I wondered what he was up to. The Germans have been requisitioning a number of buildings around the island, some to billet their troops and others for storage.

Clifton Hall could be quite useful to them, as you know it's a fair old size, the main hall with the downstairs hall and the basement", said Mrs Pettit.

"Well if they expect me to a caretaker for them, they can think again. Unless ordered there's no way I'm going to work for the Germans", asserted Mr Pettit. "Don't you be getting on the wrong side of them, I don't want you being carted off to Germany".

A week later from an upstairs window, Mrs Pettit saw the same German soldier, this time he had a camera and was taking photos of the hall, including the dedication stones and the noticeboards. "Daniel, that German is back again, he's been taking photos, now he's trying the door, giving it a good push. Why don't you go across and see what he wants?"

Looking through the front sitting room window, pulling the net curtain to one side, Daniel assessed the German. He was a bit older than some of the German forces he had seen about the town. He tried to read the soldier's insignia; Daniel thought he might have been a Feldwebel. The German soldier heard the front door of the house opposite open and close behind him and turning observed Daniel hesitantly coming across the road towards him. The soldier smiled in reassurance and extended a sweeping hand towards the building. In very good English he opened the conversation, "A fine building, I think, very old, made of Guernsey granite". Daniel replied, "Yes, it is a very fine building, you can see it from the harbour, perched up here on the top of the hill". "Yes I know that", said the German, "I saw it from the seafront, a big white painted building, it took me a while to find it. One day I should like to look inside, to see the view from the upper windows looking out to the sea."

Daniel was aware that he was warming to the German, this was his first encounter with the enemy, and it was not what he expected. He wasn't ordered about, shouted at, no veiled threats, no threatening behaviour. Here was a polite German soldier, apparently just interested in the hall.

"I've got the keys in my pocket", said Daniel producing a set of keys, "would you like to have a look inside?" Together they entered Clifton Hall. Immediately the German removed his Field Grey Side Cap. The soldier walked down one of the aisles and gazed around the galleried hall. On the platform, he could see the band chairs in band formation. On the wall was a large marble shield commemorating the visit of The Salvation Army founder, William Booth, in June 1855.

In silence, the soldier dropped his hat onto a chair and picked up a songbook flicking through the pages as if he was looking for something. Replacing the book, he mounted the steps onto the platform and made his way to the rostrum, gazing out over a non-existent congregation. With both hands, he grabbed the sides of the rostrum. He stood there, pensive, deep in thought. Breaking the moment he turned around and noticed the bass drum in the corner on its stand. He strolled over to read the drum inscription, the number of the St Peter Port Corps, touching the rim of the percussion instrument.

Daniel, still standing halfway down the aisle, noted the tableau which unfolded before him. He was fast coming to a conclusion. The interest in the building, returning to take photos, the way he carefully handled the songbook, his poise when standing at the lectern, it was all pointing in one direction. This German soldier must be acquainted with The Salvation Army.

Speaking quietly across the hall, Daniel tentatively asked,"Are you Salvation Army?" There was a very long pause before the German replied, with deep emotion, "Yes, me Heilsarmee".

Dieter Weber had studied music at the University of Hamburg before the war years. Percussion being his discipline. On a Hamburg street corner, Dieter came into contact with The Salvation Army, "There was not a lot going on, folk were singing, the music coming from a piano accordion and a bass drum", Dieter related, "One of the girls invited me to a meeting which I accepted, I knew nothing at all about The Salvation Army, I thought I was being invited to a theatre show with dancing girls.

It was not the pretty girl that encouraged me into the hall, but the drum. I joined The Salvation Army in Hamburg and ended up myself playing the drum. In my heart, I knew God wanted me to be an officer in The Salvation Army, but national events made that impossible. I was able to travel to London in 1936. I went to a concert given by the International Staff Band at the Regent Hall."

Salvation Army service came to an end when Dieter was conscripted into the Wehrmacht in 1937. With his comrades, he saw military service, first in Belgium and then France. Posted to Guernsey just about the first thing he saw from the transport vessel upon entering St Peter Port Harbour was Clifton Hall with the words Salvation Army boldly written across the entire length of the building. He knew full well the significance. Dieter was not going to be on the island very long; he was part of German administration conducting a Guernsey cow headcount, he expected to go on to Jersey and complete the same survey on that island's bred of cattle.s

Daniel related to Tony the encounter, "I've met this German Salvationist, he was hanging around the hall, the wife made me go out and speak to him. Not the best of ideas, I thought. Little I could do when she pushed me in the back and out of the front door. He said Clifton Hall was a fine building and that he wanted to have a look inside, I could hardly say, 'No', to a German, so I let him in. By what he said I feel he's genuine, his name is Dieter - Dieter Weber, before the war he played in the Hamburg Salvation Army band on the drum. A very nice fellow, for a German. You may get a chance to meet him".

Because of curfew restrictions and the band not being so active, practices were held just once a month on a Saturday afternoon. In all truth, there was very little purpose in having a practice for the sake of the music, but the morale benefit made it very worthwhile. The band was struggling to get through Torchbearers inspired by the SP&S broadcast. The hall door opened, and a very timid and tentative Dieter entered. The band stopped playing. The whole band knew who Dieter was; word had quickly got around, they took their cue from the Bandmaster who motioned Dieter forward and introduced the German soldier. All that came out of Dieter's mouth was an emotional, "Guten Tag - Hello!"

Bill the bass drummer, handed Dieter the drum sticks and made way for Dieter so that he could play the percussion instrument. For the first time, the band had a drummer who could read music, who knew the difference between a hard touch and a soft one and could follow the Bandmaster's beat. It was very evident that Dieter was an excellent percussionist. "In Germany, before the war, while the Salvation Army was still permitted, we could not play pieces as difficult as this", Dieter told the band.

"He made us think, it's not his fault he had to join the German Army. Let's hope he comes through the war", said the Bandmaster at the conclusion of the practice after Dieter had left. "If only all Germans were like him", said Daniel.

That was the last Guernsey Salvationists saw of Dieter, the following week he was posted, not to Jersey but to Normandy. Dieter must've taken Daniel Pettit's address because many, many months later Daniel received a very brief letter from the German, almost a telegram. "Vielen Dank für Ihre Freundlichkeit. Ich denke oft an dich, meine Armeefamilie in Guernsey. Möge Gott Sie segnen und behalten - Dieter Weber". The letter had been stamped many times by the German censors. Translated it read, 'Thank you for your kindness. I think of you often, my Army family in Guernsey. May God Bless you and keep you - Dieter Weber'.

In 1941 German administration became aware of a situation which prevailed in the Channel Islands but not in any other part of Europe which was under their control. The Salvation Army was still active. It was the newspaper advertisements which was their undoing. A one-page letter from the German Feldkommandantur 515, noting the press adverts, instructed the movement to cease their activity. There would be no punishment on this occasion, and there was no prospect of any appeal.

Bandmaster Robilliard and Gerald met at the hall and began the process of mothballing. "If they want, let some of the chaps look after their instruments at home, it could well prove to be the safest place", suggested Gerald. "That's fine by me", said the Bandmaster, "that might be okay for the smaller instruments but who has room for the new monster bass, we only just bought it in January 1940, and we've only had about six month's use". Gerald said "Do you remember the day the bass arrived from Southampton on the mailboat? It was the last thing in the cargo hold. The packing case was so big they had to use a crane to lift it up and over". The Bandmaster recalled the incident, "We had to borrow a British Railways handcart, and then pull and push the thing from the harbour, up St Julians Avenue and finally to the hall. That packing case was so big you could've lived in it."

Two instruments were needing a home for the duration, the monster bass and the big drum. Remaining in the hall would be a very old French brass baritone and a couple of beginner's cornets and the band music. "Jerry can have them when he comes looting", said the Bandmaster.

Bill played the big drum and John the side drum. It was doubtful that either was capable of reading drum music. Even so, Bill would prop the drum music on top of the drum, and give a glance at the music from time to time. Both played by instinct and inspiration. "Look up, Bill", John would say, "the Bandmaster is looking at us, I wonder what he wants"? When the Bandmaster said, "Let's pick it up at section B", neither bothered to find letter B! John said he could take the side drum home; it could fit in the under stairs cupboard. The bass drum would have to go into storage, but where?

Daniel Pettit solved the problem, "I can store them in the attic, I've got other Army stuff, and the songbooks to hide away". Like two old companions drum and bass were secreted away amongst the roof timbers, entering banding hibernation.

Like their instruments, the band members also went into banding isolation. No longer able to meet in the hall they would bump into each other in the street. The news was what everybody wanted, how the war was going, news true or false was readily exchanged. Had they received any Red Cross letters from relatives and friends who had managed to evacuate? How are they coping? Inevitably bandsmen would always get around to talking band. "I get my cornet out every day and have a practice", ventured the solo cornet player when he met up with the Bandmaster in The Arcade.

The Salvationists linked up with other churches and joined in their fellowship, the band members forming together a little musical party for Christmas to help with carols at the Carol Service. "Do you remember when we used to go around the island carol playing? We used to move from street lamp to street lamp; people would come to the door singing the carols and wishing us well. Christmas Eve was very special; we would start at one end of the town playing our way up the Pollet and down the High Street towards the Town Church. People knew we were coming and waited for the band ready to join in and sing Christmas hymns around the Christmas tree", recalled Tony.

The occupation changed many things; there was almost an absence of civilian vehicles because of the restriction on petrol, the bicycle became king of the road. The island was no longer supplied from England; provisions came in from France. In wintertime heating was always a challenge, all entertainment had to be homegrown, the confiscation of radios was a particular hardship, access to the beaches was extremely limited and pretty well denied, dual currency circulated. No contact with the outside world; the news you received was censored by the Germans, although many people had clandestine homemade 'cat whisker' radio sets.

Islanders saw the immense fortification of the island, built by imported slave labour, requiring substantial troops to garrison the German Army military structures. Island life was dominated by just about everything German and all the while the local civic administration had to contend with the rules and regulations of the German oppressor.

One day was to bring change and swing the conflict in favour of the islanders: D-Day, 6th June 1944. "Have you heard the news?", a very excited Daniel asked Tony as they met in the High

Street. "Do you think there is anybody on the island who hasn't heard, you could hear the gunfire from first thing in the morning. I'm told German troops were scurrying around all over the place they could not believe landings hadn't taken place on the island", replied Tony.

Whilst the war wasn't over by Christmas 1944 the islanders believed the end of the war was the event they could soon celebrate. German troops now were being held in a 'pocket' from which they could not escape. German troops freely admitted that the war was over and hoped for the day when they could return to their homeland. Both groups were going to have to wait for nearly another year.

Channel Island liberation was to be one of the last acts of the war. Total and unconditional surrender in Europe was signed on 7th and 8th May, to be effective by the end of 8th May. On Wednesday 9th May 1945, Guernsey was liberated.

The Bandmaster was not prepared to allow this significant glorious event to pass without celebration. "We will give a band concert on Saturday afternoon and will play in the bandstand at Candie Gardens, I need to get the chaps together, but that should not be a problem".

In preparation, Gerald unlocked the hall door and entered the hall, the first time he had done so in three years. The hall had been requisitioned by the Germans and used as a furniture store. Crammed into the main hall were tables and chairs, cupboards, beds, settees and other miscellaneous items of domestic furniture.

Just off the lower hall was the bandroom. Jerry had taken the brass baritone and with it the two training cornets. In the band cupboard, the band music journals were in place just as the day they had been abandoned.

With no useable main hall, it was suggested that the band organise a pre-concert get together checking instruments and music. "We've got permission to use the bandstand so we might as well all meet up in the morning and set up", instructed the Bandmaster.

For Daniel, it meant climbing the attic steps into the loft to bring down the monster bass and the drum. The monster bass had survived but not the drum; the skins had perished, the wood was no longer drum-shaped and cracked. The Bandmaster and Daniel surveyed the disaster. The afternoon band concert would be bass drumless.

The afternoon performance was an enormous success. The crowd applauded every item and even clapped halfway through when the band broke down completely. People gave generously to the band and when the collection was counted the takings included, not only English money, Guernsey money, French Francs but also German Marks.

The Guernsey Press reporter wrote an excellent review of the concert. The missing bass drum did not go unnoticed; he was critical on that point, the band not having a bass drum. "I'm sorry to say the drum was a victim of the occupation", was the Bandmaster's quote, "when funds allow we will certainly purchase a new one, but many other things must come first, there is a lot of rebuilding to be done, and the bass drum is pretty low down the list".

Six months later, as Daniel arrived back home from work, he noticed parked outside his house was a British Railways delivery wagon. "You got something there for me, Charlie?", asked Daniel, "I'm not expecting anything". "Well it is certainly addressed to you, look at the docket. It's come from London. It's a fair old size, what have you been buying on the black market?". "Don't be stupid, give me a hand to get it off the lorry, we will put it in the hall, I can open the crate in there later. I'll have my tea first, Tony can help me unpack it when he comes in for band practice".

Later that evening, Daniel and Tony set about opening the wooden crate, and in the midst of all the straw packing, they lifted out the familiar shape of a bass drum. The drum was beautiful, decorated in the traditional Salvation Army pattern, draped flags, with the name of the Corps, the Corps number and in the centre The Salvation Army crest.

There was an added German inscription. In liebevoller Erinnerung an Dieter Weber - 1909 - 1944 (In loving Memory of Dieter Weber - 1909 - 1944).

The Final Drum Beat

The Final Drum Beat is a short story based on fact. The names of the people have been changed. The chronology is correct.

William and Catherine Booth spent part of their honeymoon on Guernsey, William preached in Clifton Hall.

The monster bass was stored opposite the hall for the duration of the occupation.

St Peter Port Salvationists did play and sing in a hospital to the German wounded. (Reported in the local press).

I have a copy of the original letter sent by the Germans to the local Corps closing the movement.

A German military band performed concerts on precisely the same spot that St Peter Port Corps held the Saturday evening open air.

It was reported, though never confirmed, that in one of the German bands which visited the island they had two Salvation Army trombones identified by the crest on the bell.

A German soldier with links to The Salvation Army was stationed in Guernsey and linked up with L'Islet Corps members and attended house prayer meetings.

The German Salvationist from Hamburg was stationed on Jersey. (Information recorded by Jersey Salvationists who met him frequently).